.W345

2010

Non-Governmental Organizations in World Politics

Non-governmental organizations (NGOs) from Amnesty International and Oxfam to Greenpeace and Save the Children are now key players in global politics. This accessible and informative textbook provides a comprehensive overview of the significant role and increasing participation of NGOs in world politics.

Peter Willetts examines the variety of different NGOs, their structure, membership and activities, and their complex relationship with social movements and civil society. He makes us aware that there are many more NGOs exercising influence in the United Nations system than the few famous ones.

Conventional thinking is challenged in a radical manner on four questions: the extent of the engagement of NGOs in global policy-making; the status of NGOs within international law; the role of NGOs as crucial pioneers in the creation of the Internet; and the need to integrate NGOs within mainstream international relations theory.

This is the definitive guide to this crucial area within international politics and should be required reading for students, NGO activists, and policy-makers.

Peter Willetts is Emeritus Professor of Global Politics at City University, London. His previous publications on NGOs include *Pressure Groups in the Global System* (London: Pinter, 1982) and the edited volume *"The Conscience of the World": The Influence of Non-Governmental Organisations in the UN System* (Washington DC: Brookings Institution, 1996).

Routledge Global Institutions
Edited by Thomas G. Weiss
The CUNY Graduate Center, New York, USA
and Rorden Wilkinson
University of Manchester, UK

About the series

The "Global Institutions" series is designed to provide readers with comprehensive, accessible, and informative guides to the history, structure, and activities of key international organizations as well as books that deal with topics of key importance in contemporary global governance. Every volume stands on its own as a thorough and insightful treatment of a particular topic, but the series as a whole contributes to a coherent and complementary portrait of the phenomenon of global institutions at the dawn of the millennium.

Books are written by recognized experts, conform to a similar structure, and cover a range of themes and debates common to the series. These areas of shared concern include the general purpose and rationale for organizations, developments over time, membership, structure, decision-making procedures, and key functions. Moreover, current debates are placed in historical perspective alongside informed analysis and critique. Each book also contains an annotated bibliography and guide to electronic information as well as any annexes appropriate to the subject matter at hand.

The volumes currently published are:

The volumes currently under contract include:

The UN Human Rights Council
by Bertrand G. Ramcharan (Geneva Graduate Institute of International and Development Studies)

International Aid
by Paul Mosley (University of Sheffield)

Maritime Piracy
by Bob Haywood

The International Monetary Fund (2nd edition)
Politics of conditional lending
by James Raymond Vreeland (Georgetown University)

The UN Global Compact
By Catia Gregoratti (Lund University)

Security Governance in Regional Organizations
Edited by Emil Kirchner (University of Essex) and Roberto Dominguez (Suffolk University)

Responsibility to Protect
Perspectives from the Global South
by Thomas G. Weiss (The CUNY Graduate Center) and Rama Mani (University of Oxford)

UN Institutions for Women's Rights
by Charlotte Patton (York College, CUNY) and Carolyn Stephenson (University of Hawaii)

For further information regarding the series, please contact:

Craig Fowlie, Publisher, Politics & International Studies
Taylor & Francis
2 Park Square, Milton Park, Abingdon
Oxford OX14 4RN, UK

+44 (0)207 842 2057 Tel
+44 (0)207 842 2302 Fax

Craig.Fowlie@tandf.co.uk
www.routledge.com

Non-Governmental Organizations in World Politics

The construction of global governance

Peter Willetts

Routledge
Taylor & Francis Group

LONDON AND NEW YORK

First published 2011 by Routledge
2 Park Square, Milton Park, Abingdon, Oxon, OX14 4RN

Simultaneously published in the USA and Canada
by Routledge
270 Madison Avenue, New York, NY 10016

Routledge is an imprint of the Taylor & Francis Group, an informa business

© 2011 Peter Willetts

Typeset in Times New Roman by
Pindar NZ, Auckland, New Zealand
Printed and bound in Great Britain by
TJ International, Padstow, Cornwall

British Library Cataloguing in Publication Data
A catalogue record for this book is available from the British Library

Library of Congress Cataloging in Publication Data
Willetts, Peter.
Non-Governmental Organizations in World Politics: the construction of
global governance / Peter Willetts.
   p. cm. — (Routledge global institutions; 49)
  Includes bibliographical references and index.
  1. International organization. 2. International cooperation.
3. Non-governmental organizations. I. Title.
  JZ1318.W545 2010
  341.2—dc22   2010026785

ISBN13: 978-0-415-38124-6 (hbk)
ISBN13: 978-0-415-38125-3 (pbk)
ISBN13: 978-0-203-83430-5 (ebk)

Contents

Illustrations

Figures

Tables

Boxes

Foreword

The current volume is the forty-seventh new title—two have already gone into second editions—in a dynamic series on "global institutions." The series strives (and, based on the volumes published to date, succeeds) to provide readers with definitive guides to the most visible aspects of what many of us know as "global governance." Remarkable as it may seem, there exist relatively few books that offer in-depth treatments of prominent global bodies, processes, and associated issues, much less an entire series of concise and complementary volumes. Those that do exist are either out of date, inaccessible to the non-specialist reader, or seek to develop a specialized understanding of particular aspects of an institution or process rather than offer an overall account of its functioning. Similarly, existing books have often been written in highly technical language or have been crafted "in-house" and are notoriously self-serving and narrow.

The advent of electronic media has undoubtedly helped research and teaching by making data and primary documents of international organizations more widely available, but it has also complicated matters. The growing reliance on the Internet and other electronic methods of finding information about key international organizations and processes has served, ironically, to limit the educational and analytical materials to which most readers have ready access—namely, books. Public relations documents, raw data, and loosely refereed websites do not make for intelligent analysis. Official publications compete with a vast amount of electronically available information, much of which is suspect because of its ideological or self-promoting slant. Paradoxically, a growing range of purportedly independent websites offering analyses of the activities of particular organizations has emerged, but one inadvertent consequence has been to frustrate access to basic, authoritative, readable, critical, and well-researched texts. The market for such has actually been reduced by the ready availability of varying quality electronic materials.

For those of us who teach, research, and practice in the area, such limited access to information has been frustrating. We were delighted when Routledge saw the value of a series that bucks this trend and provides key reference points to the most significant global institutions and issues. They are betting that serious students and professionals will want serious analyses. We have assembled a first-rate line-up of authors to address that market. Our intention, then, is to provide one-stop shopping for all readers—students (both undergraduate and postgraduate), negotiators, diplomats, practitioners from non-governmental and intergovernmental organizations, and interested parties alike—seeking information about the most prominent institutional aspects of global governance.

NGOs in world politics

We could not have found a better-placed scholar than Peter Willetts to write this volume on a controversial and challenging topic that many people have compared, unfavorably, to herding cats. Currently Emeritus Professor of Global Politics at City University, London, Peter has researched this topic extensively including two earlier and well-regarded books dealing with non-governmental organizations (NGOs).[1]

His subtitle, *The Construction of Global Governance*, tells the reader why the editors are enthusiastic to have this title finally appear in our series. It was one of the first topics that we deemed essential to appear on our masthead. Why? Because long gone are the days when students of international relations could only focus on the 250 or so existing intergovernmental organizations as the primary players in international society. While we have plenty of titles in this series on them, formal institutions such as the United Nations or the World Bank or NATO (North Atlantic Treaty Organization) no longer occupy center stage for students of international organization. They share an ever more crowded governance stage not only with nearly 200 UN member states but also with both civil society and for-profit corporations: including some 7,500 international NGOs and 10,000 single-state NGOs with significant international activities as well as some 75,000 transnational corporations and their 750,000 foreign affiliates.[2] This panoply of institutions may not yet represent a "post-Westphalian" world, but this new reality clearly is inadequately reflected in state-centric analytical perspectives that dominate most theoretical treatments of important actors in world politics.

Peter's thorough treatment here focuses on the network of transnational and local NGOs as well as social movements that make civil society one of the most challenging and complex topics in international relations today. His work clearly walks the reader through the political, legal, historical, and social dimensions of NGOs, including such challenging questions as "Are they democratic?"

While UN Charter Article 71 made room for non-governmental organizations from the very outset of the world organization, the nature of that ever-changing relationship was a minor concern for both analysts and international officials. "Until recently, the notion that the chief executive of the United Nations would have taken this issue seriously might have caused astonishment," wrote then Secretary-General Boutros Boutros-Ghali in the foreword to an edited volume on the subject of UN–NGO interactions. "The United Nations was considered to be a forum for sovereign states alone. Within the space of a few short years, however, this attitude has changed. Non-governmental organizations are now considered full participants in international life."[3] This book was one of the first to grapple with such a challenging a topic, but Peter Willetts now has gone further in his treatment of a subject that has evolved significantly in the last decade and a half.

We thoroughly recommend *Non-Governmental Organizations in World Politics* to all interested not only in the study of world politics, international organization, and global governance but also to those keen to understand why global politics operates the way it does. As always, we look forward to comments from first-time or veteran readers of the Global Institutions series.

Thomas G. Weiss,
the CUNY Graduate Center,
New York, USA

Rorden Wilkinson,
University of Manchester, UK
July 2010

Acknowledgments

This book aims to present what I have learnt from 30 years of studying non-governmental organizations and to take the subject forward, by arguing why it is essential to consider NGOs as significant participants in all aspects of world politics. On such a long journey, I have a great debt to many who helped me along the way. Many classes of students made me aware of the need to clarify what is meant by an NGO. The skepticism of British academics in the 1980s about the significance of NGOs pushed me into obtaining a broad knowledge of the variety of ways in which NGOs participate in world politics. John Groom and Paul Taylor were important exceptions at that time, in being supportive and publishing my first analysis of international institutions. In the 1980s, my colleagues in the British International Studies Association Working Group on International Relations Theory and, since 1991, those in the Environment Working Group provided a friendly, critical forum that assisted in the development of my "issue-based approach," an embryonic version of constructivism. My doctoral students in the 1990s, Mandy Bentham, Tom Bigg, Mira Filipovic, Peter Hough, and David Humphreys, proved that an issue-based approach, encompassing both governments and NGOs in the politics of international regimes, could provide deeper understanding of global policy-making than a traditional state-centric approach. The British government's Department for International Development provided a research grant that made it possible to attend sessions of the UN Commission on Sustainable Development, the Council of the Global Environment Facility, and the IMF, World Bank Spring Meetings in 2001 and 2002. Roberto Bissio and Ian Peter provoked exploration of NGO influence upon the creation of the Internet. Helen Hawthorne prompted me into integrating my own work with the constructivist literature, by placing NGOs at the center of the development of global norms. Tom Davies provided support and intellectual challenge. Finally, thanks are due to the series editors, Thomas Weiss and Rorden Wilkinson, for their encouragement and their endless patience in being willing to wait too many years for the slow production of the manuscript.

This book is dedicated to James Rosenau for his pioneering work on transnational relations that stimulated me in the late 1970s to start down the road of asking how NGOs relate to the United Nations.

Abbreviations

AFL	American Federation of Labor
APC	Association for Progressive Communications
ARPA	Advanced Research Projects Agency
ARPANET	Advanced Research Projects Agency Network
BBS	bulletin board system
CBD	Convention on Biological Diversity
CBO	community-based organization
CERN	European Council for Nuclear Research
CHR	Commission on Human Rights (ECOSOC subsidiary body)
CITES	Convention on International Trade in Endangered Species of Wild Fauna and Flora
CONGO	Conference of Non-Governmental Organizations in Consultative Relationship with the United Nations
COP	Conference of the Parties (to an international treaty)
CRIES	Regional Co-ordinating Agency for Economic and Social Research (Nicaragua)
CSD	Commission on Sustainable Development (ECOSOC subsidiary body)
CSI	Christian Solidarity International
CSO	civil society organization
CSW	Commission on the Status of Women (ECOSOC subsidiary body)
ECOSOC	Economic and Social Council (of the United Nations)
ELCI	Environment Liaison Centre International
ENDA-TM	Environment and Development Action in the Third World
FAO	Food and Agriculture Organization of the United Nations
FCCC	Framework Convention on Climate Change
FIFA	Fédération Internationale de Football Association
FONDAD	Forum on Debt and Development
FTP	file transfer protocol

GAVI	Global Alliance for Vaccines and Immunisation
GEF	Global Environment Facility
GONGO	government-organized non-governmental organization
Habitat	United Nations Human Settlements Programme
HURIDOCS	Human Rights Information and Documentation Systems International
IAEA	International Atomic Energy Agency
IBASE	Brazilian Institute for Social and Economic Analysis
IBFAN	International Baby Food Action Network
ICA	International Co-operative Alliance
ICAO	International Civil Aviation Organization
ICBL	International Campaign to Ban Landmines
ICC	International Criminal Court
ICCROM	International Centre for the Study of the Preservation and Restoration of Cultural Property
ICDA	International Coalition for Development Action
ICJ	International Court of Justice
ICOMOS	International Council on Monuments and Sites
ICRC	International Committee of the Red Cross
ICSU	International Council for Science (formerly International Council of Scientific Unions)
ICT	information and communication technology
IDOC	International Documentation and Communication Centre
IFC	International Facilitating Committee
IFRC	International Federation of Red Cross and Red Crescent Societies
IFW	International Federation of Women
IGC	Institute for Global Communications (the US member of APC)
IGO	intergovernmental organization
IGY	International Geophysical Year
ILO	International Labour Organization
IMF	International Monetary Fund
IMO	International Maritime Organization
INGO	international non-governmental organization
INSTRAW	United Nations International Research and Training Institute for the Advancement of Women
IPPF	International Planned Parenthood Federation
IPU	Inter-Parliamentary Union
ISO	International Organization for Standardization
ISP	Internet service provider
ITU	International Telecommunication Union

IUCN	International Union for the Conservation of Nature and Natural Resources (also known as the World Conservation Union)
IUSSP	International Union for the Scientific Study of Population
JANET	Joint Academic Network (United Kingdom)
MANGO	Micro-Computing for NGOs (Zimbabwe)
NGLS	Non-Governmental Liaison Service (a UN system, inter-agency body)
NGO	non-governmental organization
NPL	National Physical Laboratory (United Kingdom)
NPT	Non-Proliferation Treaty
NRA	National Rifle Association (USA)
NSFNet	National Science Foundation Network (USA)
OCIMF	Oil Companies International Marine Forum
ODA	Official Development Assistance
OECD	Organisation for Economic Co-operation and Development
OEN	Ontario Environmental Network
OSCE	Organization for Security and Co-operation in Europe
PC	personal computer
PrepCom	Preparatory Committee (usually of a UN conference)
PVO	private voluntary organization
SCAR	Scientific Committee on Antarctic Research (a committee of the ICSU)
SCOPE	Scientific Committee on Problems of the Environment (a committee of the ICSU)
TCP-IP	Internet Protocol Suite, including the Transmission Control Protocol and the Internet Protocol
TNC	transnational corporation
TRP	Transnational Radical Party
UDHR	Universal Declaration of Human Rights
UN	United Nations
UNAIDS	Joint United Nations Programme on HIV/AIDS
UNCED	United Nations Conference on Environment and Development (Rio de Janeiro 1992)
UNCHE	United Nations Conference on the Human Environment (Stockholm 1972)
UNCTAD	United Nations Conference on Trade and Development
UNDCP	United Nations International Drugs Control Programme
UNDP	United Nations Development Programme
UNEP	United Nations Environment Programme
UNESCO	United Nations Educational, Scientific and Cultural Organization

UNFPA	United Nations Population Fund
UNHCR	Office of the United Nations High Commissioner for Refugees
UNICEF	United Nations Children's Fund
UNIDIR	United Nations Institute for Disarmament Research
UNRWA	United Nations Relief and Works Agency for Palestine Refugees
UNSSOD	United Nations General Assembly Special Session on Disarmament
UPU	Universal Postal Union
WEDO	Women's Environment and Development Organization
WELL	Whole Earth 'Lectronic Link
WFTU	World Federation of Trade Unions
WHO	World Health Organization
WILPF	Women's International League for Peace and Freedom
WIPO	World Intellectual Property Organization
WMO	World Meteorological Organization
WSIS	World Summit on the Information Society
WTO	World Trade Organization
WWF	World Wide Fund for Nature (changed from the World Wildlife Fund in 1961)

Introduction

A book about all non-governmental organizations (NGOs) in all parts of the world would in effect cover all social and political activities of all people. The title of this book might at first glance appear to suggest such a gigantic task is being attempted. However, the subject matter is much more focused. It covers the relationships of NGOs with each other and with governments, when they are seeking to influence *global* political decisions. This statement contains an implied assumption that global politics can be analyzed as a distinct level of analysis, separate from politics within individual countries. Orthodox approaches to international relations deny the existence of global political systems. However, political scientists have no problems with analyzing the politics of each country as a distinct level of analysis, separate from regional or local government. Just as we can understand federal politics within the United States without a detailed knowledge of politics within Texas and every other state, so also we can study global politics without a detailed knowledge of politics within the United States and every other country. Just as we can understand NGO influence upon the US Congress, so also we can study NGO influence upon the United Nations. Thus, this book is mainly concerned about NGO activities at the global level: their relationships across country boundaries and within international organizations. The reader will find virtually no mention of local or national NGOs trying to influence their own government, nor of NGO projects within individual countries.

This book is about global *politics* and not about other aspects of NGOs and their operations. Politics within countries is sometimes seen in narrow terms, as the relations between political parties and what determines whether or not government leaders remain in office. By extension, international politics is then the relations between governments. Clearly, the study of NGOs must comprise much more than the world of governments and diplomacy. This book adopts a broader concept of politics, as the process by which any group of people reach a collective decision, which they expect to be respected by all the members of the group. Global politics covers any process by which a claim is made that people in different countries should respect a joint decision. Such decisions are sometimes made in country-to-country relations, but they are predominantly made within international organizations. Thus, the primary focus of this book is the way in which NGOs have exercised influence at the global level: through participation in the politics of international organizations, through their international legal rights and obligations, and through the nature of global communications via the Internet.

Now that there is much wider awareness of, and interest in, the global activities of NGOs, it is commonplace to ask whether it is legitimate for NGOs to have significant influence. Is it democratic? Who do NGOs represent? Some activists and analysts respond with a naive anarchism, in which NGOs are regarded as "the voice of the people" and governments are oppressive. They argue for the establishment of a "People's Assembly" on a global basis. If NGOs could provide at least an input to global policy-making or at most have some direct decision-making authority, it would be a step towards a more progressive and/or a more peaceful democratic world. Underlying such arguments, there is confusion about the nature of democracy. It has three fundamental components. The governments must be responsible to the population they rule, through free and fair elections, in which the electorate can choose who should hold office on the basis of the policies that they advocate. In addition, in between the elections, there must be a free flow of information about the decisions the government takes and freedom for individuals and groups to discuss and evaluate those decisions. Lastly, there must be some system of communication for groups within civil society to have their voice heard and to make demands upon the government, in order to influence the policy-making process. There is no possibility in the foreseeable future of global policy-making being subject to democratic control through global elections to a global assembly. Nevertheless, we do now have global democracy in the second sense that global international organizations are for the most part completely transparent and in the third sense that global civil society has access to policy-making processes.

NGOs may wish to claim legitimacy because they have millions of supporters and can at times mobilize support in demonstrations and in public debate. However, such claims can never make NGOs, individually or collectively, more legitimate than democratic governments. Many NGOs are too small to make any claims to be representative. Many NGOs, including very influential organizations such as Human Rights Watch, Oxfam, or Greenpeace, have supporters but not members. These NGOs have no internal democracy and their leaders are not directly responsible to anyone but themselves. Most, but not all, of the religious NGOs would deny internal democracy should make any contribution to their witness to their moral positions: for them democracy is not a basis for spiritual authority. Some NGOs, such as Amnesty

International or trades unions and professional bodies, do determine their policy through their own internal democratic policy-making institutions, but this does not give them a higher democratic legitimacy than an elected government. However large they are, they are still a self-selecting minority within a much larger civil society.

Thus, there is democratic legitimacy to the claim that all international organizations (including international NGOs) should be transparent, with policy papers and policy debates being accessible to all members of civil society. The Internet now makes it cheap and simple to be completely transparent and the United Nations has set the gold standard of 100 percent transparency with its many, well-indexed websites. There is also democratic legitimacy to the claim for voices from global civil society to be heard in global policy-making. There are practical limitations on the number of contributions that can be made by civil society at a particular time and place. Generally, the news media, NGO publications, and the Internet, among them, allow all voices to speak, even though some may by drowned out by the overall volume. In addition, the system of consultative status, as described in Chapter 2, allows the major strands of thought in civil society and the major types of organized interests to be heard within the formal proceedings of the UN. Any claim for NGOs individually or collectively to have a vote in existing policy-making bodies, or to have a new People's Assembly with decision-making authority, would not be democratic. Indeed, it could be nothing but anti-democratic elitism or corporatism. We do not have a fully democratic world, but the main problems lie at the country level rather than the global level. NGO activity at the global level, notably through the extension of the global human rights agenda, is shining some light into non-transparent societies and making some demands upon governments that do not respect their citizens' right to engage in policy debates. NGOs contribute significantly to democracy, but they have no right to be considered as the sole channels through which democracy can be practiced.

Before it is possible to discuss the role of NGOs in global politics, international law, and global communications it is necessary to be clear what we mean by an NGO. Chapter 1 addresses this question. The reader is alerted to abandon preconceptions about NGOs gained from personal experience with particular NGOs or from common prejudices about NGOs. If we are considering NGOs in global politics, then the only reasonable basis to proceed is to ask what organizations the UN accepts or refuses to accept as NGOs. This is not just because the UN itself is the primary focus of a great deal of NGO political activity but also because UN policy and practice have been a major influence on all other international organizations. This approach produces some surprising results. For example, neither trades unions nor religious organizations consider themselves to be NGOs, but they can only participate in the UN by registering themselves as NGOs. Also, it cannot be assumed that I or the reader endorses all NGOs. Indeed, it is argued in Chapter 1 that this is impossible because NGOs are so diverse.

Chapter 2 demonstrates how NGOs have fought for and gained the ability to participate in and to influence all aspects of global politics. It starts by outlining the official consultative arrangements for NGOs with the Economic and Social Council (ECOSOC) of the UN. Then it is emphasized how unofficial practice has evolved over the years to give NGOs a wider range of participation rights. The evolution has widened the range of activities by which NGOs can communicate with government delegates, to include many opportunities to distribute their publications, to present their ideas at unofficial events, and to lobby for their positions to be endorsed by the UN. The evolution has also widened the range of fora, so that NGOs now are no longer restricted to questions handled by ECOSOC. The chapter presents, in summary, a comprehensive overview of the extent of NGO access to all parts of the UN system.

Chapter 3 covers NGOs in international law. It is central to this chapter and taken for granted throughout the other chapters that the term international organizations is not limited to intergovernmental organizations. NGOs also come together in their own formal, institutionalized international non-governmental organizations (INGOs) as well as less formal global networks. In addition, there is a third type of international organization, a hybrid of intergovernmental organizations and INGOs, in which both governments and NGOs are members. This means some global organizations, such as the International Conference of the Red Cross and Red Crescent Movement, are not NGOs, despite the common assumption that they are. The existence of these hybrids is part of a detailed and controversial argument that NGOs have gradually gained international legal personality.

For Chapter 4, I started to investigate how NGOs first sought to gain political benefits from global communications by using the Internet. It had been assumed they were merely early adopters of the new technology. Instead, the surprising conclusion was reached that in the 1980s NGOs made a major contribution to the creation of the Internet. NGOs were crucial innovators in bringing the Internet to the public and in making the Internet a global system. This has had a major indirect effect on global policy-making. After 1990, all global institutions have experienced much wider NGO participation because of the enhanced facilities for mobilization offered by Internet communications. In addition, NGOs gained access to global governance of the Internet, because the Internet itself was created as much by academics, NGOs, and the UN as it was by governments. The chapter does not cover policy-making on global electronic communications, but the prior story on the origins of the Internet.

After presenting the detailed evidence on the impact NGOs have made upon global politics, law, and communications, Chapter 5 moves on to ask how we should include civil society in our theoretical understanding of the nature of global politics. The answer is to merge governments, NGOs, transnational corporations (TNCs), and all types of international organizations into a pluralist analysis of global political systems. But it is not enough to say we live within multi-actor pluralist systems. There also has to be a theoretical basis for asserting NGOs are able to exercise influence over the other political actors. A constructivist analysis of the mobilization of support for values and norms is essential to explaining how NGOs that lack the ability to coerce others and lack access to substantial economic resources can nevertheless change policy-making outcomes. Relating pluralism to constructivism takes the theoretical debate forward, because each of the two approaches requires the other. The structures of global political systems cannot be analyzed separately from the processes of interaction within those systems. The pluralist understanding of structures, which include NGOs, and the constructivist understanding of changes in society's norms, expressed in policy-making, each substantially strengthens the other.

The final chapter is an ambitious attempt to integrate all the previous chapters into a coherent perspective on global governance. It is argued that the increased access of NGOs to the global politics of policy-making, the increased status of NGOs in international law, and the increased communication capabilities of the Internet, created and utilized by NGOs, have constructed a new system of global governance. Brief outlines of the immense change NGOs have achieved in human rights, women's issues, development, environmental politics, and arms control are given to demonstrate that NGOs do not just influence the margins of policy-making. They do contribute to the construction or the reconstruction of the overall framework for policy-making. I have no ambition to have produced a full analysis of the role of NGOs in global governance. At the end many readers may be dissatisfied with theoretical ideas that are not fully developed or the lack of detail in the discussion of global issues. It is my ambition that some readers will respond by producing their own more theoretically sophisticated and more empirically detailed studies of global political issues, carrying forward a pluralist, constructivist approach to the participation of NGOs in global governance.

1 NGOs, social movements, and civil society

Before we can study the role of non-governmental organizations in global politics, it is necessary to be clear what is meant by an NGO. The term appears to be very abstract and remote from our daily lives. Unfortunately, it is what social scientists call an essentially contested concept. For many people, to define a non-governmental organization is to take a political position, either explicitly or implicitly. NGOs are to be admired: therefore, the term can only cover admirable organizations. Alternatively, NGOs are to be condemned: therefore, the term only covers organizations with negative features. For some people, NGOs are the organizations with which they are familiar and other very different types of NGOs are not acknowledged. The only unanimous point is we cannot use the literal meaning of the term: non-governmental organizations do *not* include every organized group that is independent from governments. Another confusion is the preference of some writers and activists for the terms social movements and/or civil society. This chapter will address the question of what NGOs are and discuss how they relate to the broader concepts of social movements and civil society.

Creation of the term "non-governmental organization" by the United Nations

Until the adoption of the United Nations Charter in 1945 the term non-governmental organization did not exist. Before 1945 several different terms were used. In 1910 a group of 132 organizations, which we would now call international NGOs, came together to form the Union of International Associations. The Secretariat of the League of Nations described itself as keeping "in constant touch with a number of private national and international organizations."[1] In 1929 a group of organizations that regularly related to the League of Nations Secretariat and attended League meetings formed the Federation of Private and Semi-Official International Organizations Established at Geneva, while the representatives of "international associations" at League committees were called "assessors."[2] The League had formal relations with "international bureaux" but these were defined under its Covenant as intergovernmental bodies created by treaties. Contacts did also gradually develop over the years with private organizations, but it was in an unsystematic, pragmatic manner. There were never any permanent *official* procedures for the League to relate to private organizations.

When the UN Charter was finalized, the San Francisco conference agreed to make provision for both intergovernmental organizations and private organizations to have formal relations with the Economic and Social Council (ECOSOC) of the UN. However, the delegates were unwilling to give the same status to the two types of international organizations. Under Article 57, a new term, "specialized agencies," was defined to cover international organizations, such as the World Health Organization (WHO), "established by intergovernmental agreement" that would be "brought into relationship with the United Nations." Under Article 70, ECOSOC could make arrangements for representatives of the agencies "to participate, without vote, in its deliberations." This gave the heads of agency secretariats the same status as government delegates from countries that had not been elected as members of ECOSOC. Under Article 71, a second new term, "non-governmental organizations," was invented, but it was left undefined. The result was that "specialized agencies" and "NGOs" became UN jargon. After 1945, private international organizations quickly started to call themselves NGOs, but the term did not move outside the world of diplomacy until the 1970s. It is now widely used in public debate. On the other hand, it is not so well known that "NGOs" originated as a very broad term from the UN Charter.

Thus, the foundation stone, upon which the whole edifice of NGO influence in global diplomacy was built, is just one article in the UN Charter.

Article 71
The Economic and Social Council may make suitable arrangements for consultation with non-governmental organizations which are concerned with matters within its competence. Such arrangements may be made with international organizations and, where appropriate, with national organizations after consultation with the Member of the United Nations concerned.

There was meant to be a clear distinction between the higher status of "participation without vote" for specialized agencies and "consultation" with the NGOs. ECOSOC affirmed at its second session, by Resolution 3 (II), "this distinction, deliberately made in the Charter, is fundamental" and NGOs should not have the same rights of participation as government observers and specialized agencies. Despite the official award of a secondary status, NGOs were able to use Article 71 as the crucial lever to open the door and eventually gain a strong role as participants in international diplomacy. In 1950, ECOSOC codified its definition of what were NGOs and how it would work with NGOs, in a Statute on Arrangements for Consultation with Non-Governmental Organizations. This was revised in 1968 and again in 1996.[3] Different ways of thinking about what groups are or are not NGOs, including the UN definition of NGOs, will be discussed in this chapter. Then how NGOs participate in the UN system will be discussed in the next chapter.

Narrow definitions of non-governmental organizations in global diplomacy

NGOs are often presumed to be concerned with development, humanitarian work, the environment, or human rights. Then, they may be categorized into operational groups that run their own projects or advocacy groups that seek to influence policy. Not surprisingly, such an approach appears in the definitions used by intergovernmental organizations concerned with development. A variety of restrictive definitions of non-governmental organizations is reported in Box 1.1.

Box 1.1 Competing restrictive definitions of non-governmental organizations

- "An organization which seeks funding, hires staff, and undertakes programs, but does not realize a profit"—UN Food and Agriculture Organization (FAO) Forestry Department.[1]
- "NGOs include a wide variety of groups and institutions that are entirely or largely independent of government, and characterized primarily by humanitarian or cooperative, rather than commercial, objectives"—World Bank, 1989.[2]
- "*People's organizations* can be defined as democratic organizations that represent the interests of their members and are accountable to them ... Nongovernmental organizations can be defined as voluntary organizations that work with and very often on behalf of others"—United Nations Development Programme (UNDP), 1993.[3]
- "An NGO is a private, voluntary, not-for-profit organization, supported at least in part by voluntary contributions from the public. For Development Co-operation Report purposes, an

NGO may act as a donor (if it supplies external assistance) or as an executing or beneficiary institution. The latter are usually local NGOs"—UNDP, 1996.[4]

- "Private non-profit-making agencies, including co-operative societies and trade unions, which are active in development and national in the sense that their funds are fully or mainly obtained from sources in the donor economy"—Organisation for Economic Co-operation and Development (OECD), 2000.[5]

- "NGO has become shorthand for public-benefit NGOs—a type of civil society organization that is formally constituted to provide a benefit to the general public or the world at large through the provision of advocacy or services"—Cardoso Panel, 2004.[6]

Notes

1   UN Food and Agriculture Organization Forestry Department, Glossary and Acronyms, FAO Corporate Document Repository, undated, www.fao.org/docrep/X5327e/x5327e03.htm.

2   World Bank, Operational Directive 14.70, 28 August 1989.

3   UNDP, *Human Development Report 1993* (New York: Oxford University Press, 1993) 84–85, italics in the original.

4   Used by several UNDP country offices in their Development Co-operation Reports in the late 1990s, but now no longer available.

5   OECD, DAC Statistical Reporting Directives (DCD/DAC(2000)10), 23 May 2000, www.oecd.org/dataoecd/44/45/1894833.pdf, "Key definitions," para. 28.

6   From the glossary, in the *Report of the Panel of Eminent Persons on United Nations—Civil Society Relations, We the Peoples: Civil Society*, the United Nations and Global Governance (General Assembly document A/58/817), 11 June 2004.

Several points emerge from these definitions. As the term implies, there is general agreement that NGOs are independent from governments. It is also agreed that NGOs are not profit-making or engaged in commercial activities. Transnational corporations are definitely not NGOs. Less obviously, it is taken for granted, in the above definitions, that NGOs are established *organizations* and cannot be ephemeral groups, informal associations, or unstructured networks. Thus, the consensus only extends to negative points—what are not NGOs. Little else seems to be agreed. For the Food and Agriculture Organization, they should have operational programs, but for the others this is not essential. At United Nations Development Programme headquarters in 1993 they were seen as being altruistic, whereas for the World Bank and the Organization for Economic Co-operation and Development they could be groups cooperating to look after the interests of their own members. Sometimes NGOs are seen as raising funds from the public, but others do not mention this. Some definitions focus on the group's activities, while others focus on their objectives. Various activities such as undertaking programs, funding projects, or advocacy for general public interests, are suggested but none of the definitions mention political activities to empower disadvantaged people or research to improve understanding of what development policies succeed or fail.

Even if we accept the focus on development in these definitions, they are deficient in not leading us to expect women's groups, religious organizations, or scientists to be important NGOs. The world of NGOs goes beyond standard operational and advocacy activities to include many other, less well-known, activities, such as harmonization of technical standards, maintenance of communications systems, provision of information, professional collaboration, transnational cooperation and learning, sustaining shared values or a common identity, protecting collective interests, empowerment of the disadvantaged, cultural exchanges, and promoting communal, class, gender, or ethnic solidarity. Each of the definitions quoted above is too narrowly focused on the NGOs of concern to those who wrote the definitions. None are acceptable for a general study of NGOs.

Limiting non-governmental organizations to the virtuous

Outside the world of diplomacy, in wider public debate, NGOs are often portrayed as having high moral standing. If they are altruistic groups, concerned with the general public interest, they must be worthy of support. It comes as a shock to many that the US gun lobby, the National Rifle Association (NRA), is registered at the United Nations as an NGO. It also came as a shock to the other NGOs at the UN when the NRA joined them. Some reacted by saying: surely, the NRA is not a "true" NGO. A similar pattern of thought has been evident among environmentalists. In the run-up to the 1992 Earth Summit in Rio de Janeiro, a group of 86 NGOs set up an International Facilitating Committee (IFC) composed of representatives of the "independent sectors" to run a Global Forum and to lobby the diplomats. Other more radical NGOs formed an alternative Steering Committee. One of their major disagreements with the IFC was over inclusion of "business and industry" as an independent sector and rejection of collaboration with the Business Council for Sustainable Development. There remain very many NGO activists who see business as solely being concerned with profit-making. Hence, "true" NGOs cannot collaborate with the private sector. A third challenge has arisen with the Unification Church, popularly known as the Moonies, which has had at least four front organizations working at the UN headquarters in New York.[4] These groups have also been rejected by the NGO community. To some people, the gun lobby, business groups, or the Unification Church may be acceptable groups. To others, they are self-evidently not legitimate NGOs. Whatever one's point of view, each of these groups represents very large numbers of people and has gained recognition among the NGOs at the UN. The lesson from these events is that there is not any universal moral standard for recognition of a "true" NGO.

The above point about controversy over specific groups can be generalized. It is not possible to regard all NGOs as sharing the same values and being able to adopt common policy positions. On some occasions, in some special situations, there may be high agreement among all the NGO representatives who are present at a particular meeting. However, such self-selecting sets of NGOs will not reflect the full diversity of the world of NGOs. Similarly, invocation of "the people" or public opinion with implied assumptions that everybody is united against some "bad" policy of governments ignores the fact that no government, not even a dictatorship, can operate without support from some social groups. More extreme naive idealism, which is out of touch with reality, comes in the Cardoso Report, a UN report on its relations with NGOs, produced in June 2004. This asserts there is "a new phenomenon—global public opinion—that is shaping the political agenda and generating a cosmopolitan set of norms and citizen demands that transcend national boundaries." The report even argued that "enhancing civil society relations can also keep the United Nations in tune with global public opinion—the 'second super-power'—and enhance its legitimacy."[5] Of course, public opinion is important and it is now a factor in global diplomacy. However, there is rarely a single homogeneous public opinion within individual countries and there is never any such thing at the global level. There are multiple strands to public opinion. Consequently, there are diverse strands of thought within the NGO community.

The possibility of NGO diversity is not just a hypothetical question. It exists on many global issues. The role of transnational corporations in globalization produces divisions between those who see TNCs as the engines of growth, those who see TNCs as creating poverty through their ruthless pursuit of profits, and those who think TNCs might be beneficial but only when they are regulated. The question of global population growth unites many women's groups, development organizations, environmentalists, medical professionals, and human rights activists in support of the provision of reproductive health services, in the face of bitter opposition to birth control from the Roman Catholic Church hierarchy, some radical feminists, and ultra-conservative social groups. There is a somewhat different political division over the related question of providing abortion services. Other issues—such as the reconciliation of economic growth and environmental conservation; the balance between individual human rights, the rights of social groups and the general public interest; or the role of women in society—also produce divisions within civil society.

It may be possible to *categorize* NGOs in terms of a standard of moral acceptability, their standing with public opinion, their membership, the activities they pursue, or the issues they cover, but it is not possible to *define* what is or is not an NGO by any of these criteria. Each academic analyst and each political activist can have their own idea of what is a "good" NGO, worthy of their support, but by that person's own standards there will also be "bad" NGOs. Nobody can support all NGOs, because so many of the NGOs actively oppose other NGOs. For the same reason, nobody can oppose all NGOs, because there must be some that are in accord with their own values. There is no such thing as a "true" NGO, just as there is no such thing as a "true" person.

Broad access of NGOs to the United Nations

While the UN Charter provided for the Economic and Social Council to have consultative arrangements with NGOs, the term was not defined. Thus, as one of the many tasks required to bring this new organization into being, the United Nations had to decide which organizations would participate and what rights they would have. Even before ECOSOC could hold its first meeting in January 1946, the UN had received the first four applications from NGOs to take part in its work. They were the World Federation of Trade Unions (WFTU), the American Federation of Labor (AFL), the International Co-operative Alliance (ICA), and the International Federation of Women (IFW). The General Assembly recommended to ECOSOC that it should adopt, as soon as possible, suitable arrangements for collaboration with the WFTU, the AFL, and the ICA, and two days later ECOSOC set up an NGO Committee to work out detailed proposals. The diplomats were reluctant to assume that each and any organization that applied for consultative status would be accepted, so the International Federation of Women was not endorsed at this stage.

In June 1946, it was agreed under Resolution 3 (II) that "the arrangements should not be such as to overburden the Council"; national organizations (NGOs based in a single country) would not normally be accepted; various provisions were designed to ensure access was only given to large organizations; groups of small organizations with similar interests were asked to form joint committees for consultations; and the NGOs were to be divided into three categories, with the high-status Category A organizations having substantial participation rights. The use of this hierarchy of categories became a permanent feature of the consultative arrangements, but the naming of the categories was changed each time the NGO Statute was revised. The changes are given in Table 1.1. Interesting light is shed on the difference between the expectations about NGOs in 1946 and expectations now, by the assumption Category A "will include organizations of labor, of management and business, of farmers and consumers."

The NGO Committee was impressed by the large number of applications in the first year. Except for approving the International Chamber of Commerce, they decided in October 1946 to postpone decisions on any further individual NGOs, while they continued debate on how to limit the numbers. Then in 1947 the number of accredited NGOs was increased from four to 69. Only five were national NGOs and, until the 1970s, there continued to be fewer than ten national NGOs. As many as eight were major international women's NGOs and they were asked in March 1947 to work through a Liaison Committee of Women's International Organizations "on subjects on which there is an identity of view." This attempt at limiting numbers did not work. No other joint committees were formed, and the women's committee was finally deregistered in 1963. The UN's aspirations for NGOs to form into groups for consultation have been repeatedly endorsed but have received little response. Under the provisions of Resolution 3 (II), only nine "organizations which have a basic interest in most of the activities of the Council" were placed in Category A; the great majority, 56 NGOs, were placed in Category B, as "organizations which have a special competence"; and four

Table 1.1 Changes in the names for the three levels of ECOSOC Consultative Status

Res. 3 (II) June 1946	Res. 288 B (X) Feb 1950	Res. 1296 (XLIV) May 1968	Res. 1996/31 July 1996	Type of NGO defined for the category, since 1950
Category A	Category A	Category I	General Status	Global, large membership and work on many issues
Category B	Category B	Category II	Special Status	Regional and general *or* specialist and high status
Category C	Register	Roster	Roster	Small *or* highly specialist *or* work with UN agencies

"organizations which are primarily concerned with the development of public opinion" were placed in Category C. Categories B and C received less-extensive participation rights.

These discussions in the first two years were to be typical of the attitudes of government delegates in ECOSOC and in the General Assembly, throughout the UN's history. In general terms, there was suspicion that dealing with NGOs would be an inconvenient waste of time. However, in specific terms, most individual NGOs were championed by some governments and consultative status has been granted to all conceivable types of NGOs. In the past, applications for accreditation from certain types of NGOs have been treated with hostility by particular governments in the NGO Committee. In the 1950s and the 1960s, NGOs were caught up in the general antagonisms of the Cold War. Both communist and Western governments extended their propaganda to attacking the legitimacy of NGOs backed by the opposing side, but communist front and anti-communist NGOs remained in the system. In the same period, the politics of sexuality was just as contentious. The International Planned Parenthood Federation (IPPF) was formed in 1953 but was not able to gain consultative status until 1964 and it was initially put in the lowest category.

The apparently simple question of defining what is meant by "non-governmental" is not as straightforward as ECOSOC thought initially. In June 1946, it was enough to say, "Any international organization which is not established by inter-governmental agreement shall be considered as a non-governmental organization for the purpose of these arrangements." However, this definition was not respected when in 1950 the League of Red Cross Societies (now called the International Federation of Red Cross and Red Crescent Societies—IFRC) was accredited. The Red Cross is widely known as an NGO, but it did not qualify under a strict interpretation of the first version of the NGO Statute, because each country is legally obliged to have a national Red Cross society, under the Geneva conventions. In other words, the Red Cross and Red Crescent societies *are* "established by inter-governmental agreement."

Later, as NGOs became more prevalent and more influential in international diplomacy, some governments began to establish their own NGOs, either for the corrupt purpose of trying to gain access to funds or to provide a voice for their own policies within the NGO community. These NGOs are known as GONGOs, government-organized NGOs. They occur predominantly in authoritarian countries, but in Western democratic countries more subtle questions arise about government influence through the volume of finance provided to some NGOs. Sometimes the pressures can be more direct. There was a stir of anger and disquiet in the US NGO community when the head of the US Agency for International Development referred to US

NGOs in Afghanistan and Iraq as being "an arm of the US government."[6] Nevertheless, the overwhelming majority of NGOs sturdily maintain their independence from governments most of the time. GONGOs are not a problem, because in practice their clumsy behavior soon leads to identification of what they are.

Another question concerning who is "non-governmental" is whether political parties should be accepted as NGOs. When parties are outside the government, they are literally non-governmental. Even when a party is in government, the role of party leader may be different from that of head of government. In coalitions, minority parties sometimes act quite independently from the majority party. On the other hand, today's opposition party is often tomorrow's government. Given the complexity and diversity of the political situations that could arise, the UN does not recognize any individual political party as an NGO. This is not mentioned in the NGO Statute or in any other UN resolutions or decisions, but it is clearly the established practice, as was shown when the NGO Committee in June 1997 said the application by the French Communist Party would not be acted on by the Committee. Nevertheless, political parties can still gain access to the UN indirectly: international federations of parties have been given consultative status. The Socialist International and the Liberal International both have General Status, while the Centrist Democratic International has Special Status. In addition, the Transnational Radical Party, which links individuals from different countries and from different parties, has General Status. When parties or individuals speak collectively, in an international alliance from many countries, they cannot act as the voice of individual governments and so are accepted under the ECOSOC consultative arrangements.

From the mid-1960s, applications from human rights NGOs have often encountered explicit direct opposition. Authoritarian governments gain seats on the NGO Committee, in order to block applications from NGOs that they dislike. At times they have won a majority vote in the Committee, to reject an application, but the decision has later been overturned by ECOSOC, when it considers the Committee's report. The main success of the authoritarian governments has been in establishing a general rule restricting human rights NGOs. In 1968, when the NGO Statute was reviewed, a new clause was inserted stating:

> Organizations accorded consultative status in Category II because of their interest in the field of human rights should have a general international concern with this matter, not restricted to the interests of a particular group of persons, a single nationality or the situation in a single State or restricted group of States.

In the twenty-first century, this is regarded by human rights activists as an unacceptable restriction. However, in the world of the 1960s, when country-specific human rights mechanisms did not exist, criticizing individual countries was taboo, and national NGOs were unusual at the UN, such a restriction was an acceptable compromise for democratic governments. At the next review of the NGO Statute in 1996, the clause was amended to an extremely vague general statement.

> Organizations to be accorded special consultative status because of their interest in the field of human rights should pursue the goals of promotion and protection of human rights in accordance with the spirit of the Charter of the United Nations, the Universal Declaration of Human Rights and the Vienna Declaration and Programme of Action [agreed at the World Conference on Human Rights in June 1993].

Despite this change, the 1968 approach is still applied in practice. Global human rights NGOs have to be very careful to use well-documented information and to criticize governments by comparison with global standards embodied in human rights treaties. Small specialist NGOs who act in support of oppressed minority groups in a single country will not gain consultative status.

A closely related question is whether oppressed groups that resort to violence can be accredited as NGOs. In the 1970s, two groups obtained widespread support and were allowed to participate officially in the UN General Assembly and UN conferences, but they did so as "national liberation movements" and they were accredited as Observers rather than as NGOs. The Palestine Liberation Organization was an Observer from 1974 until 1988, when the state of Palestine was proclaimed, and the South West African People's Organization was an Observer from 1976 until 1990, when Namibia became a full UN member. Two other groups, fighting against apartheid, the African National Congress and the Pan-African Congress, were also invited to a variety of UN conferences as Observers in the 1970s and 1980s. The UN has never adopted an explicit general policy on violent groups, but from the practice it is clear that such groups are not regarded as NGOs.

In the 1990s, global environmental politics led to a new debate among governments on NGO access. Until the Stockholm UN Conference on the Human Environment in 1972, the UN paid minimal attention to environmental questions and very few environmental NGOs had any contact with the UN. After Stockholm, the UN Environment Programme was established and the Environment Liaison Centre International was also founded as an NGO forum in Nairobi. Many environmental NGOs still remained outside the ECOSOC consultative arrangements. As a result, when the Rio Earth Summit, the UN

Conference on Environment and Development (UNCED), was convened, most environmental NGOs did not qualify, via consultative status, for the right to attend. As newcomers, they had to apply for accreditation to the conference. Initially, some developing country governments were suspicious that environmental concerns would become an obstacle to economic development. At the first Preparatory Committee (PrepCom) for UNCED, in Nairobi in August 1990, a determined attempt was made to restrict NGO access to Rio and a very negative set of general principles on their role was adopted.[7] Despite this, at the remaining sessions of the PrepCom the doors were opened and 1,400 new NGOs were accredited. Hostility and suspicion gave way to a pragmatic acceptance of engagement with specific NGOs.

The Earth Summit also generated a debate within the NGO community on whether commercial organizations could be included within the arrangements for NGOs. This debate would have seemed very curious to those who established the UN system. "Business" provided one of the four groups of consultants who accompanied the US delegation to the San Francisco conference to draft the UN Charter. The only NGOs accredited by ECOSOC in the first two years were four economic interest groups and one of these was the International Chamber of Commerce, *the* major global lobby for business. On the UN list of NGOs in 2005, there were six business associations with General Status, more than 30 with Special Status and more than 200 on the Roster.[8] These figures are rather imprecise, partly because the name of an NGO is not always a clear indicator of its nature and partly because various NGOs have different mixes of commercial and other interests. For example, some engineering, legal, or research bodies represent both professional and commercial interests. From the beginning, associations representing specific sectoral interests, business lobbies on particular issues, and more general federations of commercial organizations have been accepted at the UN as being NGOs.

On the other hand, there has never been any question of allowing individual companies to have any form of recognition under the arrangements for consultative status. It has not been directly stated in any UN resolution that NGOs should not be profit-making. However, this position is universally taken for granted, as we saw in the definitions given above. Funding of NGOs did become controversial in the 1960s, but as a question of the extent to which this made them agents of governments rather than their differentiation from companies. In 1968, this debate led to the inclusion in the NGO Statute of a new clause, specifying that funding of an international NGO "shall be derived in the main part from contributions of the national affiliates or other components or from individual members." While this clause was directed at reducing government influence over NGOs, it also resulted in an indirect stipulation that companies could not be accredited. NGOs could raise some income by consultancy work or by selling reports or other products, but funding could not "in the main part" be from profit-making activities.

The principle that individual companies cannot be treated as NGOs was put to the test at the Preparatory Committee meetings for the World Summit for Sustainable Development in 2002. One company was included in the list of NGOs recommended for accreditation to the summit by the Secretariat at the second PrepCom and two more companies were included in a further list presented to the third PrepCom. Both these lists were approved. An NGO representative then queried the situation with one of the influential delegates from a small Caribbean country. Both people were surprised to find the decisions had been made without the delegates being aware that companies were on the list and that a major precedent was being set.[9] The delegate later raised the question with the PrepCom Bureau and, as a result, at the fourth PrepCom, the chair announced these accreditations were being withdrawn.[10] It is unclear whether the Secretariat was deliberately trying to establish a procedure for bringing companies directly into the UN consultative arrangements or whether an overburdened official did not realize the significance of including them in the lists. Either way, the governments clearly vetoed bringing individual companies directly into policy-making processes.

When Kofi Annan became Secretary-General in January 1997, he initiated a sustained, wide-ranging program to reform the structure and operations of the UN. A major goal of the reforms was to increase the engagement of the UN with both civil society and the private sector. Annan attended the World Economic Forum of business leaders at Davos each year and in January 1999 he announced a Global Compact to associate companies with the UN. This was formally launched in July 2000, with companies being asked to endorse, implement, and promote nine "universal principles": respecting human rights in their own work; not being complicit in human rights abuses by others; upholding the rights of trades unions; eliminating forced labor; abolishing child labor; eliminating discrimination in employment; supporting a precautionary approach to environmental questions; promoting environmental responsibility; and encouraging the use of environmentally friendly technology. Later, at a Global Compact meeting in June 2004, a tenth principle, working against all forms of corruption, was added.[11]

Many NGOs were outraged by the idea of the Global Compact. Fears were expressed that the NGO voices would be submerged by companies gaining equal access and greater influence.[12] Some of the most notorious companies, such as Exxon and Monsanto, are not involved in the Compact, but for the anti-business NGOs their general suspicions were confirmed by the inclusion of Nike in July 2000 and Nestlé in February 2001. By mid-

2006, only six of the 136 large NGOs with ECOSOC General Status had endorsed the Compact. There has been a positive response from the global trades union movement and from two major human rights NGOs, Amnesty International and Human Rights Watch. The environmental movement has been divided, with the World Conservation Union, the World Wide Fund for Nature, the World Resources Institute, and the Rainforest Alliance endorsing the Compact, but Friends of the Earth, Greenpeace, and the World Rainforest Movement refusing to do so. This division is between reformist, insider NGOs, who are willing to work with business, and radical, outsider NGOs, who are not willing to work with business. Very few NGOs address corruption, but the major one in this field, Transparency International, is working with the Compact. In the NGO development community, only Oxfam and Save the Children have signed up. The first Global Compact Leaders Summit was organized at the UN's headquarters, with Kofi Annan in the chair, in June 2004. The event divided the NGO community, with 12 insider NGOs participating and 15 outsider NGOs sponsoring a counter-summit on the day before.[13] Thus, companies are not only excluded from having consultative status but also the majority of NGOs have refused to work with them in the UN's alternative mechanism, the Global Compact, and some are actively hostile.

To summarize, the Economic and Social Council of the UN will give access to the consultative arrangements to almost all organizations that are non-violent, non-criminal, and non-commercial. The involvement of governments with NGOs in international organizations does not prevent these hybrids from being accepted. Individual political parties, human rights NGOs specializing in a single country, ethnic minorities, and individual companies cannot gain consultative status, but international federations including these types of organizations can be recognized as NGOs. As a result, people from the excluded groups can participate as fully as anybody else, provided they are willing and able to attend under the auspices of some wider international NGO. At various times there have been controversies over the politics of sexuality, human rights, the environment, and engagement with business, but in each case the controversy has been resolved by including all the relevant organizations in the NGO community. The UN is open on all issues. There is only one current exception: advocacy of pedophilia puts a group beyond consideration. Some NGO leaders complain that the ECOSOC NGO Committee will refuse to endorse other types of controversial NGOs. In a few rare cases, this has happened, but the Committee decision has subsequently been overturned by ECOSOC itself granting consultative status. Sometimes the process of gaining recognition can be frustratingly bureaucratic and time-consuming, but all sections of global civil society can and do gain access to the UN.

Non-governmental organizations in domestic politics

In the analysis of the domestic politics of individual developed countries, it is common to refer to interest groups and promotional groups and the term NGO tends to be limited to development and environmental groups that are focused on foreign policy questions. Interest groups, also known as sectional groups, are business associations, trades unions, professional bodies, and other groups of people acting to maintain joint activities or common financial concerns. Promotional groups, also known as advocacy groups, enter politics to win support for a particular set of values. In the United States, they tend to be known as public interest groups or private voluntary organizations (PVOs), while in Britain they may be called pressure groups. The distinction between interest groups and pressure groups is not clear-cut. All private groups, even altruistic ones, have some interests to protect. Similarly, all private groups are likely to have some common values. Thus, all private groups may apply pressure on governments, for their own economic benefit or to promote values. However, there are never any references to pressure groups in the world of diplomacy, because it is taboo to suggest that supposedly sovereign state-actors are subject to pressure. In the practice and in the study of global politics, all these pressure groups are called NGOs when they operate in the UN system.

There is another distinction—between insider groups and outsider groups—that captures an important difference between the strategies of different groups. Insider groups work within the policy-making bureaucracies and lobby politicians behind the scenes, sometimes achieving great influence without attracting attention in the news media. Outsider groups concentrate on mobilizing public support, organizing demonstrations, and gaining coverage in the media. The boundary is blurred, because insider groups may also seek to have a large membership, to add weight to their lobbying, while outsider groups will also lobby politicians, to enhance their political credibility. Logically, an insider/outsider label is more appropriate to describe each type of *activity*, but in practice it is effective for indicating the style and the image of a group. While the distinction was developed for the study of domestic politics, it can also be applied to pressure groups operating in the UN system.

In the analysis of the politics of developing countries, it is quite common to see NGOs as external actors based in Northern countries. In the case of international NGOs, the false argument is made that they are Northern, simply because their headquarters are based in a Northern country. On this logic, the UN and all the UN specialized agencies would be Northern rather than global organizations. The argument seems somewhat less ridiculous for international NGOs that were founded in Northern countries and initially had very few Southern members or none at all. By the late twentieth century, many of the old European NGOs were transformed into truly global NGOs. Now, when an international NGO has a majority of its members from developing countries, has a governing body representing all global regions, and perhaps has a chief executive from the South, it cannot possibly be labeled a Northern NGO simply because its headquarters are in Europe. Any global organization is likely to be located in Europe or North America, because communications to these countries are better than in the South, because the headquarters facilities are often subsidized by the government or by other organizations, because the legal and political status of NGOs is more secure in Northern countries, because there is easier access to the global news media and because NGOs often wish to cooperate with or influence other global organizations based in the North. Of course, some NGOs are completely or predominantly Northern, just as some are completely or predominantly Southern. Thus, it is reasonable to describe Oxfam International as Northern and the Third World Network as Southern, although both operate on a global basis. Nevertheless, it is political nonsense to make any general link between NGOs and the North.

The term civil society was first used widely in the UN system, as an alternative to NGOs, at the World Summit for Social Development in March 1995. Given the concern of this summit with poverty eradication, gender equity, social exclusion, and people-centered development, it is not surprising that there was a focus not only on government policies but also on change within society. Many of the summit's recommendations were addressed to "all actors of civil society."[14] Subsequently, use of the term civil society organization (CSO) has become common, but it is rarely defined. One UN report did try to assert that CSOs are different from NGOs "as they may not be registered ... are not always structured and often their members are not officially recognized."[15] However, this is a very poor basis for distinguishing between organizations. Many governments do not have any system for registering NGOs, many NGOs have a minimal structure, and many NGOs do not have members. There is a different distinction that is often implicit in usage of the terms. As we have seen, in the UN until 1996, NGOs were overwhelmingly international NGOs. In contrast to this, society is a concept that has been, until recently, limited to individual countries or the more local level. The idea that there is a global civil society is still highly contested.[16] Thus, there is a tendency to assume NGOs are larger, formal, multinational organizations and CSOs are smaller, informal, national or local organizations. The distinction becomes sharper when people refer to community-based organizations (CBOs), which are usually seen as being local to one city, town, or rural area.[17] Nevertheless, there is no general agreement about any criteria that might distinguish NGOs from CSOs or CBOs. It is simpler to use the one term NGOs, and to distinguish global, regional, national, and local NGOs.

Those who do want to brand NGOs as being from the North often refer to organizations in the South as CSOs or CBOs. Such language even penetrated the UN at the highest level in the Cardoso Report on United Nations–Civil Society Relations. It is common among anti-Western nationalists in developing countries, particularly in Africa, to regard NGOs as illegitimate foreign groups who, at the worst, represent a new form of imperial influence. There seems to be an unwillingness to recognize African, Asian, or Latin American community groups, faith-based groups, cooperatives, trades unions, professional associations, federations of small businesses, environmental campaigns, or women's groups for what they are—indigenous developing-country NGOs. A more subtle argument that these national NGOs are subject to external influence, when they seek funding from Northern governments or foreign NGOs, does have some validity. Much depends on the ratio of external funds to domestic funds and whether conditions are imposed on the use of the funds. National NGOs may also be members of international NGOs or networks and, as a result, subject to foreign influence. However, this is a two-way process, in which Southern NGOs also influence the perceptions and priorities of Northern NGOs. Whatever the balance of these arguments may be for the various groups, in different countries, CSOs and CBOs in developing countries are simply Southern NGOs.

Non-governmental organizations, non-state actors, and transnational actors

For decades after the UN was formed, the term NGO remained diplomatic jargon and was a mystery to those outside the world of diplomacy, because it seemed so vague and abstract. Also, little attention was given by international relations academics to the work of NGOs. NGOs started to be recognized in the 1970s, but usually academics preferred to discuss non-state actors or transnational actors.[18] Non-state actor is sometimes used to cover organizations, such as the United Nations or the European Union, even though this is inappropriate for organizations whose members are "states." Non-state actors is a loaded term, because it privileges "states" and downgrades other actors. One might reasonably argue, in the same manner, that "non-governmental" privileges governments and downgrades NGOs. However, the term NGOs is widely recognized and often used with positive connotations. Because "non-state" is ambiguous and clearly implies a less influential actor, use of "non-state actors" should be abandoned. We can instead refer to governments and transnational actors, including NGOs, interacting in various types of international organizations.

A transnational actor is defined in academic usage as any private group from within one country that engages in activities in another country, involving another private group, the foreign government, or an intergovernmental organization. Thus, transnational actors include not just NGOs but also companies, criminals, and terrorists. Outside the academic world, the meaning of "transnationals" is more limited. Until recently, it has usually been shorthand for transnational corporations. Now it is also common to refer to transnational terrorism. The term NGOs only moved into general use in the 1980s, as there came to be regular media coverage of development, environmental, human rights, and women's issues in global politics. Unfortunately, as was argued above, it is often forgotten that NGOs cover a much wider range of groups than those reported in the media. To this day, the term NGOs is mainly used for groups that engage in transnational activities. Even groups that never deal directly with the UN and only have an indirect impact through joining NGO networks become transnational actors, by virtue of the networks being transnational. However, we can go further than this. Any private group, anywhere in the world, has access to postal services, telephones, and Internet cafés, which allows it to take part in transnational political communications. Therefore, a group that today is not transnational can chose tomorrow to be transnational.

To conclude, the actors in the politics of each country include the government departments, companies, and NGOs, as legitimate actors, along with criminals and terrorists, as illegitimate actors. Then the governments engage in bilateral and multilateral intergovernmental diplomacy, while some of the private actors may choose to engage in transnational relations. Not all NGOs go transnational and not all transnational actors are NGOs, but all NGOs are potential transnational actors. When they do engage in global politics, NGOs are thereby classified as transnational actors.

NGOs and social movements

Writers on global institutions refer to the impact of NGOs, but writers on globalization usually refer to social movements. This term is taken from work in political science and sociology on long-term social and political change within each country. Analysis of social movements concentrates on the mobilization of individuals to form a shared identity and to support radical challenge to the status quo. The classic example was the rise in a class identity to sustain the labor movement's demands for full employment, improved working conditions, and greater provision of social welfare. Widespread mobilization on civil rights, nuclear disarmament, development, the environment, and feminist questions, from the 1960s onwards, is seen collectively as the expression of new social movements, in contrast with the earlier class-based mobilization. Some add a normative dimension by referring to progressive social movements or anti-systemic movements, but others also recognize the rise of racism and religious fundamentalism as social movements. For a while in the 1990s, some analysts claimed class and the new issues had been merged under the "global backlash" of the "movement of movements": the anti-globalization movement.[19] During the Seattle demonstrations against the World Trade Organization (WTO) in December 1999, this was illustrated, when an alliance between environmentalists and trades unions was humorously proclaimed in the slogan "Turtles and Teamsters United at Last."[20]

Sidney Tarrow has defined movements as "collective challenges by people with common purposes and solidarity in sustained interaction with elites, opponents and authorities."[21] It is always implied, but not so often stated explicitly, that a movement has to be large and generally representative of a sector of the population or of society as a whole. Despite the apparent clarity, there are problems with the concept. How many people are required to turn a group into a movement? Who are the members of the movement? What is the minimum degree of involvement: is it active participation in demonstrations, passive membership of an organization, or simply support for significant change? Even when there is general agreement on the long-term goals, social movements usually contain divisions between reformers and radicals. Quite often there are also fundamental differences in the basic goals of those working together in a campaigning coalition. What is the necessary minimum breadth of common purpose, ideological coherence, and political unity?

For the purposes of this chapter, the important question is how individual people, NGOs, and social movements relate to each other. NGOs cannot be separated from movements, because some of their activities are contributions to movements. NGOs are simultaneously less than social movements and more than social movements. They are less, because many NGOs will be smaller in size and more specialized in their concerns than a movement. For example, Birdlife International is only part of the environmental movement. On the other hand, they are more, because some individual NGOs and the NGO community as a whole cover a wider range of issues than a single movement. For example, the Women's Environment and Development Organization (WEDO) covers at least three movements: women's rights, the environment, and development. In addition, the biggest NGOs may cover a larger proportion of society than small movements. At times, NGOs are seen as being limited to very formal, bureaucratic organizations that are complicit in maintaining the existing order, rather than offering a fundamental challenge to it.[22] The hostility of activists in radical movements towards their own image of NGOs sometimes can be intense. I observed a demonstration outside the World Bank headquarters in Washington DC, on 29 April 2001, at which chants expressing hostility to the Bank were mixed with chants against NGOs. The idea of NGOs being pillars of the status quo is yet another example of observers imposing their own limited perspectives on what is meant by an NGO.

The role of NGOs within movements is fundamental. Tarrow makes the crucial point, "Although it is individuals who decide whether or not to take up collective action, it is in their face-to-face groups, their social networks and their institutions that collective action is most often activated and sustained."[23] In other words, NGOs (Tarrow's "face-to-face groups") cannot be contrasted and separated from social movements. NGOs provide the leadership and communications structures that enable movements to be mobilized. Friends of the Earth, Greenpeace, the World Wide Fund for Nature, Birdlife International, the World Resources Institute, and other similar groups are each simultaneously effective NGOs and parts of the wider environmental movement. A social movement consists of a network of NGO employees and activists, who articulate a set of common values and common policies that challenge the dominant social norms and/or official policy in a particular issue-area, *plus* the members or active supporters of those NGOs, *plus* members of the general public who to some extent identify with those NGOs and take some form of personal action to generate social change.

NGOs and civil society

At the United Nations, the term civil society has been used to refer to all sectors of society taking part in political debate. From the mid-1990s onwards, the UN Development Programme and the World Bank have preferred to talk about their relationships with civil society rather than with NGOs. Since 2000, the same term started to appear in UN documents. Its usage generally implies a desire to engage with a wider range of groups, with the inference that NGOs are only part of civil society.[24]

Various political actors who have expressed antagonism towards NGOs have each given preference to a "civil society" discourse, as a way of claiming there are groups beyond the established NGOs who should be given greater priority. Developing country governments and nationalist leaders may call for greater participation from Southern civil society, in contrast to supposedly Northern NGOs. Radical and populist groups, in both the North and the South, see social movements as being more progressive than supposedly conservative groups co-opted by the UN and prefer the implied populism of the term civil society. Union leaders see themselves as having greater legitimacy, as they represent millions of members and are subject to democratic policy-making processes. Religious leaders claim to speak for faith-based communities with millions of believers and to be articulating universal moral truths. Leaders of indigenous people claim to speak for all their people and the values embodied in ancient cultures. Unions, faith-based groups, and indigenous people can assert their differences from other NGOs, by talking of civil society. Various social welfare, environmental, and development activists have a political bias towards promoting grass-roots participation in policy-making. Without there being any obvious reason, such activists often assume community-based organizations (CBOs) or civil society organizations (CSOs) are somehow very different from NGOs. In the UN Development Programme, the World Bank and in the wider Official Development Assistance (ODA) donor community, including development ministries, there is a desire to expand their existing extensive relations with development and environmental NGOs into other sectors of society, which is expressed by shifting their emphasis to civil society. Each of these different political actors is imposing limitations on what may be considered an NGO and failing to recognize its all-encompassing usage, as technical jargon in UN diplomacy. Southern civil society groups, the organizations leading social movements, CBOs, unions, faith-based groups, and indigenous people's groups are all part of civil society. They are also all represented at the UN by accrediting themselves under the consultative arrangements for NGOs.

At the country level, we may separate policy-making activities within governmental institutions from public debate about what the policy should be: that is, we separate the public sector from civil society. There remains just the private life of the individual and the family, though, as feminists remind us, the private is political, in as much as social relations structure private relations. Civil society consists primarily of organizations, which vie with each other to gain influence over the norms of social behavior and decisions on public policy. In addition, when individuals direct their attention to public debate, for example through writing letters to newspapers, exchanging comments on issues with friends or through voting, they then become part of civil society. Similarly, at the global level, civil society is the realm of public debate about global norms and global policy. With the advent of mass ownership of computers and mobile phones, many—but not all—individuals can now be part of global civil society, as easily as the civil society of their local community. Salman Pax, a Baghdad blogger, Redwood Mary, a feminist environmentalist, or those demonstrating against the Iranian government can report on major news events, with unconventional personal accounts, that move in unpredictable ways around the world. However, individuals rarely, if ever, have any impact unless their information and ideas are taken up and propagated by organized groups. Both at the country level and at the global level, we can simplify political analysis by assuming that civil society only has a significant effect through NGOs.

Some NGOs have been annoyed to find that, on the UN website, the term civil society generally brackets them with private sector commercial organizations. They have strongly asserted that society must be divided into three: the public sector, the private sector, and civil society, excluding the private sector. In contrast to this, the UN Secretariat and some governments refer to civil society as including both NGOs and the private sector. The conflict and confusion on this question is shown in the Cardoso Report on the UN's relations with civil society. The Panel's terms of reference, upon their appointment by Kofi Annan, placed the private sector within civil society. Given the deep hostility of many NGO activists to transnational corporations, the Panel made a safer political decision in putting commercial organizations into a separate category. They invented a term that was new in the world of diplomacy. They referred to three "constituencies": civil society, the private sector, and the state.[25] ECOSOC practice straddles this debate, in that individual companies cannot be accredited, but commercial associations do have consultative status. Similarly, NGOs who wish to engage with the private sector will usually argue for "multi-stakeholder dialogue" notably on environmental questions. In so doing, they simultaneously distinguish themselves from the private sector and include it in politics. There is no analytical method for resolving this dispute about the definition of civil society and there is no clear consensus among governments at the UN nor within the NGO community on either side of the dispute.

What matters for the study of global politics is that at the UN in New York, in contrast to the politics within countries, individual companies do not exercise political influence. In the wider UN system, companies can have an impact on specialized agencies, such as bankers at the International Monetary Fund or shipping companies at the International Maritime Organization. In New York, business people such as Bill Gates or Ted Turner may be important as philanthropists. Economic sectors collectively can lobby through business NGOs, but they are not in practice very active. The only institutionalized links with companies are through the Global Compact, in which political influence is flowing in the opposite direction. The UN Secretariat and NGOs are pressing companies into implementing UN-defined principles, in their commercial practices. Thus, the fear among some NGOs that the UN Secretariat's inclusion of the private sector within civil society will weaken the political influence of NGOs is fear of an imaginary danger.

In the 1990s, the collapse of the communist regimes in Eastern Europe, followed by the collapse of apartheid in South Africa, led to a revival of academic interest in the concept of civil society. The academic literature in sociology and political science focused on the country level was similar to the approach in the UN, in adopting a very broad concept to encompass the whole arena of debate about social norms and public policy. Like the UN, there have also been divisions on whether civil society includes or excludes the private sector.[26] Four different, but comparable, strands of political activity have required acceptance of the concept of civil society in the study of global politics from the 1970s onwards. Women's groups increased the density of their transnational connections and the effectiveness of their lobbying in UN policy-making. Human rights groups raised issues that were *by definition* primarily concerned not with relations between governments but with the claims made by individuals and social groups to their rights to act independently and challenge oppressive behavior by governments. Environmental groups increasingly gave priority to global questions and saw their social movement as linking the local to the global, against governments which gave insufficient attention to either level. Then, the anti-globalization movement arose and promoted an ideology of the common struggle of all humanity for global equity. In response, a new literature on transnational social movements and global civil society arose to address these issues.

As with NGOs and social movements, some writers wish to insist on a normative dimension to civil society. This has been done with great clarity in analytical work by Civicus, a transnational NGO based in South Africa. They associate civil society with the values of "trust, tolerance, democracy and civic-mindedness." It has been an "adversarial role … that has been the defining feature of civil society's relationship to state and market actors." Civil society is able to develop "consensus around a set of civic norms and a collective definition of the public good." Bodies such as the Ku Klux Klan and the Mafia are not part of civil society because the "one criterion that none of these organizations meets is the normative one" and "civil society does not include all organizations that comprise a society's associational life."[27] Several academic analysts share the activist perspective of Civicus. Richard Falk has long argued for "World Order" on a normative basis and more recently has expressed his ideals in terms of "a normative project to achieve humane governance." As part of this he identifies "emergent realities" of "creative energies" in a global civil society, growing through "transnational citizens associations" with "transformative political visions" and "the vision of cosmo-politan democracy" in "transnational initiatives that have begun to construct the alternative paradigm of a global civil society."[28] Neera Chandhoke claims "global civil society actors legislate and mandate a normative and thus a mor-ally authoritative structure for the national and international community."[29] David Chandler sees global civil society as bringing the realm of morality into international relations, previously dominated by amoral states.[30] He also argues confidently that "few people would argue against the normative or ethical concept of civil society or global civil society."[31]

In this Chandler is wrong: major writers do argue against making the concept a normative one. The editors of the first edition of the *Global Civil*

Society Yearbook assert a purely normative definition of civil society tends to become tautological. It is good simply because it only includes those whose values we think are good. They ask "are nationalist and fundamentalist movements part of civil society? Where and how do we draw the boundaries?" and conclude that the normative content of the concept is too contested to go beyond a descriptive definition.[32] Robert Fine not only criticizes "identifying civil society with ethical life" because this "avoids confrontation with the uncivil nature of civil society" but also he warns "civil society theory contains within itself elements of that which it most opposes." The dangers of totalitarian communism or fascism are present when one "opens the gates to the hunt for the Alien or Other deemed responsible for [civil society's] 'deformations'."[33] Fine's position is a restatement of the accusation that Rousseau, in arguing for obedience to the general will for a good society, was opening the doors to totalitarian leaders who legitimize their leadership in terms of morality and pursuit of the public good. John Keane alludes to a similar position: global civil society "contains no 'self-evident truths' ... indeed any attempt to project a particular bundle of norms as candidates for 'Common World Values' ... appears both reactionary and divisive." Keane goes on to make the important point, "Global civil society is at best bonded together by norms that are strongly procedural—commitments to due process of law, political democracy, social pluralism."[34]

We may conclude it is perfectly reasonable for individual political actors to propose their values *should be* universal. It is not at all reasonable for anybody to claim their values *are* universal. While recognizing there are no universally accepted values, we can take Keane's point a step further. All writers on civil society emphasize the free association of individuals in groups and free processes of political debate. Thus—for those who do not have a normative view of civil society—communists, fascists, nationalists, fundamentalists, or any other groups considered to be undesirable are part of civil society, when they engage in normal political debate. Equally, *by definition*, they are not part of civil society when they obstruct political debate and, in particular, when they resort to violence against their political opponents. On this basis, there is a limited normative component of civil society. Violent criminals and terrorists are not part of civil society. This conclusion from the academic normative debate matches precisely the practice in ECOSOC's consultative arrangements.

Thus, for the study of global politics, we may reduce global civil society to the sum of all the activities of all NGOs that have some form of transnational relations. As we have seen, many political actors will object to the conclusion that global civil society consists of NGOs. It would appear self-evident that civil society includes CSOs. However, this is no more than an argument about vocabulary. The UN can move from "NGO consultations" to "civil society hearings." This is sometimes done on an ad hoc basis, in order to bring in a wider range of participants than the NGOs who are already accredited with ECOSOC. For example, in 2006, at the General Assembly annual review of its Declaration of Commitment on HIV/AIDS, in addition to the ECOSOC NGOs, nearly 800 CSOs were accredited.[35] However, if these CSOs were to be given any form of permanent accreditation, they would have to be accepted under the existing arrangements for NGOs. Logically, it would be possible to have two sets of rules, one for NGOs and one for CSOs, but that would require the creation of a definition of the difference between the two. Nobody at the UN has ever suggested this should be done, for the obvious reason that there is no basis to distinguish between them. Another possible response, to the new fashion for civil society, would be to rename the NGO Statute as a statute for civil society. This would only make it evident that NGOs and CSOs are one and the same. In practice, at the UN, "NGOs" usually means NGOs that have consultative status and "CSOs" usually means NGOs that do not have permanent consultative status.

Conclusion

This book will use the following definition. *An NGO is any organization that has, or is eligible to have, consultative status with the Economic and Social Council of the United Nations.* Thus, the question, what is an NGO?, becomes: what are the requirements for a group to be recognized by the UN? Because consultative status is granted almost automatically to the overwhelming majority of groups that apply to ECOSOC, this is a broad definition. The groups may vary in size from mass organizations that mobilize large segments of civil society to small numbers of people. They may speak on behalf of the poor and the oppressed or they may represent privileged élites. They may engage in advocacy; run operational programs; provide a great variety of public services; promote and sustain many types of social, economic, and political cooperation; or raise funds for other organizations to spend. They may perform these activities for part of society or for society as a whole. They are not limited to groups concerned with women's rights, general human rights, the environment, development, peace, or other progressive causes. Their values may be of any type: whether progressive, conventional, or reactionary; religious or secular; nationalist or cosmopolitan. They may be in favor of globalization or part of the anti-globalization movement. They are not different from, but part of, social movements. If they seek change, their strategies may be radical or reformist. They can act as insider or outsider groups. They may be wholly or partially government-funded or refuse to accept government funds. They may be established by governments, collaborate to varying degrees with governments, or be in conflict with some or all governments.

Similarly, they may be established by commercial interests, collaborate with business, or totally reject the capitalist system. Most groups are seen, by most others, as being legitimate social and political actors. However, even when we exclude criminal groups, such as the Mafia or terrorists, some of the NGOs at the UN are not regarded as legitimate by some other NGOs. They may be from the North, from transition societies, or from the South. Their geographical scope may be global, regional, national, or local. They establish the relationships that give concrete reality to civil society. Some analysts may wish to define certain civil society groups, notably faith communities and trade unions, as being separate from the world of NGOs, but, for the purposes of studying global politics and diplomacy, there is no logical basis for making such distinctions. There can be no generally agreed definition of a "true" NGO that excludes other groups. There is no such thing as a typical NGO. NGOs are any organized groups of people that are not direct agents of individual governments, not pursuing criminal activities, not engaged in violent activities, and not primarily established for profit-making purposes.

2   The access of NGOs to global policy-making

This chapter will outline how non-governmental organizations gain access to the diplomatic processes in the United Nations and what they are able to do to influence the outcomes. The first success of NGOs was achieved in 1945 at the San Francisco conference that agreed the text of the UN Charter. They lobbied for the inclusion of a new article, to obtain the right for NGOs to be involved in the formal proceedings of the UN. The result, Article 71, was a radical innovation, in providing for NGOs to participate in intergovernmental diplomacy. On the other hand, it was cautious and limited, in vaguely referring to consultation and in restricting the role of NGOs to the work of the Economic and Social Council (ECOSOC). We will start by examining how ECOSOC established an NGO Committee to handle applications for consultative status and to supervise the consultative arrangements. It will again be necessary to refer to the three versions of the Statute on Arrangements for Consultation with Non-Governmental Organizations, originally agreed in 1950 and amended in 1968 and 1996.[1] We will see that since 1970 a wider range of activities has been developed, going far beyond the official procedures listed in the Statute. In addition, NGO participation has been extended beyond ECOSOC to all parts of the UN system. The reader may wish to skip one or more of the sections on NGO access to the less well-known parts of the system, such as the operational programs, the global conferences, the treaty bodies, or the specialized agencies. However, a comprehensive overview has been given, in order to sustain the claim there is access throughout the system and NGOs have some influence on all policy questions.

The work of ECOSOC's NGO Committee

One of the first decisions of ECOSOC in 1946 was to establish an NGO Committee to oversee the consultative arrangements. Initially, the Committee was dominated by the "Big Five" (China, France, the Soviet Union, the United States, and the United Kingdom). Its composition changed significantly in the

Table 2.1 Composition of ECOSOC's NGO Committee

Regional Group	Seats 1966–81	Seats since 1981
Africa	2	5
Asia	3	4
Eastern Europe	2	2
Latin America and the Caribbean	2	4
Western Europe and Others	4	4
Total Committee Membership	13	19

1960s, when the impact of African countries joining the UN worked its way through all the principal organs. First of all, ECOSOC was increased in size from 18 to 27 members in 1965. Then, the next session of the Council increased the size of its NGO Committee to 13 members, with a further increase to 19 members in 1981. These changes did much more than simply increasing the size of the Committee. In 1966, for the first time, it became representative of the UN's membership as a whole, with a formal requirement for the seats to be divided out between the regional groups. The political effect was to change the NGO Committee, from one in which there had always been a clear Western majority, to one in which there would always be a majority from the developing countries.

From the beginning, the role of the NGO Committee has been to evaluate applications for consultative status, to consider requests from existing NGOs for reclassification to a higher status category, and to manage NGO relations with ECOSOC. From 1968, it has also been required to review reports by NGOs on their work and to decide whether controversial NGOs should be deprived of consultative status. On four occasions, in 1946, in 1949–50, in 1967–68, and in 1993–96, the Committee has been expected to be a major forum for negotiations on the nature of the consultative arrangements. Each of these responsibilities will be considered in turn.

Applications for consultative status

Deciding which organizations should have consultative status and which should not still takes up the majority of the Committee's time. The text of the NGO Statute suggests an NGO must have a formal institutional structure. From 1946, there was supposed to be "an established headquarters, with an executive officer" and from 1968 policy-making was supposed to be determined by "a conference, congress or other representative body" with an executive organ responsible to it, under a "democratically adopted constitution." In practice, the majority of NGOs do not possess the formal policy-making structures required by the Statute, but this has been no barrier

to accreditation. For most NGOs, it is not these neglected political requirements but bureaucratic procedures that have been the main obstacle to gaining
consultative status.

From 1946 to 1972, the Committee met regularly in conjunction with
ECOSOC sessions. The aim was to complete its work prior to ECOSOC
opening, so that new applicants for consultative status could, if approved, take
part in ECOSOC's work straightaway. In 1973, this approach was adversely
affected by a general decision of ECOSOC requiring its subsidiary bodies
only to meet once every two years. This meant the non-consideration of an
application, due to a backlog of work or referral for further information, could
lead to the NGO having to wait four years or even six years before they gained
accreditation. Then, in July 1995, ECOSOC requested the Committee to meet
annually again. However, a year later, the Statute was revised to allow a new
category of NGOs, national NGOs, to apply, resulting in a steep increase
in the volume of work. In 2003, the NGO Committee was able to improve
the situation by becoming the UN's first "paperless committee" with the
delegates using laptops.

The formal application by an NGO must include answers to a questionnaire
about their work, copies of their annual reports, and full details of their funding. Members of the Committee can and do pose questions to the applicants
about aspects of special concern to them. For example, the Chinese government is vigilant in blocking any NGO that suggests Tibet is not part of China.
There will also be detailed probing on the NGO's finances, if the sources of
their support are not clear from the application documents. Although human
rights NGOs may be harassed, when they are persistent, they can expect to
be accredited eventually. For example, in the 1980s, the Lawyers' Committee
for International Human Rights (now known as Human Rights First) made
no progress with its application across five sessions of the NGO Committee,
but finally gained Category II status in 1991.

A second aspect of the mandate is the need for the NGO Committee to
decide, when NGOs are accepted, in which category they should be placed.
They do not always gain what they request. The NGOs were from the beginning divided into three categories. The categories have been renamed, but the
current definitions, in ECOSOC Resolution 1996/31, carry through the essential political features of the distinctions made in 1950. General Consultative
Status covers global NGOs:

> [O]rganisations which are concerned with most of the activities of the
> Council and its subsidiary bodies ... have substantive and sustained
> contributions to make ... and are closely involved with the economic
> and social life of the peoples of the areas they represent and whose
> membership, which should be considerable, is broadly representative

of major segments of society in a large number of countries in different regions of the world.

Special Consultative Status covers important NGOs that are more limited in their scope:

> [O]rganisations which have a special competence in, and are concerned specifically with, only a few of the fields of activity covered by the Council and its subsidiary bodies, and which are known within the fields for which they have or seek consultative status.

The wording for the two categories does not explicitly allow for NGOs that cover a wide range of issues, while being limited in their geographical scope. However, one of the minor amendments made in 1996 was to add the words "in different regions of the world" to the definition of General Status. This means the previous practice of awarding no more than Category II status to regional NGOs should in principle continue, limiting them to Special rather than General Status.[2] The third category of NGOs was originally defined from 1946 to 1950 as "organisations which are primarily concerned with the development of public opinion and with the dissemination of information." In response to the unexpected large number of rather specialist NGOs who were interested in relating to the UN, it was decided in 1950 to expand the definition of the third category, now known as the Roster, to other organizations

> which the Council, or the Secretary-General of the United Nations ... considers can make occasional and useful contributions to the work of the Council or its subsidiary bodies. ... This list may also include organisations in consultative status or similar relationship with a specialised agency.

In 1968, the Secretariat lost the right to include NGOs on the Roster. While no significant changes in these definitions were made in 1996, a major change in their application was agreed. NGOs that are based in a single country (known as "national NGOs") are now encouraged to apply for Special Status or a place on the Roster. Prior to 1996 this had only been permitted for a few exceptional cases.

During the 1950s, each side in the Cold War objected to NGOs that appeared to support the other side. However, this was an uneven contest, as Western NGOs could be criticized but not blocked by the communist governments. On the other hand, the Western countries had enough votes to prevent new pro-communist NGOs being accredited. After the deepening of the crisis over apartheid in South Africa in the 1960s, the developing countries paid detailed attention to any connections between NGOs and South Africa, but did not systematically object to all work in the country. Thus, Oxfam was respected for its assistance to poor people who were victims of apartheid, but the International Police Association was struck off the list in 1985, after it was discovered it had 850 policemen from South Africa as individual members. In recent years, only a narrow focus on the rights of specific ethnic or national minorities and the politics of pedophilia have been systematic barriers to acceptance.

Requests by accredited NGOs for reclassification

Alongside the new requests for consultative status, the Committee also receives requests from NGOs that are already accredited to be reclassified from the Roster to Special Status or from Special Status to General Status. In principle, if the NGO Statute was fully respected, an NGO would only be upgraded if and when it was able to show it had expanded the global coverage of its membership or it had expanded its range of activities. In practice, reclassification is regarded by both NGOs and governments as an increase or decrease in the status of the NGO concerned.

The clearest example of the change in the political climate affecting an NGO's classification is for the International Planned Parenthood Federation (IPPF). It was formed in 1953, but in the 1950s it faced deep hostility from many governments, particularly in Catholic countries. In this period, whenever it was suggested that family planning might be discussed at the World Health Organization, some governments threatened to leave the WHO if this were to happen. In the early 1960s, under the impact of the Second Vatican Council, the Catholic Church started to reform and it was widely expected that the opposition to family planning might be modified. As a result, IPPF gained consultative status in 1964, but it was initially put in the lowest category. In September 1965, the International Union for the Scientific Study of Population (IUSSP) organized the Second World Population Conference in Belgrade. It brought home to the wider public how fast the world's population was growing. When Pope Paul VI issued an Encyclical Letter, *Humanae Vitae*, in July 1968, strongly reaffirming opposition to family planning, criticism of papal authority arose, even among Catholic theologians. During the ECOSOC review of the classifications of all NGOs that took place in 1969, IPPF was promoted to Category II. Finally, in May 1973 IPPF was promoted to Category I, so that it was a high-status participant at the World Population Conference in August 1974.

The highest status used to be reserved for the most prestigious global NGOs. In 1948, only nine of the 69 NGOs had gained Category A status. By 1968, this had increased to just 12 of the 377 NGOs. Thereafter, the numbers slowly climbed to reach 41 NGOs in Category I from the total of 969 accredited NGOs in 1993. The review of NGOs in 1993–96 led to a doubling of the numbers in General Status to 80 in 1996 and a trebling from 1993 to reach 120 in 2000. Thereafter the numbers increased slowly, reaching 136 by 2005 and stabilizing at that level. No sooner had the new version of the NGO Statute been agreed in 1996, tightening the 50-year-old definition of General Status NGOs, than its provisions began to be violated regularly. By 2005, among the supposedly global NGOs 14 were clearly regional and 15 were national. Other NGOs, such as the International Council of Environmental Law and the Organization of World Heritage Cities, were global, but were too specialist to be "concerned with most of the activities of the Council." In other words, from 2005 onwards, somewhere between one-fifth and one-third of the General Status NGOs were not eligible to be in that category and should have been in Special Status or on the Roster.[3]

Arrangements for NGO written statements and hearings

The next question after deciding which NGOs should be consulted was what would be meant by consultation. In the early years, there were two main forms of activity. Written statements could be submitted to the Secretariat, who would translate them into the UN's official languages and circulate them as official UN documents. In the first eight years, there were on average about 50 statements per year.[4] In the days when the UN had a smaller membership and a smaller agenda, this was a worthwhile contribution to the diplomatic process. Despite the massive increase in the number of NGOs since then, the right is now rarely exercised at ECOSOC by any of the major global NGOs. In addition to written statements, requests could be made for oral "hearings." In the early years, NGOs made their speeches concerning Council business to open meetings of the NGO Committee, which then provided written summary records in a report to the Council. There is evidence of some influence upon ECOSOC, because delegates did at times refer to points made in the NGO hearings. On one occasion, the hearing led the NGO Committee to recommend a draft resolution, which was later adopted by ECOSOC. The role of the NGO Committee was changed in 1968 with respect to hearings, when it ceased acting as an intermediary, and NGOs now address ECOSOC directly.

In 1946 the World Federation of Trade Unions had made demands for much more extensive participation rights, including full membership of ECOSOC with the right to vote. Although there was no support among government delegates for such a radical demand, the status of the WFTU was sufficient for it to win the right for Category A NGOs to request the addition of an item to the agenda. When ECOSOC agreed to such a request, the NGO was allowed to open the debate on the item and to respond to comments made by governments. In recent years, NGOs have been more interested in setting the global agenda of public debate through the news media than in adding items to the formal agenda of ECOSOC and this right is rarely exercised. Nevertheless, the existence of this right is granting an extraordinary privilege to the higher status NGOs. It is inconceivable that the US Congress or the British House of Commons would ever take the comparable step of granting the right to pressure groups to initiate a debate on the floor of the house.

The provisions for participation, in the current version of the NGO Statute, are summarized in Table 2.2 below. While these formal provisions were used and regarded as being important in the early years of the UN, we will see below that they now only represent a limited aspect of NGO engagement with multilateral diplomacy. Of the five types of participation, only the ability to make oral statements during the debates is used to the maximum obtainable extent in all forums by NGOs. Much depends upon the relative sympathy of the chair towards NGOs and the evolution of the established practice for the particular committee, in determining the frequency and timing of NGO contributions. Submission of written statements for circulation as official UN documents is not used at all in some fora, but it is used extensively in the Human Rights Council. The significance of the Statute lies less in the specific text and more in the overall assertion that NGOs have participation rights. This is of immense symbolic importance. It legitimizes the physical presence of NGOs in the UN buildings, their political presence in the policy-making

Table 2.2 Official NGO participation rights in ECOSOC and its subsidiary bodies

Participation Right	General Status	Special Status	Roster
Receive all documents	Yes	Yes	Yes
Attend all meetings	Yes	Yes	Yes, for meetings within their field
Propose agenda items	Yes	No	No
Written statements (a) in Council and (b) in subsidiary bodies	(a) 2,000 words (b) 2,000 words	(a) 500 words (b) 1,500 words	If invited, the same as Special Status.
Oral hearings (a) in Council and (b) in subsidiary bodies	(a) Yes (b) Yes	(a) If no other body covers the issue (b) Yes	(a) No (b) If invited

processes, and any activities they undertake to influence delegates—within the limits of diplomatic decorum.

Loss of consultative status

In 1968, a whole new section on "Suspension and Withdrawal of Consultative Status" was added to the NGO Statute. The key provision specified an NGO may lose accreditation:

a   if there exists substantiated evidence of secret governmental financial influence to induce an organisation to undertake acts contrary to the purposes and principles of the Charter of the United Nations;

b   if the organisation clearly abuses its consultative status by systematically engaging in unsubstantiated or politically motivated acts against States Members of the United Nations contrary to and incompatible with the principles of the Charter;

c   if, within the preceding three years, an organisation had not made any positive or effective contribution to the work of the Council or its commissions or other subsidiary organs.

The NGO community was initially very worried by this change, as they feared their freedom to criticize governments would be circumscribed by the threat of expulsion from consultative status. In practice, the ability of NGOs to operate in a critical manner has steadily expanded, even in the field of human rights. Nevertheless, each of the three criteria has been of significance.

The prohibition on secret government funding was originally included by developing country governments who suspected Western funding would be used to support opposition groups in their countries. In practice, the danger for the UN comes from developing country governments themselves setting up "government-organized NGOs" (GONGOs), to gain a voice within the NGO community and to pursue their policies at the UN. There may be a few GONGOs that have slipped through the net, but they have not been struck off. The provision is more important in preventing GONGOs being accredited, when they submit their applications.

The second criterion on "politically motivated acts" is vague and meaningless as it stands. It can only be understood in terms of human rights NGOs being required to have a general international concern and not a special focus on a single government. On this basis, the Indian government has been able to block applications from the World Sikh Organisation and the Chinese government has blocked a variety of Tibetan-oriented NGOs. However, the ability to prevent country-specific NGOs from gaining consultative status does not protect governments from criticism. General human rights NGOs can and sometimes do accredit, as their representatives, people from countries with a poor human rights record. There are limits to what can be done with such a procedure. When Christian Solidarity International (CSI) put forward John Garang, the leader of the Sudan People's Liberation Army, to speak at the Commission on Human Rights in March 1999, there was a storm of protest. The matter was referred to the NGO Committee and on its recommendation ECOSOC decided to revoke the consultative status of CSI. Even the US government representative who voted against this decision was severely critical of CSI allowing Garang to "deliver an intemperate speech" and, along with several European Union countries, had suggested a penalty of suspension for their "transgression."[5]

Another case of a similar kind produced much more controversy. The Russians were furious when in April 2000 the Transnational Radical Party (TRP) put forward Akhiad Idigov at the Commission on Human Rights. He made the mistake of introducing himself as the European representative of President Aslan Maskhadov of Chechnya. The Russian delegate immediate interrupted on a point of order and Idigov corrected himself to say he was speaking on behalf of the TRP. However, he went on to accuse the Russians of genocide and to claim Chechnya was an independent state. A few weeks later, the Russians took the initiative in the NGO Committee and called for withdrawal of the TRP's consultative status, with wild accusations that it supported terrorism, promoted drug trafficking, and condoned pedophilia. The TRP replied that it was devoted to the Gandhian principle of non-violence, did not support secessionism, and had done no more than discuss drugs and pedophilia as social issues. On 23 June 2000, the NGO Committee endorsed a compromise "consensus" recommending suspension of the TRP for three years. This was not a genuine consensus, as the US delegation dissociated themselves from the decision. The following month, the United States and delegates from the EU fought back in ECOSOC. They succeeded in having the question referred back to the Committee, on the grounds that an NGO is supposed to be given written reasons for its suspension and have an opportunity to respond. Two Committee meetings were held in July solely on this question and, as the Russians introduced new information, the TRP was given a further chance to reply in September. After all this attention to due process, the NGO Committee reaffirmed its original decision, but ECOSOC in October decided not to endorse the suspension of the TRP. In the final Committee vote, the majority of the developing countries had sided with Russia and only Chile and Romania voted with the United States and the two EU countries. The result in ECOSOC was different, because only 18 of the 34 developing countries voted with Russia.[6] The TRP had had a narrow escape.

The debates on the Chechens caused such deep divisions, because they pitched the principle of sovereignty against the principles of human rights.

The Transnational Radical Party maintained its consultative status, albeit by narrow margins, because it was genuinely engaged on a broad range of human rights concerns and because it was able to mobilize very strong support from some European governments, notably the Italian government. In the same period, other more specialist NGOs were rejected by the NGO Committee without ECOSOC overturning the Committee's decision. In 2000, applications from the Assyrian National Congress, the Tamil Centre for Human Rights, and the North American Taiwanese Women's Association were rejected. Applications from the Kashmiri American Council and Vishva Hindu Parishad (the World Hindu Council) were not rejected, but simply deferred for further consideration, year after year.

The third criterion for suspension is not making any "positive or effective contribution" to ECOSOC's work. This would appear to offer potential for protracted disputes, but it has actually been applied in a simple bureaucratic manner. Since 1968, NGOs have been required to make reports on their work every four years. The failure to make an effective contribution has become the failure to submit a quadrennial report. Different penalties have been applied to different NGOs. Sometimes an NGO is reclassified to a lower status. Sometimes an NGO has its status suspended for a year or even withdrawn permanently. This does have the advantage of deleting from the list NGOs that have become defunct. There has been varying practice on whether particular NGOs are given extra time to submit their reports. In recent years, the reporting process has also been used by various delegations on the NGO Committee to harass individual NGOs, by criticizing their activities and requesting further information, before the report is accepted.

There is another source of problems, which is not mentioned in the NGO Statute. NGO representatives do not always behave in a manner appropriate for a diplomatic forum. Incidents have occurred in which delegates have been subject to verbal abuse or physical harassment at the meetings of the Commission on Human Rights in Geneva. Heckling has occurred in the General Assembly. Most of these cases have been handled by the NGO concerned apologizing and promising never again to accredit the individuals involved in the incidents. In one case, two representatives of the Peruvian group, Tupac Amaru, rushed towards the US delegation and unfurled a banner. In a second, more extraordinary case, a representative for A Woman's Voice International was alleged to have produced and activated a Taser gun. In both cases, the NGO was suspended for one year. Most NGOs were extremely worried by these incidents, because there was widespread talk of drawing up a code of conduct for NGO behavior. After a while the debate on a code of conduct was quietly forgotten, but NGOs became much more careful about who they accredited and security around UN buildings was greatly increased.

Reviews of the overall arrangements for consultation

The NGO Committee has also been responsible for reviewing how the consultative arrangements operate. Sometimes there are minor procedural changes that simply modify the Committee's practice, such as setting deadlines for the receipt of new applications for status. In addition, there have been much more substantial formal reviews of the whole text of ECOSOC's Statute for NGOs, resulting in new versions of the Statute in 1950, 1968, and 1996. The most remarkable aspect of these reviews is how little has changed. The second and third reviews were long and arduous, with major divisions between those governments who wished to support NGO participation and those who sought to impose restrictions. The outcome from such a process was to make few changes to the established text. Much of the wording of the current Statute can be traced directly back to the first ECOSOC resolutions in 1946–47.

Only one change has been of political significance. Until 1996, national NGOs were not normally accredited. In particular, a national NGO could not gain consultative status if it was a member of an international NGO that was already accredited. Thus, it was decided in 1991 the various Save the Children national associations would lose their Category II status after the International Save the Children Alliance obtained Category I status. The change in 1996 was based on the false perception that the majority of accredited NGOs should be regarded as being from the global North. It might have been more accurate to say that global NGOs were likely to be represented at the UN by people who live in New York and hence NGO representatives were disproportionately from the North. The aim of giving access to national NGOs was to increase participation by developing country NGOs. The initial perverse effect at the end of the 1990s was to produce a set of national NGOs among whom the largest category was NGOs from North America. Then, a little later, many of the new NGOs from the South, notably from Cuba and Tunisia, were regarded as being GONGOs, government-organized NGOs. Now after more than a decade a much wider range of countries is represented, but it is a tiny fraction of the potential number of applicants. In practice, as developing country activists can attend UN events through their connections to international NGOs, the crucial question is not the accreditation of national NGOs. The really important factor is whether a potential participant can fund travel to and accommodation in New York or Geneva.

A few months after the third review was completed, Kofi Annan took over as Secretary-General in January 1997. He was the most ambitious reformer the UN has ever seen. In particular, he was a strong supporter of civil society participation in the UN, but his early initiatives obtained insufficient support among the government delegates. In September 2002, Annan appointed a Panel of Eminent Persons on UN–Civil Society Relations, known as the Cardoso Panel, and it reported in June 2004. Because the Panel was over-ambitious, intellectually incoherent, and politically insensitive, it too made little impact upon the legal and procedural status quo.[7]

Current NGO participation in ECOSOC and related institutions

The practices for NGO participation developed in the early years of the UN are reflected in the NGO Statute, but the new practices developed in more recent years are not mentioned. When the third version of the Statute was produced in 1996, it was not updated to reflect the richness and diversity of current activities. Indeed, to have done so might have risked putting a block on innovation. Written statements may not be circulated very often as formal UN documents, but a variety of written materials is provided by NGOs for the government delegates. The corridors in the UN headquarters building are very wide and large tables are placed along the walls near to the doors of the meeting rooms. During debates on major global issues, these tables are stacked with NGO leaflets, reports, position statements, and newsletters. Many delegates browse through the display, taking what interests them, on their way into the meeting. Oral statements during the *formal* debates are not sufficient for achieving political influence. Even when NGOs can speak in every meeting during the session of a commission, only a small propor-tion of the NGO representatives have the opportunity to speak and the time allocated is only a few minutes for each speech. Nevertheless, speeches at *informal* events can offer a real opportunity for dialogue. During the long lunch breaks and at the end of the day a variety of lectures, seminars, and debates is held as "side events." These are initiated by governments, notably the EU, the Group of 77 developing countries, or the United States, or by the major NGOs in the subject or occasionally by the Secretariat. They may be held in the smaller committee rooms in the UN building, at various NGO buildings, principally Church Center, which is just across the road from the UN headquarters, or in a government's Permanent Mission to the UN.

Until the advent of the Internet, the right to receive copies of UN documents was crucial for NGOs to have a basic understanding of what was happening in the UN. Now the UN must be a leading contender for holding the world's biggest non-commercial website. Special pages are set up in advance of the sessions of all important bodies, with a full guide to the main documenta-tion and the facility to download all the major reports, background papers and the records of previous meetings. NGO representatives can arrive a few days before the session opens and be as well briefed as the average govern-ment delegate. The Internet is not only useful in preparing for attendance at the session but also it has the advantage that involvement and influence is open to those who are not present at the UN. NGOs can use the Internet to communicate back home, feeding stories to the news media, or asking supporters to lobby their government in the capital city. NGOs can establish much larger coalitions to endorse policy statements, by use of e-mail list servers, discussion forums, their own websites, and websites for broader networks of NGOs. The advent of the Internet has in effect made the UN as transparent as any political system can be and also made it easier for groups around the world to have their voice heard at the UN.

It is important to distinguish between the official provisions of the NGO Statute and the actual practice. Generally, the rights spelt out in the Statute are the minimum an NGO can expect. Sometimes, if they are not used, they can become moribund. More often, practice will evolve and become more generous to NGOs than is provided for by the Statute. In ECOSOC itself, the participation rights are generally only used by a few of the General Status organizations and by the Conference of Non-Governmental Organisations in Consultative Status with the United Nations (CONGO) on behalf of all the recognized NGOs.[8] However, they are used extensively in ECOSOC's commissions, its other subsidiary bodies and other political processes related to ECOSOC. There is a total of more than two dozen subsidiary bodies. Some, such as the Group of Experts on Geographical Names, may have a significant impact in their obscure field, but attract little attention, beyond a few highly specialist NGOs. The main bodies are listed in Table 2.3.

The functional commissions and other subsidiary bodies of ECOSOC

When the UN was formed, the functional commissions were expected to offer "non-political" advice to ECOSOC, which would be a policy-making and coordinating body. In the early years, most of the commissions remained obscure and to quite an extent operated as independent forums for experts. Since the early 1970s, they have attracted a great deal more public attention, especially from NGOs, and have become significant intergovernmental policy-making bodies. Their importance is greatly increased prior to major global conferences, when they may act as the preparatory bodies, and afterwards, when they are mandated with a "follow-up" role. The NGO Statute spells out the rights of NGOs in these commissions, but the different practices that have developed within each commission are rather more important than the precise text of the Statute. It should also be noted that the commissions generally do not pay attention to the distinctions between the three categories of NGOs.

Table 2.3 The main subsidiary bodies of the Economic and Social Council

Functional Commissions
  Commission for Social Development
  Commission on Crime Prevention and Criminal Justice
  Commission on Human Rights (only from 1946 to 2006)
  Commission on Narcotic Drugs
  Commission on Population and Development
  Commission on Science and Technology for Development
  Commission on Sustainable Development (since 1993)
  Commission on the Status of Women
  Statistical Commission

Standing Committees
  Committee for Programme and Coordination
  Committee on Non-Governmental Organizations

Other Bodies
  Committee for Development Policy
  Committee on Economic, Social and Cultural Rights
  United Nations Forum on Forests (since 2001)
  Permanent Forum on Indigenous Issues (since 2002)

In the Commission on the Status of Women (CSW), there is an especially strong relationship between the NGOs and the governments, not least because the majority of representatives on both sides are women. In some countries, the government delegates hold consultations in the capital city, before each session of the CSW, with a national network of women's NGOs. The delegates often have strong personal links with women's NGOs. Sometimes, NGO people are appointed as government delegates. These links have made it easy for NGOs to communicate with the delegations and to influence the decision-making processes. The CSW has also evolved a more extensive range of events than is usual in many other UN bodies. The sessions start with two high-level roundtables organized by the NGO Committee on the Status of Women and the UN Secretariat's Division for the Advancement of Women. The roundtables focus on a key issue for the session, with the debate led by ministers and a few selected NGOs also making contributions. Then there is a series of panels, which are rather like academic seminars with presentations by government experts, international civil servants, academics, and NGO specialists, the balance depending on the topic. One of the functions of the panels is to float ideas on "emerging issues" with the result that their proceedings will at times influence the agenda for the following year's session. The roundtables and panels are recorded as being part of the official proceedings of the CSW. In addition, there is an extensive program of more than 250 unofficial "parallel events" during the two-week session. Some of these are sponsored by governments, in their own name or in collaboration with NGOs, and are held in the UN building. Other events are solely under the auspices of NGOs and are mainly held in Church Centre. In addition, there are extensive opportunities for NGOs to lobby the delegates.

One outcome from the Rio Earth Summit was the establishment in February 1993 of a Commission on Sustainable Development (CSD) under ECOSOC's authority. The CSD was mandated to review the implementation of *Agenda 21*, the main policy document adopted at Rio. It included a section on "Strengthening the Role of Major Groups" with separate chapters on the "partnership" relationships required between governments and nine sectors of society.

The list of Major Groups is arbitrary in including, for example, women, but not men; young people, but not the elderly; indigenous people, but not other minority groups; and trades unions, but not professional associations. It is strange to include local authorities, which are governmental bodies, among the social groups. It is also logically incoherent that one of the nine Major Groups of NGOs is "non-governmental organizations." Nevertheless, the concept of Major Groups passed permanently into UN diplomacy on all environmental questions. Despite the apparent innovation, all the participants in the Major Groups must still have been approved by ECOSOC for consultative status or for accreditation to the Earth Summit, or to subsequent conferences.

The CSD sessions open with stakeholder dialogues, in which several of the Major Groups organize the speakers to initiate the debate at the opening meetings on the year's special topic. These dialogues can directly influence ministries concerned with sustainable development, because government desk officers responsible for the special topic are flown in, to supplement the permanent delegation. The layout of the debating chamber is symbolically important. During the stakeholder dialogues, the NGOs arranged in their Major Groups are seated in the center and the governmental delegates are seated around the edge.

Table 2.4 The specification of "Major Groups" in the *Agenda 21* chapter headings

24)	Global action for women towards sustainable and equitable development
25)	Children and youth in sustainable development
26)	Recognizing and strengthening the role of indigenous people and their communities
27)	Strengthening the role of non-governmental organizations: partners for sustainable development
28)	Local authorities' initiatives in support of *Agenda 21*
29)	Strengthening the role of workers and their trade unions
30)	Strengthening the role of business and industry
31)	Scientific and technological community
32)	Strengthening the role of farmers.

Source: *Agenda 21*, Section III (UN General Assembly document A/CONF.151/26), 14 August 1992.

During the subsequent policy debates, the seating is returned to normal, but a few NGOs can still make statements at the end of each meeting.

Other commissions and other subsidiary bodies of ECOSOC do not usually receive so much attention from NGOs and several do not have the same sense of the centrality of the NGOs to the proceeding as in the Commission on the Status of Women, the Commission on Sustainable Development or the Commission on Human Rights (discussed below). Nevertheless, when a commission is acting as the preparatory committee for a major global conference, (such as the population conferences or the "social summits"), there can then be very high levels of NGO engagement. Similarly, when bodies become the negotiating forum for a global treaty, such as the Open-Ended Working Group of the Commission on Human Rights that drafted the Convention on the Rights of the Child, then NGOs can become deeply involved in the proceedings and have a significant influence on the text of the treaty.[9] In some subsidiary bodies, a smaller number of more specialist NGOs may be intensely involved. For example, the UN Forum on Forests, established by ECOSOC in October 2000, follows the practice of the CSD in relating to Major Groups, but fewer NGOs attend. The Permanent Forum on Indigenous Issues is interesting in that political problems about the status of indigenous people/peoples were avoided by constructing a forum of independent experts. This enabled the 16 members to include eight nominated by governments and eight nominated by indigenous people's organizations. This is the only body within the UN that gives NGO representatives the status of *members* rather than observers or consultants, but officially it is not membership of an intergovernmental body.[10]

There are no standard procedures (other than the NGO Statute) and no consistent patterns to delineate the full range of NGO participation in ECOSOC bodies. The experience with the CSD and the Convention on the Rights of the Child negotiations are instructive. In each case, at the very start of the political process, many government delegates were highly suspicious of NGOs and did not wish to engage with them. As each side learnt from their interactions, the hostility of the delegates gradually declined, until after some years important new procedures became routine and NGOs gained privileges in the respective issue-areas that they do not have elsewhere. Progress for NGOs does not come from the overall reviews and changes to the Statute but from the steady evolution of practice.

The Human Rights Council

Until 2006, the Commission on Human Rights was an ECOSOC subsidiary body. As a result, the ECOSOC Statute for NGOs used to apply to its deliberations and NGOs were a strong presence at its sessions. When the General Assembly by Resolution 60/251 abolished the Commission on Human Rights and replaced it by a Human Rights Council from June 2006, primary responsibility for human rights questions was transferred from ECOSOC to the General Assembly. The question arose whether NGOs could still be involved. Because of the crucial leadership role of NGOs in the UN's work on human rights, the new Human Rights Council would have had no credibility unless it too had established formal consultative arrangements with NGOs. It was decided that participation of NGOs would be based on the NGO Statute and previous practice. This was a radical change for the UN, in formally extending consultative status, on a permanent basis, to a General Assembly body, for the first time in its history.[11]

NGO involvement in human rights questions has been the most vigorous and most controversial aspect of the UN's relations with NGOs. In the next chapter it is argued this amounts to a revolution in international law, by violating the sovereignty of states. In the final chapter, a summary is given of the wide-ranging political achievements of the human rights NGOs. We should also note that this is the issue-area where outside the intergovernmental world NGOs have exceptionally high status. The news media rarely cover any human rights questions without reporting on the positions taken by NGOs. The role of NGOs in the global politics of human rights cannot be stated too strongly. Without their work, the UN Charter would not have mandated anybody to discuss human rights, the treaties would not have been drafted, the political mechanisms would not have had any sources of information, the High Commissioner would not have been established and oppressive governments would have continued to be able to shelter behind sovereignty.

Operational programs of the United Nations

There are several programs—variously known in official documents as funds, programs, offices, or institutes—which focus on operational activities around the world. The programs are semi-autonomous units, with distinct mandates, their own budgets and their own directors, who are important political leaders. Nevertheless, each of these programs is legally an integral part of the UN. Their mandates are dictated by the General Assembly; their administrative budgets are part of the main UN regular budget; and their directors are part of the UN Secretariat. The most prominent ones, in the order in which they were established, are:

- UNICEF: United Nations Children's Fund, 1946
- UNRWA: United Nations Relief and Works Agency for Palestine Refugees, 1949
- UNHCR: Office of the United Nations High Commissioner for Refugees, 1949

- UNDP: United Nations Development Programme, 1965
- UNFPA: United Nations Population Fund, 1967
- UNDCP: United Nations International Drugs Control Programme, 1971
- UNEP: United Nations Environment Programme, 1972
- INSTRAW: United Nations International Research and Training Institute for the Advancement of Women, 1976
- Habitat: United Nations Human Settlements Programme, 1977
- UNIDIR: United Nations Institute for Disarmament Research, 1980.

All of these were established by the General Assembly and have their own executive committee, board, or council, to oversee their activities.[12] With two exceptions, they all report to ECOSOC. However, because the General Assembly oversees ECOSOC and is responsible for the budgets of all UN bodies, it may also review the work of these programs. UNRWA and UNIDIR report directly to the General Assembly.

One aspect of being relatively autonomous is the ability of each executive to decide independently how they will relate to NGOs. They all cooperate extensively with NGOs in their operational activities, but the role of NGOs in relation to the policy-making sessions of the executives varies considerably. UNHCR has an especially close relationship with the Red Cross. UNEP and Habitat each have a Governing Council, which meets in Nairobi, and their rules have always explicitly provided for NGO participation. In addition, the Environment Liaison Centre International has its headquarters in Nairobi and provides a strong NGO network to support access to both councils.

UNICEF from the beginning had a unique relationship with NGOs, because transnational relief activities for children were under way in the aftermath of the military conflict in Europe, before the UN had even been formed. Unlike any other UN program, when UNICEF was established it issued an appeal to the public for funds and many NGOs responded energetically. This group of NGOs eventually evolved into the NGO Committee on UNICEF, which became the focus for consultative relations between NGOs and UNICEF's Executive Board. In addition, UNICEF National Committees were formed in many countries and they still "contribute roughly one third of UNICEF's over-all income."[13] In the 1950s, 1960s, and 1970s, there were extensive exchanges between the NGO Committee on UNICEF, the National Committees, individual NGOs, and UNICEF's Board and secretariat. Gradually, from the 1980s these relations declined. Project-oriented NGOs concentrated more on relations with UNICEF at the country level, and advocacy NGOs focused more on the negotiations on the text of the Convention on the Rights of the Child and then the implementation of the convention. UNICEF is exceptional in being a UN body that used to have strong relations with NGOs at the central policy-making level, but now no longer does so. However, there is still occasional close cooperation on an ad hoc basis, particularly for global conferences on issues affecting children.[14]

In December 1993, the General Assembly passed Resolution 48/162, a long and complex resolution, on restructuring the UN's social and economic work, including specifying new mandates for the governing bodies of UNDP, UNFPA, and UNICEF. One result of this was to impose upon the executive boards of these three bodies an obligation to amend their rules of procedure to allow for NGOs "to participate in the deliberations without the right to vote." UNICEF's Executive Board was surprisingly reluctant to respond to these instructions. Negotiations had to continue through a Working Group and three sessions of the Board in 1994 before a text was agreed. The outcome of this obscure abstract debate was an important political shift, from easy denial of NGO access to a presumption they would attend UNICEF's Board.[15] UNDP and UNFPA simply refused to follow the General Assembly's instructions. They have a joint Executive Board, which went through three and a half years of debate to amend its rules of procedure. The new rules still carry the presumption that NGOs will *not* be involved in its work, unless "it considers it appropriate" to "invite" them to participate on "questions that relate to their activities."[16] In practice, the Board's reports have no mention of NGOs being invited to attend. It is an extraordinary anomaly that the section of the UN that has the highest level of operational collaboration with NGOs has no consultative processes in its central policy-making.[17]

United Nations conferences

International conferences are convened either by ECOSOC or by the General Assembly for two main reasons: to discuss new global issues or to negotiate the text of treaties. In addition, there have been conferences covering trade in commodities and others to pledge funds for UN programs. On the principle that conferences are autonomous diplomatic events, they are not bound to follow UN practices. Indeed, the very reason most of them are convened is to initiate a new political or legal process, outside the confines of existing institutions. This means each conference has to decide its own structure, agenda, and rules of procedure. While conferences have legal autonomy, they are subject to substantial political influence from the general norms of UN practice and from the politics of UN preparatory processes.[18]

Until the 1970s NGOs generally had considerably fewer rights at conferences than in ECOSOC, while since the mid-1980s they have increasingly had a higher political status and better participation opportunities than in ECOSOC. Participation in debates has increased from a single token speaker on the last day trying to represent the whole NGO community, to some forums allowing NGOs to make brief interventions every morning and afternoon. Access to decision-making has changed from a minor role in the main plenary bodies to significant influence in the committees and NGO representatives quite often taking part in the small working groups where the more difficult questions are thrashed out. In some fields, such as human rights, population planning, and sustainable development, NGOs have changed from being peripheral advisers of secondary status in the diplomatic system to being high-status "social partners" at the centre of policy-making.[19]

Before the 1970s, UN conferences were generally low-key events and some were more like academic conferences than intergovernmental political events. A substantial change occurred when Maurice Strong was appointed to be the Secretary-General for the 1972 United Nations Conference on the Human Environment (UNCHE) in Stockholm. First of all he mobilized the scientific NGOs to consolidate the existing research on threats to the environment in reports that would be accessible to non-specialists. Then, he sought public engagement, initially by involving women and young people. By the time of the conference, the UN, the Swedish government, and NGOs were collaborating in organizing an NGO Forum. The conference became a major political event, not only for diplomats but also for NGOs, the news media, and hence the general public. The Forum provided a ferment of ideas in NGO workshops and other public events. Friends of the Earth organized the production of a daily newspaper, *ECO*, for the period of the conference. This provided publicity for the Forum, NGO articles on the broad issues, and news reports on the official proceedings. As a result, some of the diplomats and UN officials, including Strong, attended some of the events at the Forum. In particular, NGOs raised the question of the threat to whales, both in Forum events and in a demonstration in Stockholm. The question was added to the UNCHE agenda and a resolution passed, calling for a ten-year moratorium on whaling.

NGOs exercised influence on the official conference through four channels: public debate in the news media, open access to the forum, consultative status at the official conference for some ECOSOC NGOs, and individuals from NGOs being appointed as government representatives at the conference. The Stockholm conference became the model for a new type of global conference. Twenty years later, the 1992 Rio Earth Summit made a mark by massively increasing the scale of NGO participation and by being the first global political event to be covered on the Internet. Then, the World Summit on Sustainable Development in Johannesburg in 2002 went further with more extensive NGO participation in the preparatory process and the main event. NGOs were involved, mainly via the Major Groups, in six thematic "partnership" plenary events—the general debate, four roundtables, and a "multi-stakeholder" event—all of which were part of the official conference proceedings. In addition, there was a diverse range of unofficial civil society events.[20]

After Stockholm, NGOs became more deeply involved in the planning of conferences and at all the major conferences they organized their own forum. They expected to and were able to influence the official proceedings. Gradually, the UN developed more complex political processes to plan conferences, with several sessions of preparatory committees, and gradually it became taken for granted that NGOs would have access to these processes. From the early 1970s, there was a steady evolution in accreditation of NGOs. Attendance at UN conferences moved from being dependent upon invitations issued by the Secretariat, through "relevant" NGOs being allowed to apply, to all NGOs recognized by ECOSOC having an automatic right to register. By the 1980s it was standard to allow other "interested" NGOs to apply.

The evolution in the practices for NGO accreditation and participation in UN conferences was finally codified in Part VII of ECOSOC Resolution 1996/31, the third version of the NGO Statute approved in July 1996. This embodied an immense political shift. Instead of the preparatory committee arguing about each application and NGOs being blocked if a small number of governments opposed them, the UN Secretariat is now expected to make a positive recommendation for accreditation, as long as the NGO "has established its competence and the relevance of its activities." When the Secretariat recommends rejection, it must give reasons and the NGO has a right of reply. Then, the preparatory committee is expected to take a decision within 24 hours and, if it does not, the default position is for the NGO to be given "interim accreditation." Thus, the standard position now is for all genuine NGOs—genuine by the criteria in the NGO Statute—to be accredited.

Treaty bodies managed by the United Nations

When governments commit themselves to legally binding agreements, these may be called treaties, conventions, covenants, articles of agreements, constitutions, statutes, or charters. For simplicity, we can refer to them all as treaties. Many of the major global treaties on arms control or on environmental questions contain clauses for conferences of the parties to the treaties (COPs) to meet regularly to review progress in their implementation. They also provide for a small secretariat to carry out any monitoring processes, conduct research, and organize the COPs. Although these are often the product of conferences organized by the UN and although the UN often provides premises and runs the secretariat, they are legally not part of the UN. They are the responsibility of the particular group of countries that have ratified the relevant treaty and this never coincides exactly with the membership of the UN. Nevertheless, because UN practice establishes global norms for diplomatic behavior, these independent conferences have in recent years also given access to NGOs.

At the COPs for the conventions on endangered species, biodiversity, desertification, climate change, and the other environmental questions, there is very open access for NGOs. The text of each of the four main conventions simply specifies that an NGO only has to inform the secretariat of its wish to be represented and it will be admitted unless at least one-third of the treaty parties object. The NGOs are also given the higher status of "Observer" on a par with UN specialized agencies and governments of countries that have not ratified the convention. At the Copenhagen Climate Change Conference in December 2009, for example, nearly a thousand NGOs were present. The range and balance of these NGOs was rather different from the standard attendance at UN events. In particular, there was a large number of commercial associations (but not individual companies) from the energy sector and from sectors that are high users of energy. The environmental NGOs coordinated strategy and strengthened their political impact by working through the Climate Action Network. More radical NGOs collaborated in a loose coalition as the climate justice movement, through Friends of the Earth International, Climate Justice Action, and other networks. However, the scale of NGO and media interest became a disadvantage. The number of people in the second week of the conference was more than double the 15,000 official capacity of the building, so access was restricted, causing resentment among those who were excluded.[21]

The situation is somewhat different for treaty bodies on other issues. The human rights treaties do not have regular COPs. On the other hand, they have elected committees that review regular reports on implementation of the treaty provisions by the governments. It might appear from the text of these treaties that there is no role for NGOs in the reviews. However, the committees have extended their own procedures, by inviting governments to answer questions on their reports and inviting NGOs to provide information so that the questions are challenging and penetrate through any bland complacency in the reports. The Convention on the Rights of the Child has gone the furthest in embodying a role for NGOs, because under Article 45 they are expected as "other competent bodies" to provide "expert advice on the implementation of the Convention." Governments are required to report regularly to the Committee on the Rights of the Child, which oversees the Convention, and in many countries NGO coalitions prepare alternative reports, to present to pre-sessional working groups in Geneva. NGOs are also invited "to participate in the pre-session working group tasked with making the agenda for the meeting."[22]

In the area of disarmament and arms control, substantial NGO participation in treaty review conferences is a more recent phenomenon. During the

Cold War, the 1968 Non-Proliferation Treaty (NPT), preventing the spread of nuclear weapons, was the only global treaty requiring continual political attention, but for 20 years NGO input was little more than rhetoric, at their own fringe meetings. The Acronym Institute in 1994 started to seek more focused and more professional NGO contributions. Then the Women's International League for Peace and Freedom (WILPF) created the Reaching Critical Will project in 1999, with the aim of promoting and facilitating the engagement of a wider range of NGOs in UN processes related to disarmament, especially nuclear disarmament. The NPT fifth review conference in 1995 decided to strengthen its processes and these two NGOs obtained a new procedure for one "informal" meeting devoted to NGO contributions, at each session of preparatory meetings and the main conference. They also were allowed to make their publications available on tables in the corridor. However, NGOs were still excluded from the detailed committee work and found it difficult to obtain copies of documents. Development of the WILPF website in 2000 meant access to documents was greatly improved. WILPF also produced a daily conference newspaper, *News in Review*, on the website and in print at the meetings. Despite there now being better access, the accreditation of NGOs to these conferences cannot be taken for granted. In a peculiar departure from UN practice, under the NPT rules, even those NGOs accepted in previous conferences have to reapply for each new conference. In the period after the Cold War, during George Bush Sr.'s term as US president, many more governments wanted to mobilize support from NGOs, in order to maximize the coalition against the Bush administration. Large NGO networks became important in the diplomacy to create the treaties to ban landmines and cluster munitions. The resulting treaties refer explicitly to the role of NGOs in implementing the treaties and give NGOs Observer status at their review conferences. The change from the NPT to the more recent treaties is substantial.

United Nations specialized agencies

It was emphasized earlier that funds and programs are part of the UN, while agencies are independent from the UN. This is even true for agencies, such as the United Nations Educational, Scientific and Cultural Organization (UNESCO), that have the words "United Nations" in their formal title. The 19 agencies are established by distinct treaties, conventions, constitutions, or agreements. Their membership is determined by which governments ratify these treaties, as a separate act from ratifying the UN Charter, and none of them has exactly the same membership as the UN. They have separate secretariats and separate budgets. The term "UN specialized agency" is reserved for independent global institutions that have signed an agreement to cooperate with the UN through ECOSOC. The International Atomic Energy Agency (IAEA) and United Nations Conference on Trade and Development (UNCTAD) behave politically as if they were agencies, but they are actually part of the UN.

At times attempts are made to suggest the agencies should standardize their relations with NGOs, but this is unlikely to happen, because the agencies jealously guard their independence and are reluctant to change well-established practices. NGOs have their strongest relations with the Global Environment Facility and the four large agencies, International Labour Organization, FAO, UNESCO, Food and Agriculture Organization and WHO, which have large budgets and large operational programs in developing countries. They work with these agencies both at the project level within countries and at the central policy-making level. The ILO is a special case: it is constituted so that trades unions and employers from each member country are seated in its annual General Conference and have full participation rights, including the right to vote. In addition, other NGOs have a consultative relationship with the ILO, similar to their role in the UN. UNESCO also felt the need for an exceptionally strong relationship with NGOs, to the extent that for some decades it subsidized some of the major international NGOs concerned with its work, by providing them with offices in UNESCO's headquarters building and assisting with their administrative costs. The WHO differs in being much more sensitive about relations with transnational companies and their international NGOs. As the WHO runs a campaign called Tobacco or Health it would not have relations with tobacco manufacturers. There are similar controversies that prevent it giving NGO status to company associations from other industries. In sharp contrast to the WHO, the small, specialist, technical agencies have especially close relations with company associations.

The World Bank and to a lesser extent the International Monetary Fund (IMF) and the World Trade Organization (WTO) have strong relations between their staff and NGOs, but do not allow any direct access to the policy-making boards. Bank staff started holding specialist workshops with NGOs in the 1970s and in the 1980s this was institutionalized into a World Bank–NGO Committee, which met on an annual basis for a wide-ranging policy review. During this period, NGOs exercised substantial policy influence, especially on standards for environment impact assessment and popular participation in projects. The Committee, which consisted of a small number of self-selecting NGOs, gradually lost its legitimacy when larger numbers of NGOs became active on global development questions. It stopped meeting at the end of the 1990s and was eventually replaced in 2003 by a Civil Society Policy Forum, held in conjunction with the spring and fall meetings of the Bank and the Fund. This meets for a period of four or five days, holding 40–50 policy dialogue sessions, on the basis of proposals from NGOs, foundations, or

Table 2.5 Independent agencies in the UN system

The major specialized agencies

International Labour Organization
Food and Agriculture Organization of the United Nations
United Nations Educational, Scientific and Cultural Organization
World Health Organization

The financial specialized agencies

International Monetary Fund
The World Bank Group

The technical specialized agencies

International Civil Aviation Organization
International Fund for Agricultural Development
International Maritime Organization
International Telecommunication Union
United Nations Industrial Development Organization
Universal Postal Union
World Intellectual Property Organization
World Meteorological Organization
World Tourism Organization

Other autonomous UN entities

International Atomic Energy Agency
United Nations Conference on Trade and Development

Inter-agency or joint programs

World Food Programme
Joint United Nations Programme on HIV/AIDS
Non-Governmental Liaison Service

Other global bodies cooperating with the UN

International Sea-Bed Authority
Global Environment Facility
World Trade Organization

---

staff of the Bank or the Fund. The Forum has had two advantages over the previous Committee. There is open access, allowing engagement with many more NGOs. In addition, the association with the IMF meetings has opened up a dialogue between NGOs and the IMF's staff. A similar forum is held each year by the WTO in Geneva. From the early 1990s, the Bank gradually became much more transparent in making its documents publicly available on the Internet. In 2009, the Bank made a radical shift towards complete public access for all documents, with effect from 1 July 2010. The Fund started to publish policy documents concerning its lending activities from January 2001, with "voluntary but presumed" permission from governments. From

January 2010, consent no longer has to be explicit, but is on a "no objection" basis. However, this still leaves the Fund much less open than the full freedom of information at the Bank. The WTO also keeps many documents secret. Thus, there is immense variability in the ability of NGOs to gain access to information, to relate to staff, and to exercise influence within the economic institutions.

One other part of the UN system is worthy of special note. The Non-Governmental Liaison Service (NGLS) was established in 1975 as an inter-agency program. This status enables it to be rather more independent and imaginative in promoting engagement between NGOs and the UN system than is possible for most international civil servants. It publishes a highly informative newsletter, *Go Between*, two or three times per year; a series of reports on key special events at the UN; handbooks to brief NGOs about the UN system; and guides to obtaining access to particular events. While it is of value to all NGOs, its main focus is to achieve higher levels of participation by NGO representatives from developing countries. The inter-agency status of NGLS allows it to convene annual meetings of all the staff in the UN system who are responsible for relations with NGOs, to encourage them to learn from "best practices."

NGO participation in the General Assembly

Since 1950, the NGO Statute has specified NGOs shall have "appropriate seating arrangements and facilities for obtaining documents" at the General Assembly. In spite of this, NGOs have been unable to gain formal participation rights at its regular sessions. The question was last debated seriously during the 1993–96 review of the Statute. At the end of the review, developing countries were pushing hard for ECOSOC to recommend NGO participation in the General Assembly. The US delegation was bitterly opposed and so ECOSOC only asked the Assembly to "examine" the question. For a few years, the Canadians and some NGOs tried to keep the question alive, but they made no progress. The explanation of US government opposition seems to be that they wanted no precedent to suggest NGOs might participate in the Security Council.[23]

Although the principle was maintained that NGOs have no political rights in the General Assembly, they still are able to exercise influence. The mere fact of being in the building to attend meetings enables NGO representatives to speak to delegates in the corridors and the restaurants. In many cases, there will already be mutual recognition from personal relationships established at ECOSOC commissions and other bodies which do accredit NGOs. In addition, there are many ad hoc ways in which they are allowed to participate on particular occasions. First, since the 1970s, when the General Assembly has held a special session, to handle one specific issue, NGOs have been accredited. In the 1990s, a series of special sessions was held as "plus five" follow-up reviews of major UN conferences. In such situations, when NGOs had been a vigorous presence at the original conference, it was politically untenable to exclude them from the reviews, five years later. This process went the furthest when, five years after Rio, statements were made by representatives of Major Groups in most of the plenary meetings of the Nineteenth Special Session, called in June 1997 to review progress with *Agenda 21*.

The sensibilities of delegates are less in subsidiary bodies of the General Assembly. From the 1960s, the Special Committee Against Apartheid worked closely with NGOs in order to increase the pressure against the apartheid regime. There has also been a curious practice of allowing NGOs to speak in a Main Committee, but pretending they have not done so, by formally "suspending" the meeting for the few minutes when the NGO person is speaking. More recently, the possibility has arisen of the General Assembly officially authorizing NGO involvement in subsidiary bodies. When it established a committee in December 2001, to draft a Convention on the Protection and Promotion of the Rights and Dignity of Persons with Disabilities, the resolution merely invited NGOs to make "contributions to the work." The Commission on Human Rights responded in April 2002, by applying pressure for the drafting committee "to adopt working methods which allow for full participation by relevant non-governmental organizations." The General Assembly relented and in July 2002 it authorized participation in the committee by representatives of ECOSOC NGOs and other interested NGOs. However, it carefully ended the resolution by asserting the "arrangements shall in no way create a precedent."

Two subsidiary bodies of the General Assembly *have* engaged with NGOs on a permanent basis. The first of these, the Conference on Disarmament, has done so very cautiously. NGOs did not have ready access to debates on disarmament in the early years, because ECOSOC has no direct responsibilities in this area and during the Cold War most of the significant negotiations started outside the UN. Nevertheless, the Quakers gained consultative status in 1948 as the Friends World Committee for Consultation and established high respect for their quiet work for peace behind the scenes. The situation improved for NGOs when, during the period of détente, the General Assembly agreed to convene a Special Session on Disarmament (UNSSOD I) in 1978. Prior to this session, the Quakers organized 23 seminars for delegates from 58 smaller countries. NGOs were allowed access to the preparations and to UNSSOD itself, including the holding of an NGO Day when 25 NGOs addressed the General Assembly. Afterwards, the new permanent forum, the annual Conference on Disarmament, accepted NGOs could be present and provide "communications" that would be "made available to delegations on request" and "a list of all such communications" would be circulated, but they could *not* make speeches.[24] In the early years, the NGOs interested in disarmament were poorly organized. UNSSOD had improved the situation and further substantial improvement occurred through WILPF's Reaching Critical Will project. However, it was not until February 2004 that NGOs obtained a decision giving them the right to display their publications at the Conference on Disarmament and to have an informal meeting devoted to their presentations, following the practice at the NPT conferences.[25] Thus, despite being limited in the Charter to economic and social questions under ECOSOC, NGOs now have the ability to influence disarmament debates and arms control negotiations, under the auspices of the General Assembly.

The other subsidiary body of the Assembly that has officially recognized NGOs on a permanent basis is the Human Rights Council. As was mentioned above, the Council was intended to be of much higher status and authority than the previous ECOSOC Commission. It is bringing the full vigor of NGO activities to a body at the level of a principal organ. Although this change in 2006 made no difference to the involvement of NGOs in the politics of human rights, it did establish a precedent that NGOs could have extensive participation rights in a body that reports directly to the General Assembly.

Kofi Annan's attempts to strengthen the UN's relations with global civil society, through appointing the Cardoso Panel, were partly aimed at bringing NGOs more into the General Assembly's work. However, neither government delegates nor NGO representatives took seriously many of the proposals in the Panel's report. In particular, the naive proposal to move the accreditation of NGOs from ECOSOC to the General Assembly was dismissed by all except the EU and the Australian government. In the debate on 4–5 October 2004, many developing country governments argued that any role for NGOs in the General Assembly would undermine its "intergovernmental nature," but others supported involvement of NGOs, particularly if there could be increased participation by developing country NGOs. This left sufficient room for maneuver to achieve agreement in December 2004 on an experiment with "Informal Interactive Hearings" in June 2005, prior to the summit-level meeting in September. They were held under a special, carefully crafted, compromise set of procedures. NGOs were welcomed to the Hearings at a plenary meeting, but the five debates were "Informal" and hence were not part of the General Assembly's official proceedings. NGO contributions were not recorded in the verbatim records, but summaries were forwarded to the September summit. One taboo was broken. Renate Bloem, President of the Conference of Non-Governmental Organizations in Consultative Relationship with the United Nations, was one of the three speakers at the opening meeting. She thus became the first-ever NGO representative to address a plenary meeting of a regular session of the General Assembly. The Hearings did result in the introduction of new language into the September summit's Outcome Document, particularly on sustainable development, on women's issues, and on human rights. Following the breakthrough in 2005, there has been a series of hearings and roundtables associated with the General Assembly, devoted to specific issues on its agenda. They have covered international migration and development, implementation of the Programme of Action for the Least Developed Countries, UNICEF's World Fit for Children program, HIV/AIDS; Interreligious and Intercultural Understanding, and Africa's development needs.

Taken together, the general access to the building, the participation in Special Sessions, the involvement in the Main Committees, the participation in a few subsidiary bodies, and the recent development of hearings have not significantly modified the legal position. NGOs still have no permanent, general, recognized, formal participation rights in the General Assembly itself. Looked at differently, the political change has been enormous. NGOs can now reasonably expect to exercise influence on all policy-making in the General Assembly on sustainable development questions, women's issues and human rights. They cannot confidently expect to affect policy-making on other issues, but with skill, knowledge, planning, and good communications it is worth making the attempt.

NGO participation in the Security Council

It was assumed for decades that there was no possibility of NGOs having any role in the UN Security Council. Officially, that is still the situation. However, various methods have been adopted on a pragmatic basis to enable Security Council delegates to gain information and understanding by hearing testimony. In March 1992, during the crisis over the disintegration of Yugoslavia, Ambassador Arria of Venezuela met a priest from Bosnia. Arria was President of the Security Council and he felt the other members should hear what the priest had to say, so he invited them all to meet over coffee in the Delegates Lounge. Thus, the members of the Security Council met without there being an official meeting. Whenever this is done, it is know as an Arria Formula meeting.[26] Shortly afterwards, debate started about reform of the Security Council and, in 1995, James Paul, the Executive Director of Global Policy Forum, took the lead in forming an NGO Working Group on the Security Council. This quickly established itself as a forum for debate and interaction between NGOs and diplomats interested in reforms to produce a more transparent and accountable body. In 2000, a group of women's NGOs formed a distinct NGO Working Group on Women, Peace and Security, to campaign for women's issues to be given direct consideration in the responses to conflict situations.

The first attempt to use the Arria Formula to cover a meeting between NGOs and Security Council members met significant opposition, but a meeting still went ahead on 12 February 1997 under the auspices of Ambassador Somavia of Chile. Oxfam, Médecins sans Frontières, and CARE provided a briefing on the refugee crisis and conflicts in the Eastern Congo and neighboring countries. The Somavia Formula, focusing on delegates with responsibility for humanitarian questions, could not easily be repeated for further meetings. Later the same year, Ambassador Monteiro of Portugal, who had been collaborating with the Working Group for some time, decided to invite Pierre Sané, the Secretary-General of Amnesty International, to an Arria Formula briefing on human rights and armed conflict. Initial opposition was overcome by calling it an "ad hoc event" and the meeting was held on 15 September 1997, with Sané arguing that the breakdown of human rights provides early warning of potential conflict. Disagreement about NGO access continued until some key personnel changed and the next meeting was held in April 2000. From then onwards some three or four meetings per year have been held. The strongest examples of NGO influence on the Security Council are Resolution 1314 (2000) on Children in Armed Conflict and Resolution 1325 (2000) on Women, Peace and Security, both of which were passed shortly after Arria Formula meetings on the topic.[27]

Conclusion

If we summarize the practice, it is plain the NGO Statute does not provide the main framework for deciding which NGOs should or should not be granted consultative status. The default position is for any national or international NGO to be accepted. Some rules, such as being established for more than two years or being open about their funding, will generally be enforced. Other rules and general abstract arguments are simply used as weapons on a pragmatic basis, depending on whether each government feels the particular NGO will be hostile or sympathetic to their position. This occurs in specific ways, as when individual human rights NGOs are denied accreditation or struck off the list. Hostility to NGOs can also occur for more general reasons. The West supported environmental NGOs gaining access to the Earth Summit, against hostility from developing country governments, who were worried that environmental issues might become constraints upon development. The developing country governments have supported development NGOs wanting access to the World Bank and the IMF, against hostility from the US delegation, who were worried that US dominance of these financial institutions might be threatened.

Once an NGO has gained consultative status its representatives are admitted to all meetings of ECOSOC and its official subsidiary bodies. The rights to participate are generally only used in the full Council by a few NGOs. However, they are used extensively in the subsidiary bodies and here the status classifications make little difference to what can be done. The consultative arrangements have evolved steadily, especially since the 1970s. First, the relationships have become more intense. In a great variety of bodies, new methods of interaction between governments and NGOs have been adopted. Some of these are incorporated into the official proceedings, while others remain unofficial "side-events." Second, the relationships have become more extensive. Participation now has expanded from economic and social issues to virtually all issues, in virtually all parts, of the UN system. Relations evolved with UN specialized agencies from the 1940s onwards in parallel to, but separate from, the arrangements with ECOSOC. Starting in the 1970s, NGOs have become a significant presence in UN conferences, in treaty bodies, and on the fringes of the General Assembly. Since the late 1990s, NGOs have increasingly been granted access, but no *right* of access, to the General Assembly and the Security Council. Further evolution is to be expected, but this is not likely to be the result of further attempts to amend the NGO Statute nor ambitious plans for reform proposed by the Secretariat. On specific issues it will seem important to include NGOs in the policy-making process. At specific meetings the chair and various respected individuals will suggest new forms of interaction. Gradually, what is innovatory will become normal. The last bastions to resist formal relationships with NGOs will be the International Monetary Fund and the Security Council.

The most important variables determining the rights of NGOs are not the formal rules, but the status, the expertise, the communication skills, and the trust established in personal relationships between NGO representatives and government delegates. Four variables tend to determine the actual extent to which governments allow the NGOs to participate. The smaller the decision-making body, the less it has a public profile, the more technical the subject matter, and the more experienced are the NGO representatives, the more likely it becomes that the NGOs can take a full part in the discussions and exercise significant influence. Sometimes issues will not fit into such a pattern. When there is a high-level decision-making body, with a high public profile, high levels of public concern about an issue, such as climate change, can also result in significant NGO influence. Usually, this will require a two-pronged strategy. Technically competent and experienced NGO "insiders" gain support from more radical "outsiders" who campaign on the streets and in the media.

It must be remembered that NGOs are always vulnerable to devices for excluding them, when a majority of the government delegates want to meet in private or when the individual in the chair is hostile to NGOs. One response has been to exclude NGOs by declaring a meeting to be "informal." Because NGOs have increasingly been admitted to informal meetings, delegates sometimes resort to "informal-informals" to exclude NGOs. Another pressure on NGOs arises when the UN security staff tighten up security measures. Since September 2001, the permanent NGO representatives based in New York have felt insulted that they can no longer use the diplomats' entrance to the UN headquarters but have to pass through security at the public entrance. Continual pressure by CONGO has failed to reverse this change. When individual delegates instruct security staff to deny access for NGOs to particular events, this can usually be overcome by an appeal to the secretariat for the meeting. Finally, there is a severe practical problem for NGO representatives traveling from developing countries: they have to submit applications for a US visa three months in advance and applications are sometimes rejected arbitrarily. Nevertheless, all these problems only have a marginal impact on NGO participation.

The impact of NGOs can rarely be seen on a particular day at a specific meeting. Even when an identifiable victory is achieved, it is the result of years of research, communicating with supporters, promoting debate in the media, and lobbying of delegates. This chapter has demonstrated that the global political system has been changed, so the NGOs do now have the access to be able to use their lobbying skills.

3 The status of NGOs in international law

There is a normative debate, in which some people are loosely in favor of all non-governmental organizations, some wish to define "true" NGOs as the only ones worthy of support, and some are hostile to all NGOs, identifying them as participants in an unjust social and political system. There is also a second, quite separate, analytical debate over the question whether NGOs need to be included in the study of international relations. In this chapter, the question will be examined from the perspective of international law and in the next chapter from the perspectives of political science and sociology. International law was for three centuries, from the Peace of Westphalia in 1648, defined simply as the law covering the relations between states. It is a radical challenge to conservative academics and conservative practitioners to discuss the status of NGOs. It is in the nature of lawyers to emphasize the historical traditions on which law is based, the relevance today of precedents from the past, certainty in its interpretation, and the need for continuity in its practice. Nevertheless, law is not static and over time radical changes can occur. It is now absolutely incontestable that since the Second World War international law has evolved to include legal persons other than states. The question is whether the evolution has gone so far as to include NGOs.

This chapter will start by illustrating how the concept of international legal personality has been extended to include intergovernmental organizations. Then, it will be argued that there has been a long period of evolution in the international status of NGOs, starting with a few anomalous cases gaining privileges of statehood. The politics of the UN has also evolved to engage many NGOs in a manner that challenges the traditional view of state sovereignty. A third change has been the conferring of rights and responsibilities upon NGOs by international treaties. Then special attention will be given to hybrid international organizations that have both states and NGOs as members. Finally, it will be argued that Economic and Social Council's (ECOSOC) NGO Statute has gained the status of customary international law and confers international personality to those NGOs accredited under its provisions.

Intergovernmental organizations in international law

Until the creation of the United Nations, it was generally agreed the only subjects of international law were states and intergovernmental organizations (IGOs) were no more than the sum of the activities of their member states. The door was opened for many IGOs to be international legal persons by recognition first being given to the UN. From a contemporary perspective, it is surprising to note that the drafters of the UN Charter in 1944–45 did not themselves feel able to accord *international* legal personality to the UN. Article 104 contains a more limited obligation on UN members to give the UN "legal capacity" within their *domestic* law. However, attitudes soon changed and, in February 1946 by Resolution 22 (I) A, the General Assembly approved the text of the Convention on the Privileges and Immunities of the United Nations, which asserted the "United Nations shall possess legal personality." Despite this, following the assassination of Count Bernadotte in September 1948, while he was acting in Jerusalem as the UN Mediator in Palestine, the General Assembly by Resolution 258 (III) requested an advisory opinion from the International Court of Justice (ICJ) on whether the UN has "the capacity to bring an international claim against the responsible … Government." The ICJ unambiguously came to the conclusion, with its Opinion in April 1949, that the UN "is an international person … a subject of international law."[1]

Despite the increasing recognition of intergovernmental organizations as subjects of international law in diplomatic practice in the 1950s, the Vienna Convention on Diplomatic Relations of April 1961 only refers throughout to "the sending State" and "the receiving State." It does not even explicitly cover the activities of permanent missions established by many governments at the headquarters of the UN in New York, its Office in Geneva and specialized agencies in other cities. Furthermore, the wording does not cover diplomatic missions staffed by UN or agency personnel. Similarly, for the purposes of the Vienna Convention on the Law of Treaties of May 1969, a treaty was defined as meaning "an international agreement concluded between States" and an international organization meant "an intergovernmental organisation." However, the 1969 Convention did acknowledge the existence of "other subjects of international law" who were capable of making agreements with legal force, even though these agreements would not be covered by the 1969 Convention. By March 1986, it became possible for the global diplomatic community to give full recognition to the 1949 ICJ Opinion and the Vienna Convention on the Law of Treaties between States and International Organisations or between International Organisations was agreed. The text of the 1986 Convention directly matched the text of the 1969 Convention, article by article, simply modifying the wording so that all the provisions on inter-state treaties could apply to any written agreements

concluded by the UN, its agencies, or any other intergovernmental organization. Not only did the 1986 Convention unambiguously treat all IGOs as being
subjects of international law but also it referred to "subjects of international
law other than States or international organizations" and hence opened the
possibility of NGOs, transnational corporations, and individuals being parties
to international agreements and subjects of international law.[2]

Evolution in the practice covering NGOs

Against this background of the slow acceptance of intergovernmental
organizations, it is not so surprising to find non-governmental organizations
are seldom accepted as subjects of international law. Nevertheless, there is a
variety of unusual circumstances, some going back before the UN was formed,
by which particular NGOs have had a special legal status. In addition, several
treaties allocate special responsibilities either to specific NGOs or to NGOs
in general. Beyond this, there is a diverse range of important international
organizations in which states accord NGOs equality of status. All these points
provide the strongest evidence of practice within a wider argument that the
general acceptance of NGOs amounts to an evolution of customary international law, under which NGOs have become capable of possessing legal
personality. Each of these developments will now be considered in turn.

A set of special cases: NGOs gaining privileges of statehood

In political terms, the Catholic Church is directly comparable with the
Anglican Communion, the Lutheran World Federation, the Baptist World
Alliance, and other transnational churches that are among the NGOs accredited to ECOSOC. In legal terms, the Catholic Church is different. Due to
the historical legacy from its temporal role in the Holy Roman Empire,
it is treated as if it were a state. It engages in diplomacy, with embassies
(apostolic nunciatures) in many countries. In most Catholic countries, the
Papal Nuncio has precedence over other ambassadors and is Dean of the
Diplomatic Corps. Under the title of the Holy See, the Catholic Church has
ratified treaties on human rights, on diplomatic practice, and on arms control.
It has joined a few intergovernmental organizations, with full membership
rights, as the Holy See or as the Vatican City State—the Organization for
Security and Co-operation in Europe (OSCE), UN Conference on Trade and
Development (UNCTAD), the International Atomic Energy Agency (IAEA),
World Intellectual Property Organization (WIPO), the Universal Postal Union
(UPU), and the International Telecommunication Union (ITU)—but it is
not a member of the UN. By virtue of its membership of UN agencies, it
has been automatically invited, on the same basis as governments, to all

special conferences convened by the UN, since the formula was adopted of inviting "all states." It differs only slightly from other NGOs, in that it does have sovereign control of a tiny amount of territory, the Vatican, which is less than one-fifth of a square mile (0.4 sq km) in area. When it comes to the politics of UN conferences on population questions, many of the other NGOs are angry at the privileged position and political influence accorded to this one NGO.

The Sovereign Order of Malta is another, less well-known, historical anomaly. The Knights of St. John of Jerusalem are a Catholic monastic order dating back to the eleventh century. They were formed to care for pilgrims in Jerusalem and later became a military order, gaining control of Rhodes in 1310. The Knights moved to Malta in 1530 and remained in control there until Napoleon took over the island in 1798. This period, as rulers of Malta, led to the alternative secular title, the Sovereign Order of Malta. From the mid-nineteenth century, they have engaged in "charitable works for the sick, the needy and refugees."[3] The Order now works throughout the world, as if it were a humanitarian NGO, and cooperates closely with the Office of the UN High Commisioner for Refugees (UNHCR). However, it is still treated as if it were a state and has formal diplomatic relations with accredited missions in over 100 countries. It has never had NGO status at the UN, but it is an Observer at the General Assembly and uses this status regularly to contribute to debates on humanitarian questions and sustainable development.[4]

The International Committee of the Red Cross (ICRC), despite its name, is not an international body established in all the different countries where it works. It is purely a Swiss NGO, which employs individual people from many countries and operates from Geneva on a transnational basis. It was of immense historical significance in establishing the Red Cross movement and lobbying successfully in the nineteenth century to create a new domain for international law. Because of this historical leadership role, the ICRC has a special status in the four Geneva conventions of 1949. For example, 13 articles of the Third Convention on the treatment of prisoners of war and 18 articles of the Fourth Convention on the protection of civilians during military operations and in occupied territories make specific mention of the ICRC. All four conventions include provisions for the ICRC to act like a state in providing "good offices" when there are disagreements about interpreting the texts. Sovereignty of states is limited by the obligations to provide access for ICRC delegates to all "places of internment, detention or work" for prisoners of war or civilians. In the conventions, the ICRC may care for the sick and wounded and/or provide food, medical, and clothing supplies. These responsibilities have led more than 60 states to conclude agreements with the ICRC for its staff to be immune from judicial processes and for any disputes to be settled by international arbitration. Menno Kamminga concludes, "all these agreements qualify as treaties under international law."[5] Thus, the ICRC has a central role in the implementation of these important intergovernmental treaties.

It is even more impressive that, from the first convention in 1864, through the consolidation and updating of the four conventions in 1949, to the adoption of additional protocols in 1977 and 2005, the ICRC has taken the leading role in *creating* the draft legal texts, which are submitted to governments for approval. Certainly, in political terms and arguably in legal terms, this gives the ICRC, as an NGO, a role superior to any individual state in the creation of international humanitarian law.

The UN General Assembly has long had the practice of issuing permanent invitations for various political actors to be Observers at its sessions. The specialized agencies gained Observer status as part of their agreements to cooperate with the UN, with the first four being approved in December 1946. Then, the regional intergovernmental organizations gradually followed. The first ones were the Organization of American States in October 1948 and the Arab League in November 1950. Now there are over 50 IGO Observers, not including the specialized agencies. Switzerland became the first non-Member State with a permanent Observer mission in November 1948 and over the years 14 other states, which are now all full UN members, had this status for some years. In the 1970s, liberation movements also had their claim to statehood boosted by being made Observers.

Given the historical background, there were no objections when the Holy See, the ICRC and the Order of Malta joined the IGOs and states with Observer status in the General Assembly. The unusual nature of the decision in October 1990 to make the ICRC an Observer, although it was unambiguously an NGO, was recognized by saying the status was granted "in consideration of the special role and mandates conferred upon it by the Geneva Conventions."[6] The door appeared to be opening more widely to NGOs when in October 1994 the International Federation of Red Cross and Red Crescent Societies also became an Observer, although—unlike the three previous cases—it had no special legal status. As soon as the Federation was proposed, the US delegation took counter-action and the General Assembly agreed to place a block on any more NGOs being recognized. They formally decided that "the granting of Observer status should in future be confined to States and to … intergovernmental organizations."[7] While this decision in December 1994 apparently closed the door, two more exceptions were added a few years later. The World Conservation Union (IUCN) gained Observer status in December 1999 and the Inter-Parliamentary Union (IPU) in November 2002. The ICRC, the Federation, the IUCN and the IPU each had to give up their consultative status as ECOSOC NGOs when they joined the ranks of the states and the IGOs in the General Assembly.

The challenge to state sovereignty from human rights and environmental NGOs

The UN Charter contains a fundamental contradiction. One the one hand, it asserts the sovereignty of states and, in particular, Article 2 (7) says, "Nothing contained in the present Charter shall authorize the United Nations to intervene in matters which are essentially within the domestic jurisdiction of any state." On the other hand, due to the lobbying of NGOs at San Francisco in 1945, the Charter referred seven times to the promotion of human rights and specifically required ECOSOC to establish a Commission on Human Rights (CHR). The problem is that any real engagement with human rights is dealing with questions that are fundamentally the internal affairs of a state. Initially, at its first session, the CHR resolved this contradiction in favor of sovereignty, by asserting that "it has no power to take any action in regard to any complaints concerning human rights."[8] The turning point came when in May 1970, by Resolution 1503, ECOSOC decided that complaints could be reviewed to determine whether there were "particular situations which appear to reveal a consistent pattern of gross and reliably attested violations of human rights." Then, over the following decade the situation was transformed, by the adoption of a variety of special procedures covering topics, such as torture and disappearances, or the record of particular countries. A series of human rights treaties were negotiated and came into force. Finally, in the 1990s, the post of High Commissioner for Human Rights and the International Criminal Court (ICC) were established.

Now there are treaty mechanisms that give international legal rights to individual people, enabling them to bring violations of their human rights by their own governments to review by intergovernmental committees. The Convention Against Torture and the Statute of the ICC have gone the furthest in undermining sovereignty, because government leaders can be imprisoned for acts they performed when they were in government. Finally, in 2006, the CHR was replaced by a higher-status Human Rights Council, reporting directly to the General Assembly. Under its Universal Periodic Review mechanism, every UN member has their human rights record reviewed, within a four-year cycle, with NGOs contributing to the review process. The principle of sovereignty has been overturned in favor of each government's relations with its citizens being subject to international review and in favor of sovereign immunity being lost with respect to torture, genocide, crimes against humanity, and war crimes. The crucial point is that every one of these developments was initiated and promoted by NGOs. Without NGOs, there would have been no international law of human rights.

Individual governments do not have the sovereign capacity to implement policy to prevent damage to the environmental global commons—air and water pollution, ozone depletion, loss of biodiversity, deforestation, and climate change. *Agenda 21*, the main policy document produced at the 1992 Earth Summit, acknowledged the irrelevance of sovereignty in achieving sustainable development, as "no nation can achieve this on its own." A distinct concept of Major Groups was developed to define the role of NGOs in the implementation of *Agenda 21*. The section on Major Groups described their "commitment and genuine involvement" as "critical" and "broad public participation in decision-making" as a "fundamental prerequisite."[9] The corollary of such arguments is not just that governments should collaborate with the Major Groups, but they *cannot* act without them.

The arguments found expression subsequently at the UN in the categorization of NGOs into Major Groups at all bodies dealing with sustainable development questions: the Commission on Sustainable Development, the UN Forum on Forests, General Assembly special sessions called to review progress with *Agenda 21*, and further global conferences. Each of these bodies is noteworthy for NGOs having a higher frequency of interactions with governments (both formally and informally), a more diverse range of interactions, and a higher status in the proceedings than is accorded within the UN on other issues. The format for the more prestigious interactions is known as a multi-stakeholder dialogue, in which NGOs are expected to collaborate and express common positions for their Major Group. This process is transferring the concept of interest groups and the practice of government consultations in domestic politics to the global bodies. It is breaking the distinction between domestic politics and international politics. Thus, in global environmental politics a distinct set of arrangements, which are not fully compatible with non-interference and sovereignty, have been institutionalized

NGOs serving on intergovernmental committees

While NGOs have from the beginning of the UN's work been able to extend their consultative status with ECOSOC to all of ECOSOC's subsidiary bodies, for decades there was never any willingness to suggest that NGOs could have direct involvement in intergovernmental decision-making processes at the UN. NGOs could not have a negotiating role and they could not have any responsibility for designing programs or allocating budgetary resources. Because this was taken for granted, individual NGOs could not be elected or nominated as participants on smaller policy-making committees. The situation has changed a little, with innovations in some fields where NGOs have special expertise to offer.

The UN Educational, Scientific and Cultural Organization (UNESCO) has a World Heritage Committee, established by a special treaty in 1972 to protect cultural and natural heritage sites of global significance. Three NGOs, the International Centre for the Study of the Preservation and Restoration of Cultural Property (ICCROM), the International Council on Monuments and Sites (ICOMOS) and the World Conservation Union (IUCN) "may attend the meetings of the Committee in an advisory capacity." They also are expected to participate in "the implementation of its programmes and projects" and assist the secretariat to "prepare the Committee's documentation and the agenda of its meetings."[10] They are privileged compared with states, in that states have to be elected to the Committee, whereas the three NGOs are permanent participants. Their role in preparing documentation and the Committee's agenda means they can have substantial influence on its work.

A more radical step was taken in July 1995 when the arrangements were endorsed for a new inter-agency body, the Joint United Nations Programme on HIV/AIDS (UNAIDS), to oversee all AIDS activities in the UN system. Five NGOs were "invited to take part in the work of the Programme Co-ordinating Board" by ECOSOC Resolution 1995/2. An official from UNAIDS has been quoted as saying these NGOs are on the Board "not observers, but as members—this was the first time this has happened in the UN system."[11] Not surprisingly, the ECOSOC resolution formally recorded that the arrangements were "not to be regarded as setting a precedent." Outside the UN system, in another area of health policy, a wider, more innovative partnership was established through the leadership of the Gates Foundation in 2000. The Global Alliance for Vaccines and Immunisation (GAVI) brings together governments, vaccine manufacturers, other private sector groups, public health and research institutes, UNICEF, WHO, the World Bank, and NGOs. The main policy-making body is the Alliance Board, consisting of five developing country governments, five industrialized country governments, one research institute, two vaccine manufacturing companies, and one representative from civil society. The rarity of arrangements such as these examples with UNESCO, UNAIDS, and GAVI serves to emphasize the significance of the following section on hybrid international organizations.

The lessons from practice

It is relatively easy to dismiss any one of the above special situations, such as the Catholic Church being treated as a state, and to say it is an anomaly, which does not affect the general picture. It is more difficult to argue we are only dealing with anomalies when we note it is not solely a small number of historical curiosities. The range of special situations is increasing. Successive restrictive boundaries are being crossed. NGOs now violate the sovereignty of states, most obviously in the field of human rights, but also in a more subtle manner in environmental politics. NGOs have, as of right, moved beyond the Charter limitation of consultative status with ECOSOC to a role in the Human Rights Council under the authority of the General Assembly. NGOs are slowly gaining new rights, from agenda-setting and participation in committees to responsibilities under treaties. The total number of NGOs involved in these new legal situations is substantial and they affect all states. Furthermore, the evolution has occurred in global institutions and hence (except for some small states who are not members of all institutions) all the changes have been accepted by all states. Overall, the breadth and depth of the change in practice since the UN was formed would have been unimaginable and incomprehensible to an international lawyer in 1945.

NGOs and states in hybrid international organizations

From 1945 until recently, the term international organization was predominantly used to mean a permanent inter-state institution that holds formal diplomatic meetings on a regular basis.[12] Most current textbooks on international organizations make a basic distinction between intergovernmental organizations and international non-governmental organizations (INGOs). Some then concentrate overwhelmingly on IGOs and ignore INGOs.[13] Others do cover both IGOs and INGOs, make comparisons between them and ask how they relate to each other, but treat the distinction as a simple, straightforward dichotomy.[14] However, there is a logical possibility of a third category of international organizations. Governments and transnational actors can come together in a *hybrid* international organization. Some authors mention this possibility and then ignore its significance. Only Clive Archer briefly gives the question more than passing attention, but he treats hybrids as a form of INGO.[15] In so doing, Archer is privileging the intergovernmental world, by treating all deviations from the "normal" as a single category. When we come to the practice of international diplomacy, there is not even any language to express the concept of an IGO-INGO hybrid.

In the early years of the UN the question of hybrids was not addressed. When the NGO Statute was revised in 1968, it was decided formally and explicitly that consultative status could be granted to any "organizations which accept members designated by governmental authorities" with the proviso "that such membership does not interfere with the free expression of views of the organization." Consequently, this little-known reference allows hybrid international organizations to be hidden within the ECOSOC lists of NGOs. We have already noted the diplomatic confusion whereby four organizations have been able to give up their consultative status as NGOs with ECOSOC and gain promotion to Observer status among the IGOs in the General Assembly. The confusion was at its extreme in the case of the World Conservation Union (IUCN). In 1998, the IUCN was listed by ECOSOC as having NGO Special Status, but it disappeared from the list for 1999. In a General Assembly debate at the end of 1999, granting Observer status to the IUCN was justified by asserting it was "an intergovernmental body."[16] Thus, in 1998–99 the IUCN shifted from being treated as an INGO to being treated as an IGO, when it was neither.

For the purposes of this discussion, an organization that is neither an intergovernmental organization nor an international non-governmental organization is a hybrid international organization and is defined as

> an international organization that includes in its membership *both* states, represented by government ministries and/or other governmental institutions, *and* transnational actors, which may be from a single-country and/ or multi-country, international non-governmental organizations.

The transnational actors may either be transnational corporations or NGOs, but we are concerned primarily with those involving NGOs. The crucial point about joint membership is that the NGOs do not have a secondary consultative status nor a somewhat more prestigious observer status: they are on an equal footing with governments.[17] The simple evidence of governments and NGOs having equal status within a hybrid is that each type of member has the right to vote in the highest policy-making body. There are two possible mechanisms for arranging the voting: a unicameral vote requiring a majority among any combination of all the members and a bicameral vote requiring separate majorities among governments and among NGOs. Along with the privilege of voting, one would expect to find that each member also has the obligation to contribute to the budget of the hybrid organization. As most governments have much greater resources at their disposal than most NGOs, the budget contributions are not likely to be equal, just as big countries and small countries do not make equal contributions to the UN's budget. Once we are equipped to think about hybrid international organizations, it soon becomes evident that they are present as the focal point for the global politics of some major issues.

The structure of the most important hybrid international organizations

There are many specialist international economic organizations that are hybrids, by virtue of governments in some countries engaging in commercial activities that in other countries are left to private companies. For example, the International Air Transport Association and the International Chamber of Shipping, which are both listed among the ECOSOC NGOs, have as members airlines or shipping companies that are government-owned and government-managed. Hence they are actually not NGOs but unicameral hybrids. Such organizations may be regarded as no more than curious anomalies. However, a small number of the major global organizations that have a much wider impact are also hybrids involving NGOs and not TNCs. They are worth considering in more detail.

The International Labour Organization

One UN specialized agency is only an IGO in theory, while in practice it operates as a hybrid. The International Labour Organization (ILO), under what is known as its tripartite system, gives equality of status in all its policy-making to governments, trades unions, and employers' organizations, from each member country. Legally, states are members of the ILO, but decisions are taken with each member having two government representatives, one union representative, and one employers' representative, voting on a unicameral basis. For some countries, on some decisions, unions and employers may not wish to, or feel able to, vote independently, but others can and do vote in all the possible combinations, including unions or employers voting against their own government. This means, in principle, an International Labour Conference could adopt the text of a convention, which is an international legal instrument, with up to two-thirds of the governments opposed to the provisions of the convention. (Of course, it is politically improbable that most workers' and most employers' representatives would unite against the majority of governments, but the traditional norms of international law are violated by allowing it to be a possibility.) Put more subtly, in the ILO, employers and unions have made a major contribution to the development of a wide range of international treaty law on employment rights and health, safety, and welfare questions.

The International Conference of the Red Cross and Red Crescent

The International Committee of the Red Cross has already been mentioned as a Swiss NGO with exceptional status. The ICRC is just one part of a complex global structure, the International Red Cross and Red Crescent Movement. The emblem of the Red Cross was initially adopted not as a Christian symbol but as a reversal of the Swiss flag, to represent neutrality. Nevertheless, most Muslim countries have since 1929 used an alternative Red Crescent emblem. In December 2005, a third symbol, the Red Crystal, was adopted, to allow Israel, Kazakhstan, Eritrea, and possibly other countries to operate without using either of the established symbols. Under the provisions of the Geneva conventions, each of the 194 ratifying countries is expected to have its own National Society and 186 currently do so. The ICRC decides which societies have met the conditions to be recognized. One curious feature, for the world of NGOs, is that recognition will not be granted unless the government has passed a law affirming the independence of the society as a voluntary organization. The National Societies come together in the International Federation of Red Cross and Red Crescent Societies. These arrangements are relatively straightforward: a set of national NGOs have formed an INGO.

The work of the Movement—the National Societies, the Federation, and the ICRC—is enmeshed in the international law of the Geneva conventions. As a result, the highest policy-making body is the International Conference of the Red Cross and Red Crescent, which normally meets every four years. The Conference is a unicameral hybrid. With the National Societies, the governments, the ICRC, and the Federation each having one vote, its policy is decided by a simple majority. Interestingly, if there is not consensus, nor a vote by a show of hands, and a formal roll call is requested, then all the National Societies vote first, followed by the governments, and finally the ICRC and the Federation. Such a procedure provides a pressure upon governments to follow the lead of the Societies. Because there might at times be two more NGO votes (the ICRC and the Federation) than governmental votes, this structure in principle provides for a most extraordinary hypothetical outcome: a Conference decision could be taken by a group of NGOs voting for a proposal against the opposition of *all* governments. Of course, this will never happen, but the legal possibility does emphasize the equality of status between NGOs and governments within the Conference.

The International Conference must take sides in political conflicts when the question arises of what states are legitimate. In October 1986, this led to bitter arguments when African and other representatives, both from the governments and from the National Societies, voted to suspend the representative of the South African government, but not the National Society, from participation in the 25th International Conference. Because of this problem and conflict over the status of the Israelis and the Palestinians, the next conference due in 1991 was canceled at the last moment. The 29th International Conference made its own contribution in June 2006 to the Middle East peace process, successfully requesting the ICRC to admit both the Israeli Magen David Adom and Palestinian Red Crescent Society to the Movement. It is not just the ICRC but also the hybrid International Conference that is at the heart of international humanitarian law.

The International Council for Science

The most common occurrence of hybrids is in cooperation on highly technical questions. For example, as of the end of 2008, the International Council for Science (ICSU) was composed of 30 Scientific Union Members, which are specialist global scientific unions, and 116 National Scientific Members (representing 136 countries, as some "national" bodies cover more than one country). In the ICSU policy-making bodies, its General Assembly and its Executive Board, the two types of members each have 50 percent of the votes. Depending on the political system in each country, the National Members may be government committees or ministries, semi-independent government-sponsored councils or totally independent professional bodies. Thus, the ICSU is another unicameral hybrid, in which governments can be outvoted, because governments hold a minority share of the votes.

While ICSU may be little known, its work has sometimes been of immense significance. For example, the three scientific unions for astronomy, geodesy, and geophysics, and radio-sciences proposed the 1957–58 International Geophysical Year (IGY). This was organized by the ICSU and the World Meteorological Organization (WMO—a UN specialized agency) as a major global program of multinational and multidisciplinary collaborative research. One of the ICSU's scientific priorities was to focus on the polar regions. The IGY had an impact on the ICSU's own structure, when in March 1958 it established its Scientific Committee on Antarctic Research (SCAR). The success of the IGY led directly to the first arms control treaty during the Cold War. In December 1959, 12 countries that had established research stations in Antarctica agreed to suspend their claims to sovereignty anywhere within the territory, to keep the continent free from any military activity, and to engage in permanent scientific collaboration. The Antarctic Treaty provides for annual consultative meetings, which have resulted in the subsequent adoption of a series of more specific environmental conventions. SCAR has an important presence at the intergovernmental meetings under the Antarctic Treaty System, in providing the authoritative source of scientific advice.

Another ICSU body, the Scientific Committee on Problems of the Environment (SCOPE) has been crucial to the global politics of climate change. It was established in 1969 as the focus for the increasing collaboration between the ICSU and the WMO, particularly a series of joint programs on climate research. These two organizations along with the UN Environment Programme held a major workshop on climate issues in Vienna in 1978, followed by the World Climate Conference, in Geneva in February 1979, both of which were predominantly scientific events. The result was a joint ICSU, WMO, UNEP (UN Environment Programme), and UNESCO World Climate Programme, to gather data systematically, to model the impact of greenhouse gases on climate, and to assess the impact of climate change on both humans and ecosystems. The same organizations held another conference at Villach in Austria in October 1985. This both forged a consensus among scientists about climate change and made a direct appeal to governments to put the problem of global warming on the agenda of policy-makers. The Villach conference, along with the political shock caused by some environmental disasters, fed into the Brundtland Report, which was released in April 1987.[18] Then, in June 1987, the WMO Executive Council requested UNEP to join it in establishing a mechanism to assess the scale, timing, and impact of climate change and UNEP immediately agreed. The resulting Intergovernmental Panel on Climate Change has dominated the politics of climate change since this point. Without the leadership of the ICSU, there would have been no Framework Convention on Climate Change nor its Kyoto Protocol nor the related annual conferences to negotiate stronger responses to global warming.

The International Organization for Standardization

Another example of a technical hybrid is the International Organization for Standardization (ISO), consisting of one member from each of 157 countries, divided into three categories: 106 Member Bodies, each of which is the national body "most representative of standardization in its country"; 40 Correspondent Members, from countries which do not yet have fully developed national standards activities, but are entitled to be kept fully informed about ISO's work; and 11 Subscriber Members, from countries with very small economies, who can keep in contact about new standards.[19] In its policy-making only the full Member Bodies have the vote. Some are government ministries or agencies, while some are NGOs. Even those run by independent professional bodies have to have a close relationship with the government, because the whole point of standards is, ideally, they should be universally adopted. For example, the American National Standards Institute does no more than coordinate and accredit more than 200 distinct groups to develop and maintain nearly 10,000 standards, promoting the principles of consensus, due process, and transparency. It does not write standards itself. Nevertheless, even though all the standards are developed as voluntary documents, American federal, state, and local governments often refer to them for regulatory or procurement purposes.[20]

There is thus a complex process of interaction between governments and a diverse range of NGOs, at both the country level and the global level, to produce an authoritative set of ISO standards, having an enormous impact on production processes for a wide range of goods and services. Many ISO standards are adopted by companies and public bodies on a voluntary basis. Pring argues that on sustainable development questions these practices should be regarded as "soft law" and that over time they will become hard law, just as human rights moved from soft to hard law:

> The enormous impact ISO environmental standards will have on all industry and trade is just beginning to be appreciated. Although ISO

standards are supposedly non-regulatory, it can be expected that many countries, international bodies, financing institutions and courts will 'adopt' them either as hard law or as interpretative guidance in mining programmes, environmental regulation, contracting policies, financing approvals, and judicial liability rulings.[21]

When intergovernmental groups of regulators, such as the International Conference of Data Protection and Privacy Commissioners, seek to establish Observer status with ISO, we can envisage a new form of de facto international law, through the adoption of a non-binding international standard as binding domestic law within many countries. However, some ISO work is already hard law and embedded in international treaties. Some is highly specialized and has an impact in a very limited manner. For example, Article 3 of the Convention on the Recording of Forenames and Surnames in Civil Status Registers requires governments to use ISO standards for the transliteration of characters from Cyrillic, Arabic, Hebrew, and Greek.[22] At the other end of the spectrum, an integral part of international trade law, under the WTO, is its Agreement on Technical Barriers to Trade. The whole Agreement is based on ISO's work. It defines a standard in terms of ISO guidelines, provides that ISO standards must be used where they already exist, and provides that any new standards should be developed through the ISO.[23]

The International Union for the Conservation of Nature

The International Union for the Protection of Nature was founded in October 1948 with encouragement and support from UNESCO. It broadened its concerns and changed its name in 1956 to the International Union for Conservation of Nature and Natural Resources (IUCN), which remains its official name to this day. From 1990, it sought wider public recognition through use of the name World Conservation Union, but from 2008 it has reverted to a shortened version of its official name. It continues to promote and publish detailed scientific work, notably the famous *Red List of Threatened Species* produced by its Species Survival Commission. It also has a substantial public education program, studies habitats and runs an ecosystem management program, in the context of sustainable development, including reduction of human poverty.

The IUCN is the most important example of a bicameral voting system and has a complex system of weighted voting. The IUCN Statute specifies three categories of members. At the end of 2008, the members divided out as follows:

Category A—86 states, plus 95 government agencies from member states, and 25 government agencies from non-member states;

Category B—812 national NGOs and 90 international NGOs; and

Category C—33 smaller NGOs and government bodies that become affiliates, plus some 40 to 50 individuals who have rendered outstanding service in the field of conservation.

Only those in categories A and B have the right to vote. UN members that adhere to the IUCN Statutes have three votes, while government agencies from other countries have a single collective vote for each country. International NGOs each have two votes and national NGOs each have one vote, provided that the NGOs from one country do not obtain more than 10 percent of all the NGO votes. Then a motion is passed when it obtains, both in Category A and in Category B, a simple majority of the votes cast. In elections, the rankings obtained by the candidates in a separate count of the votes from each category are added to produce one combined ranking.[24] The point of outlining this complex system is to demonstrate how governments and NGOs each have a veto over the IUCN's decisions: neither category can act without agreement from a majority among the other category. The World Conservation Congress, the IUCN's Members Assembly, has been the global policy-making body on protecting endangered species, managing habitats, exchanging information on conservation, providing technical support for the implementation of a range of conservation treaties, and promoting field projects.

IUCN has been crucial to the development of international environmental law. Its central role in the World Heritage Convention has already been mentioned. It has a different type of role under the 1971 Ramsar Convention on Wetlands, which places obligations on contracting parties to conserve wetlands as nature reserves for migratory waterfowl. While there is an organizational structure, it does not possess legal personality. Under Article 8 of the Convention, the IUCN houses the secretariat, the Ramsar Bureau, at its headquarters in Gland and the Bureau staff are legally employees of the IUCN. Thus, the Convention establishes a set of international legal obligations, which are managed by the IUCN. In recognition of this work, IUCN and three other bodies, Birdlife International, Wetlands International, and World Wide Fund for Nature, were in May 1999 designated International Organization Partners of the Convention. They "participate regularly as observers and key actors in all meetings of the Conference of the Parties and the Standing Committee, and as full members of the Scientific and Technical Review Panel."[25]

The Convention on International Trade in Endangered Species of Wild Fauna and Flora (CITES) adopted in March 1973 has a considerably stronger organization. While the Secretariat is provided by UNEP, there is an independent budget and a program of scientific research and implementation activities. Nevertheless, much of this work is subcontracted by CITES to IUCN.[26] The

Convention on Biological Diversity (CBD) is further down the spectrum towards being a full international organization. Its Secretariat is managed by UNEP but independently located in Montréal and it has much more substantial financial resources, including access to the Global Environment Facility. However, it too has had a strong relationship with IUCN. Initially, its Global Biodiversity Programme gave guidance and support to the new CBD Secretariat. Now the CBD–IUCN relationship is less important at the global level, as the CBD has become a strong organization and IUCN has decentralized its work.

From the perspective of international law, the most important aspect of IUCN's work has been its Environmental Law Programme. This includes a Commission, which acts as a global network of lawyers from governments, NGOs, IGOs, private practice, and universities. While much of the work of the Programme has been research, maintaining databases, and training at the country level, it also has had a major role in the creation of international environmental law. In particular, it has had a role similar to the ICRC in taking the lead in initiating debate and preparing draft texts for new conventions. This was the case for Ramsar, CITES, and the CBD. It has also made significant contributions to the negotiation of other treaties on Antarctic marine conservation, on tropical timber, and on protection of the Alps.

The significance of the hybrid international organizations

There may not be a large number of hybrid international organizations, but the examples of the International Labour Organization, the International Conference of the Red Cross, the International Council for Science, the International Organization for Standardization, and the International Union for the Conservation of Nature are sufficient to show that a wide range of policy-making on important contemporary political questions is being debated in hybrids and the resulting policy is being implemented in their programs. For the purposes of this discussion, it is also important to note that each of these hybrids is central to the development of international law within their respective policy domain. The five organizations have between them initiated many conventions and treaties on labor rights, labor welfare, humanitarian law, use of Antarctica, global warming, aspects of world trade, protection of wildfowl habitats, endangered species, and biodiversity.

The general legal status of NGOs

The argument that NGOs in general have international legal personality is complex and controversial. Both Steve Charnovitz and Anthony Judge address the question, but flatly assert NGOs do not enjoy legal personality outside domestic law.[27] For some conservative international lawyers the question does not even arise. One of the major textbooks, by Ian Brownlie, even in a new edition as recent as 2008, does not discuss NGOs in any manner. He was unable to conceptualize anything about law that is not directly or indirectly related to the authority of states.[28] However, in considering this question, we are *not* asking whether NGOs are equivalent to states nor whether they have the rights and duties possessed by states. Another major textbook on international law, by Malcolm Shaw, does refer to "the wide range of participants." He acknowledges that "[t]hese include ... non-governmental organisations" but says they are not necessarily legal persons, even though they may have political influence:

> International personality is participation plus some form of community acceptance. The latter element will be dependent upon many different factors, including the type of personality under question. It may be manifested in many forms and may in certain cases be inferred from practice.[29]

Unfortunately, even though he discusses TNCs, Shaw then totally ignores NGOs. Similarly, in a subsequent chapter on "International Institutions" Shaw makes passing reference to INGOs, but then restricts his discussion to IGOs.[30] The question remains whether Shaw's criteria of "community acceptance" and "practice" do allow a wider assertion of NGO legal personality under customary international law. Menno Kamminga considers the extent to which NGOs engage in state-like activity and acknowledges their engagement in the inter-state system. He then rejects their claim to personality, not on legal grounds but on normative grounds, that not all NGOs are "praiseworthy" or democratic.[31] The failure of legal scholarship is most evident in the failure of Brownlie, Charnovitz, Judge, Kamminga, and Shaw to mention, let alone discuss, the existence of hybrid international organizations.

We have seen that some NGOs are accorded legal status under treaty law. In a few special cases, such as the International Olympic Committee, legal status can be claimed solely on the basis of an individual NGO's bilateral relations with many states.[32] The European Convention on the Recognition of the Legal Personality of International Non-Governmental Organizations, adopted by the Council of Europe in 1986, might suggest a wider acceptance. However, this is not the case, because the Convention only deals with recognition of NGOs within domestic law. We will now consider a wider argument that the UN has created legal status for NGOs.

Customary international law comes from state practice, combined with *opinio juris*, which is a widespread belief in an obligation to follow this practice. United Nations resolutions can be evidence of state practice, but this does not give legal force to all UN resolutions. Some may be hotly contested and/or flagrantly defied, after they are adopted. However, when they are adopted by consensus, have general applicability, are regularly reaffirmed, and the principles they embody are not challenged, then the resolutions do become legally binding. For example, Shaw sees General Assembly Resolution 1514 (XV), the Declaration on the Granting of Independence to Colonial Countries and Peoples, as the "transmutation of the concept of self-determination from a political and moral principle to a legal right."[33] Similarly, the Universal Declaration of Human Rights, which was adopted in 1948 as a set of political aspirations, is portrayed by Hurst Hannum as subsequently becoming central to the evolution of customary international law on human rights.[34]

The ECOSOC Statute on Arrangements for Consultation with Non-Governmental Organisations can be seen in the same light. It was adopted initially as a pragmatic set of procedures in the early years of the UN. These procedures were codified into the Statute in 1950, reviewed and reaffirmed in 1968, and reviewed and reaffirmed again in 1996. A large proportion of the text has remained unchanged since its first adoption in 1946–47. On each of the three occasions when the full NGO Statute was endorsed, even after a ferocious debate in 1967–68, the resolution was passed by consensus, without any government recording opposition to the final text. Over virtually the whole history of the UN, the status and/or the activities of particular NGOs have been matters of controversy, but the status of the Statute itself has not been challenged. Attacks upon individual NGOs almost always include claims that the NGO concerned has violated the Statute and hence these attacks implicitly confirm the validity of the Statute. Some variant on the participation rights in the Statute have become accepted practice in virtually all bodies within the UN system.

Some NGOs are small and local in their activities, never engaging in any transnational relations, and as a result there can be no basis for claiming they have international legal personality. Other NGOs may be of great political importance and have a transnational impact, but this alone is not enough to make them international persons. Thus, NGOs that participate in an Arria Formula meeting with the Security Council are only taking part in an ad hoc informal process and they will not necessarily be invited to any subsequent meetings. Even though they may have great influence on the response to a particular crisis, they have no continuous rights and responsibilities. The situation is less clear-cut when we consider NGO involvement in international diplomatic conferences, which may be in the form of a loose network rather than a permanent institution. For example, the Oslo Process, culminating in the Diplomatic Conference for the Adoption of a Cluster Munitions Convention in Dublin in May 2008, gave a very high status to the Cluster Munition Coalition in its Rules of Procedure. However, it is not the Coalition but "relevant non-governmental organisations" which are mentioned as having a continuing role in the meetings and conferences called to implement the Convention. In such a situation, the network cannot have legal personality separate from the NGOs that participate in the network.[35]

The ECOSOC consultative arrangements provide the conditions for NGOs to gain international legal personality. The combination of the multiple affirmations of the text of the NGO Statute and its continuous use for the whole of the UN's existence means that "community acceptance" and "practice" have established the Statute's provisions for NGO participation, in ECOSOC and its subsidiary bodies, as rules and procedures having the force of customary international law. Any NGO that is formally granted consultative status by ECOSOC gains specific rights within the diplomatic system, along with obligations to behave in a diplomatic manner and to report on its finances and its activities. Thus, ECOSOC-accredited NGOs, by gaining these rights and obligations, become international legal persons. Equally, NGOs accredited under the authority of comparable documents and acquiring similar rights and obligations in UNESCO, the WHO, or other UN agencies also become legal persons.[36]

Conclusion

We have demonstrated three main lines of argument that NGOs have international legal personality. First, there are the special cases. A few NGOs are anomalies in being equal to states in international diplomacy; a few exceptional NGOs are among the Observers at the UN General Assembly; much larger numbers of NGOs have a special role in the procedures for handling human rights and the environment; and a few high-status NGOs participate in intergovernmental committees. Second, although legal textbooks and legal and political language fail to recognize their existence, hybrid international organizations are constituted on the basis of NGOs having legal rights alongside states. Examination of five major hybrids demonstrated that they have made a substantial contribution to the development of international law. In these five organizations alone there are currently more than 1,500 NGOs which work in collaboration with states on a basis of equality of status and equal participation rights, including the ultimate right of voting on authoritative decisions. In these fields, the development of international law requires the explicit approval of the relevant NGOs. Such relationships, on a continual, routinized, institutional basis, are sufficient for these NGOs to be regarded as possessing international legal personality. Finally, there is a general argument that all ECOSOC NGOs gain legal personality when they are accredited under the consultative arrangements. Taken together, the three arguments provide a massive body of evidence for saying, even in strictly legal terms, that states are not the only legitimate diplomatic actors. States, transnational NGOs, intergovernmental organizations, international non-governmental organizations, and hybrid international organizations are different from each other, but all are participants in the international legal system.[37]

4 NGOs, networking, and the creation of the Internet

The Internet is usually seen as a system that enhances communications for non-governmental organizations. This chapter takes a different perspective: the desire for networking among NGOs enhanced global communications. The visionary leadership exercised by a few NGOs and their appreciation of its technology as a potential resource for mobilization helped to *create* the Internet. First of all, the common assumption that the Internet was initiated to provide a communications system for the US military will be demolished. Then, the development of networks of large expensive computers for university staff and students will be outlined. A few commercial companies also began to create their own private networks. Against this background, a totally different network based on small home computers was established by human rights, peace, and environmental NGOs. By the end of the 1980s, the NGOs had a global network, with coverage including all developed countries and the majority of developing countries. In the 1990s, the university networks, the commercial networks, and the NGO networks were combined to give us the modern Internet. The theme of the chapter is that NGOs made two crucial innovations: they were the first to offer electronic communications to the general public and they were the first to promote connections between all the different emerging networks. Because it is central to the identity of many NGOs that they should promote communication networks and because it is crucial to their role as political actors that they should use cheap communications to mobilize support they were inspired to construct a global public system.

One of the problems in making such an argument is the immense ambiguity as to what is meant by the Internet. We can coin the word *mono-net* to signify a non-public network that is only accessible from a certain type of computer or by people within a specific set of organizations or within a limited geographical area. The Internet is then a set of interconnected mono-nets. Box 4.1 contrasts three very different ways of thinking about the connections between the networks. Before 1990, the "Internet" was discussed in terms of the computer scientists' definition. This "Internet" was only *one of many* separate unconnected networks. In the late 1980s and the early 1990s, most (but not all) of these different networks were gradually connected to each other. In addition, a crucial social change occurred. Some networks started to provide access for the public and the first ones to do so were NGO networks. We now take it for granted that the Internet is a network of networks, to which the public has access. This chapter is using the third definition from Box 4.1.[1]

Box 4.1 What is the Internet?

All analysts start from the proposition that the Internet is a network of computer networks, but there is no standard definition of which networks to include.

A technical definition for computer scientists

"The Internet consists of all computers that transfer information through the TCP-IP communications protocol, now used on personal computers."

This overstates the importance of one technical standard that happened to become dominant. It also ignores the importance of networks that initially used alternative communications protocols.

The non-technical popular perception

"The Internet consists of all servers hosting websites and all computers used to read web pages."

This ignores other Internet traffic, such as e-mail. It also ignores global networking by millions of people before the World Wide Web existed.

A social definition for political scientists

"The Internet is a transnational network of computer networks used to provide human communications, with open access for any person who wishes to send or to receive information across the networks."

This emphasizes the political importance of the Internet as a global public network, not limited to any one country and not limited by who may gain access.

Military funding of research on networking

There is a widely repeated myth that "the origins of the Internet can be traced back to 1969, when the US Department of Defense created ARPANET, electronically connected computers whose transmission lines were designed to withstand a nuclear onslaught." The myth has even been propagated in academic work, by somebody as eminent as Manuel Castells.[2] Like many myths, it does have a minimal factual basis: there was some Pentagon funding. In response to the shock to the US establishment of the launch of satellites by the Soviet Union in 1957, President Eisenhower created, within the Pentagon, the Advanced Research Projects Agency (ARPA). They funded a computer science research program, to link all the major American computers in a network.[3] The second basis for the myth was the proposal by Paul Baran at the RAND Corporation to create a "distributed network" communications system containing many redundant links. He had the idea of packet-switching, sending the signals as several packets of digital information taking various routes through the network. The RAND Corporation claims "this effort would eventually become the foundation for the World Wide Web" and *Time* magazine, in 1993, ran a story saying "Baran's packet-switching network" became "the technological underpinning of the Internet."[4] However, packet-switching was made public in Britain in 1966 by Donald Davies, who was working at the National Physical Laboratory (NPL). Larry Roberts, the head of the ARPA team, learnt of Baran's work from meeting a member of Davies' NPL team. Both Baran's and Davies' theoretical work fed into the ARPANET project, but neither of them became part of the project team.

Far from the ARPA scientists being military, many were anti-establishment. Their method of work was non-hierarchical and egalitarian. The process of establishing authoritative standards was done in the modest format of a "Request for Comment" that survived by the strength of its arguments and its acceptance in the computer science community. The whole ethos was one of openness and collaborative work in the pursuit of knowledge as a collective good. All progress on the project was publicly reported, rather than made classified information. These scientists were less likely to be ideological Cold War warriors than radical hippies.

When ARPANET started in 1969 and expanded in the 1970s, it was no more than a remote time-sharing system for computer science research. Later use, as an e-mail communications network, had not been foreseen by the ARPA planners. Ian Peter has pointed out, "E-Mail is much older than ARPANET or the Internet. It was never invented; it evolved from very simple beginnings."[5] In 1975 ARPANET extended e-mail to create the first electronic discussion forum. This very simple mono-net was in no sense even an embryonic Internet. As Robert Khan put it, "When the ARPANET was first created nobody envisioned that there would be other networks connected to it."[6] The ARPA program, in its second decade, made just two permanent contributions to the modern Internet: the TCP-IP communications standard and the domain names system. The ARPA project was non-military in technical terms, in bureaucratic terms, and in sociological terms.

Universities and computer networking

Computers were being installed in the 1960s in many universities in the United States and Western Europe, and some universities in developing countries. Each machine had many users within their host university. In the early 1980s, the National Science Foundation in the United States established a series of different networks between these host computers and then created a unified NSFNet (National Science Foundation Network). As ARPANET became obsolete, its computers gradually migrated to NSFNet. During the gestation period for the Internet, the combination of ARPANET and NSFNet was widely known as *the* Internet. However, in terms of this discussion, they constituted a single-country, non-public set of mono-nets. At this time there were also similar research networks in other countries, notably the Joint Academic Network (JANET) in Britain and CYCLADES in France, which were also mono-nets.

Once the feasibility of e-mail had been established, several different communication systems developed. The first major resource for the wider academic community was Usenet. Using the ordinary telephone network to connect host computers that had the UNIX operating system, it offered a large number of discussion groups. The number of sites making Usenet available grew from 3 in 1979 to 15 in 1980 and to 150 in 1981, reaching 11,000 in 1988.[7] As each site had many users, there were at least a million individuals on Usenet by the end of the 1980s. When Usenet software was first distributed, free of charge, it was promoted as "the poor man's ARPANET."[8] In August 1983, UNIX was improved by work at University of California, Berkeley, with the addition of TCP-IP. Berkeley helped to distribute UNIX, making Usenet available to universities around the world. A similar development in the 1980s was the formation of BITNET, for universities using IBM computers. Starting from an e-mail link between the City University of New York (CUNY) and Yale in 1981, it became by August 1988 a network of some 2,300 university computers, in 32 countries.[9] It was possible to send multiple e-mails through e-mail list managers (such as LISTSERV) and to exchange files containing data or software. In the early years, both Usenet and BITNET were mono-nets, in that they were only accessible from specific types of computers. By the late 1980s, it was possible to communicate between the two and to NSFNet, by using cumbersome addressing systems.

The next big software advance for university and public use of the immature Internet was the release of the Gopher system in 1991, by the University of Minnesota. This allowed organizations to establish libraries of documents, from which other computer users could download copies. The final phase in the software development of the modern Internet was the creation of the World Wide Web, which replaced the Gopher text-only libraries. The design of the html language, which lies behind all web pages, was done by Tim Berners-Lee at the European Council for Nuclear Research (CERN), to improve access to all their news, research reports, and databases on nuclear physics. He proposed the idea in March 1989 and had produced the software and the first web page by December 1990. It required the release of Mosaic, in February 1993, by the University of Illinois, to make the web accessible to millions of non-technical users. Mosaic, the forerunner to Netscape Navigator and Mozilla Firefox, was the first user-friendly web browser for use on a PC. As a result, from 1993 to 1995, the web exploded into widespread general use.

The most striking aspect of all these developments in a variety of universities and related research institutions was the open, collaborative spirit of the innovation process. E-mail systems, Usenet, Gophers, web server software and web browsers were all immediately shared, publicized, and distributed on a non-commercial basis, as public utilities. There was a deep ideological commitment to cooperation for the public good. The only constraint on the use of the university computers and all the new software was that they should not be used for commercial purposes. The Internet remains a system which promotes open-source software, the sharing of knowledge, notably through the massive unpaid voluntary effort lying behind Wikipedia, and the free exchange of ideas, through every individual having the ability to express themselves, subject to minimal censorship.

Networking by commercial organizations

As the initial large mainframe computers of the 1960s were so expensive, many businesses started by hiring use of computers by the hour from computer bureaux. Then, as time-sharing from terminals was developed, very large companies established their own internal mono-nets, connected to company offices in different locations. For example, there were airline ticketing systems and bank cash-machines in the 1960s, inventory control and accounting systems in the mid-1970s, and the launch of the Visa credit card network in 1977. However, all of these commercial systems were private mono-nets and remain so to this day. Most transnational corporations did not pursue the benefits of networking until the late 1990s. The most spectacular delay in commercial responses to the Internet was Microsoft's failure to develop an Internet browser, until after Netscape had become highly popular.

It would have been technically feasible to have connected the growing number of commercial and other mono-nets to form a network of networks, if not a full public Internet, during the 1970s. This did not happen because it was a condition of US government research funding that the ARPANET and its successor NSFNet could not be used for commercial purposes. NSFNet's "Acceptable Use Policy" forbidding "use for for-profit activities" or "extensive use for private or personal business" continued until the NSFNet administration was disbanded and privatized, in April 1995.[10]

The commercial world made a contribution to public use of the Internet by the launch of their own networks, to sell access to any individual possessing a computer, a telephone line, and a modem. A variety of small companies started in the early 1980s to provide simple e-mail and electronic conferencing services. In the early 1990s, Compuserve, Dialcom, and Prodigy were emerging as the largest commercial Internet service providers (ISPs) and then in the mid-1990s America On-Line (AOL) surpassed them. They all limited their subscribers to the services available on their own network: they were mono-nets. AOL, for example, tried to promote loyalty, by referring to its "members" and it was not possible to send e-mail to a competitor's network. Initially, the commercial mono-net model had some success, as the big networks took the lead in providing large well-indexed websites. However, these networks were only of crucial importance for a few years. Once Google was available from 1998 onwards, there was no need for an ISP to provide more than a connection to the Internet.

Specialist commercial networks, commercial websites, and commercial profit-making ISPs were all very late additions to the Internet. They all had to conform to the system as they found it and played no part in shaping it. Transnational corporations benefit from the Internet. However, no commercial companies (other than computer manufacturers) had a significant role in the development of the Internet and none of them, not even the mighty Microsoft, has had any significant impact on the nature of the Internet, let alone control of it.

The first public networks

The launch in August 1981 of the first IBM PC made more extensive computing available to small organizations and a variety of cheaper computers became available for games. The first public networking started when individuals provided local "bulletin board systems" (BBSes) on their own home computers. Usually, the "sysops" (the people running such systems) only had one telephone line into their home, so users could only connect one at a time. Nevertheless, most BBSes could offer e-mail, file transfers (FTP) and electronic conferences. In the early 1980s, there were numerous incompatible BBSes. Tom Jennings developed something nearer to a standard BBS, when in December 1983 he provided the Fido BBS to operate within MS-DOS. It quickly became the main system on PCs and later was extended to several other popular micro-computers.

Tom Jennings went on to develop FidoNet, the first network of BBSes, which extended these public mono-nets beyond the local community. It started in May 1984 when Jennings connected his Fido BBS in San Francisco to a friend's Fido BBS in Baltimore. FidoNet was able to exchange messages between Fido hosts, sending each day's messages in a single bundle over ordinary telephone lines. These calls were made at cheap rates in the middle of the night, during a standard Fido Hour. After just six months, by the end of 1984, there were 100 nodes. In September 1985, Tim Pozar, another computer specialist, extended the benefits of FidoNet, by providing UFGATE, a gateway to link FidoNet users and those who were on UNIX systems or NSFNet. In addition, access to Usenet from FidoNet became possible. This effectively made FidoNet part of a primitive, immature Internet.

The expansion in FidoNet was dramatic, reaching some 21,000 nodes by April 1993, when the web started, and nearly 36,000 nodes at its peak in June 1995. At a very conservative estimate of 20 to 25 users per node, the *main* network must have had half a million users in 1993 (around the same number as on AOL at that time) and up to a million at its peak. The full size of the *effective* FidoNet was never known, because some nodes were entry points for local networks that were unrecognized by, and unknown to, the main system. For example, there was a local FidoNet in the Philippines from 1986, but it did not formally link to the main international FidoNet until 1991. FidoNet became important for NGOs in developing countries. By the early 1990s FidoNet had evolved from US local communities to become a global network, operating on all continents. In addition, large organizations, such as the US Forestry Service, and companies also used Fidonet to establish their own separate, private, mono-nets.[11]

Early networking by NGOs

For some, but not all, NGOs it was in their nature to adopt social and political networking and hence computer networking as an integral part of their activism. There are three political movements in which this is most evident: the human rights movement, the peace movement, and the environmental movement. All are intrinsically committed to transnational activity and each in their different ways made important contributions to the administrative and technical innovations that would eventually result in an open public transnational network, the Association for Progressive Communications (APC). However, it would be totally false to assume that all the NGO pioneers were left-wing or progressive. Racist and anti-Semitic groups were also very early users of BBSes. Liberty Bell Net went on-line in March 1984, Aryan Liberty Net also was announced by a Texan Ku Klux Klan leader in early 1984, and the White Aryan Resistance BBS was started in California in 1985. They were seeking transnational connections so that their attitudes could be expressed in countries where extreme expressions of prejudice and hate were illegal.[12]

Networking by the human rights movement

As human rights activities expanded at the UN, an increasing need was felt for networks to exchange information. By an odd quirk of history, a network for academics interested in human rights was launched in 1976 with the name Human Rights Internet, but it was not in any way computer-based. A second development came in 1979 when a group of NGOs decided to make informa-tion sharing possible. This evolved into the Human Rights Information and Documentation Systems International (HURIDOCS), which was established in 1982. It initially concentrated on making communication more precise by producing a reference work on human rights terminology and data coding. They created a database on human rights organizations and their archives, compiled a directory of computer centers, and set standards for reporting on human rights violations. HURIDOCS did not itself document human rights violations but formed a decentralized network of human rights NGOs. It also promoted networking, initially by non-electronic communications, by offer-ing training to NGOs in developing countries. HURIDOCS is now a major web-based information portal, with its own specialized search engine.

Another network originated from requests within the International Coalition for Development Action (ICDA), by their small Southern NGO members, for improved access to information. In January 1982, Chris Pinney, ICDA's chair, organized a conference in Lisbon on computer networking. After a two-year trial, using a bulletin board system, it was agreed, at a second conference in Valletri in October 1984, to create the Interdoc network. Unlike most BBSes, it had a formal organizational structure, with membership, a low-level annual membership fee, a technical advisory group, and a steering group on policy. There was also a secretariat, provided by the International Documentation and Communication Centre (IDOC), an Italian specialist group on docu-ment archiving. The goals were for the NGOs to learn about each other's work, to share knowledge on computing and networking, to improve access to each other's databases, and to improve communications, particularly on campaign issues. Signatories to the Valletri Agreement included ICDA, IDOC, HURIDOCS, five Southern NGOs, a Canadian development group, and two Dutch computing groups. Interdoc was stronger than an impersonal computer network, because it also held face-to-face conferences and work-shops. Graham Lane reports that at least 15 major events were organized in developing countries in the 1980s. One of the Dutch groups, Antenna, actively extended the reach of the network and its Director, Michael Polman, spent much time providing computer training to developing country NGOs. The core of the Interdoc network was a set of 25 NGOs, acting as intermediaries for an outer circle of developing country NGOs, including many on FidoNet. This increased the total to between four and five thousand Interdoc users.[13] While ICDA was originally focused on the exchange of information about development, Interdoc also became a major tool for human rights activists in developing countries and for the HURIDOCS network.

Amnesty International was one of the leaders in the foundation of HURIDOCS and was a very early user of the new computing technology in other ways. In particular, Urgent Action appeals were started in March 1973, to defend prisoners at risk of being tortured or executed, with an emphasis on the impact of a rapid response. While these were initially done by letters and telegrams, e-mail offered an ideal tool. In October 1987, Amnesty's National Section in the United States established an Online Urgent Action Network, based on PeaceNet (see below) and on a Compuserve "Issues Forum." Electronic appeals were made about three times per week. Amnesty was soon using this tool in other countries. For example, Laurie Wiseberg says, "An urgent action network based on e-mail was coordinated from Hong Kong in 1988, when there were sweeping arrests of social activists in Malaysia."[14]

By the time of the World Conference on Human Rights in Vienna, in June 1993, the human rights NGO community had learnt about global computer networking. They established an information center with the assistance of the UN Secretariat at the Vienna conference.[15] Access was provided to e-conferences on human rights and to important databases main-tained by Amnesty International and by Human Rights Internet. Ibrahima Fall, Secretary-General of the conference, later made a strong statement of appreciation

> for the outstanding contribution by the APC towards the success of the World Conference on Human Rights. The electronic distribution of documentation during the preparatory process and the Conference itself enabled the widest possible access to information for the benefit of all participants and especially for grassroots NGOs. Furthermore, the work-shops and briefings organised by the APC on information technology proved to be extremely useful for all NGOs.[16]

The Vienna conference did much to strengthen the human rights NGOs as a global advocacy community. It convinced them of the value of electronic communications and promoted computer networking.

For the Fourth World Conference on Women, in Beijing in September 1995, the human rights community, including the women's movement, was exceptionally well organized. An APC Women's Networking Support Programme began preparations two years in advance. Prior to the conference, they established a directory of women activists who were on-line and promoted the creation and use of new electronic conferences. They made the political point of establishing computer technology would not be a male-only field, by fielding at Beijing a team of 40 experts from 25 countries, including ten technicians, all of whom were women. They were supported by three women at GreenNet in London. The lead was taken by Latin American women, with Ecuanex, a network based in Ecuador, obtaining the funding and organizing the event and Cristina Vasconi from Nicarao, a network in Nicaragua, acting as the Technical Coordinator. There were two computer centers at the NGO Forum in Huairou and one at the main UN site in Beijing. Vasconi negotiated with the Chinese government to install a TCP-IP leased line to the NGO Forum. The APC team was divided into four groups: User Support, Information Facilitation, Political-Diplomatic Action, and Training. One problem was the lack of any computing facilities for the media, resulting in User Support having to service the media as well as NGOs. During the conference, the Information Facilitation group promoted two-way political exchanges, with grass-roots NGOs inputting to the diplomatic conference and those in Beijing using electronic communications to influence the media back home. The Political-Diplomatic Action group gained recognition of women's right of access to ICT in the final Programme of Action, to ensure computer networking would make a major contribution to follow-up activities at the UN.[17]

The human rights movement was a pioneer in adopting computer networking, but not in developing the technology. They used local BBSes, but did not extend their coverage. Their creative contribution was to demonstrate the potential value of global networks and to help to inspire more advanced networking by the peace and environmental movements.

Networking by the peace movement

We saw that computer networking for the public started with BBSes. This was ideal for peace groups who wanted to organize within the local community in the United States, particularly in Silicon Valley, California. In 1985, Mark Graham and Scott Weikart, who were professional computer experts, formed PeaceNet, by bringing together four small specialist NGOs in the

San Francisco Bay Area. In August 1986, PeaceNet offered its services on a subscription basis to a wider range of NGOs and to the general public, going on-line on 1 September 1986. Then, Weikart and Graham expanded PeaceNet to full US coverage and extensive overseas networking. They actively sought out other groups, to explain to them the benefits of e-mail and e-conferences.[18] By the end of 1988, PeaceNet was linked to another 99 NGOs from the peace movement. They included many local groups; various solidarity groups, such as for Nicaragua; some 18 religious groups, notably Quakers, Mennonites, Unitarians, and Baha'i; the leading secular US groups, the War Resisters League, SANE, and the Freeze Campaign; the leading British groups, the Campaign for Nuclear Disarmament, and the more radical Committee of 100; the respected monthly magazine *Peace News*, well-established global net-works, such as the International Peace Bureau formed in 1891, the Women's International League for Peace and Freedom (1915), and the World Federalist Movement (1947); and the newer global networks, the World Disarmament Campaign (1979), International Physicians for the Prevention of Nuclear War (1980), Computer Professionals for Social Responsibility (1981), and Peace Brigades International (1981).[19]

While it is not surprising to find peace activists adopted the Internet with enthusiasm, this was not sufficient for them to have been pioneers in network-ing. PeaceNet was itself a special type of NGO. It was a very small group of highly skilled computer experts, notably Graham and Weikart, who did no peace work themselves but were dedicated to promoting networking by peace activists. These two individuals were able to establish and operate a server, so that PeaceNet was an independent network offering the latest computing services directly to NGOs.

Networking by the environmental movement

In the United States, the creation of computer networks for the environmental movement was similar to and related to the developments in the peace move-ment. In 1982, the Farallones Institute created EcoNet, to bring together environmental NGOs, and in 1984 they were able to start a computer network. However, this local Californian initiative had a weak organizational structure and insufficient technical skills to develop further. In 1986 Mark Graham negotiated the purchase by PeaceNet of EcoNet from the Farallones Institute. For a while they operated as PeaceNet/EcoNet, but some environmentalists were not comfortable being identified with radicals among the peace activists. In June 1987, the two networks formally combined under the umbrella of a new legal identity, the Institute for Global Communications (IGC), but they agreed to operate using their separate, more recognizable names.

Another Californian mono-net, the Whole Earth 'Lectronic Link, known as the WELL, was started in February 1985 by Stewart Brand, as an offshoot from his publishing work for the counter-culture movement and sustainable, self-sufficient communes. This was a BBS system that developed over 100 e-conferences and was an important introduction to the Internet for various disparate groups: environmentalists, US radicals, fans of the Grateful Dead, computer experts, and journalists. Despite being more successful than EcoNet initially, the WELL never expanded substantially beyond its Californian origins. IGC actively promoted its services, targeting NGOs and their members around the world, whereas Brand's approach was to allow the users to develop the network in an anarchic manner. Ironically, the IGC's actively managed system gained many more participants and promoted greater diversity than the WELL's anarchic system.

In Britain, neither the political problems of relations between peace activists and environmentalists nor a focus on community networking were present. Mitra Ardron was the political pioneer who took the initiative in May 1985 to form a simple BBS on his own computer in London. In early 1986, having negotiated a special low rate charge, he transferred to a small commercial system, GeoNet, and used the name GreenNet. The network offered e-mail, use of mailing lists, e-conferences, political databases, purchase of computers at discount prices, advice on computing skills, and monitoring of news media. From the start a diverse range of NGOs were willing to work under the environment label, as their common identity. GreenNet soon included not only Greenpeace and Friends of the Earth but also Amnesty International, Survival International, International Youth Exchange, and the *New Internationalist* magazine. Initially, GreenNet was an extraordinary, innovative venture and personal gamble by Mitra, as it relied on his own funds, grants, and gifts. In October 1987, GreenNet was able to move into the headquarters of Friends of the Earth, with its own Plexus computer, to act as the hub for the network. They then opened London's first Internet café.[20]

By the end of 1988, there were 63 environmental NGOs operating on EcoNet or GreenNet. They included the major global networks, the World Conservation Union and the World Wide Fund for Nature; two important campaigning networks, based in London, the Women's Environmental Network and the Pesticide Action Network; many US and British branches of Friends of the Earth and Greenpeace; the leading US NGOs, the Sierra Club and the National Wildlife Federation; and respected British NGOs, such as the Wildfowl Trust, Panos, and the Soil Association. They could access e-conferences on 68 separate environmental topics. It was not long before the slogan "Dial Locally, Act Globally" was being widely used in both the United States and Britain.

GreenNet succeeded because NGOs were eager to gain such services. In a 1987 GreenNet brochure, Greenpeace was quoted as saying:

> GreenNet allows us to monitor UPI, AP [the major US news agencies] and Washington Post stories as they develop. Often we can correct an error, add an opinion, or catch a misquote before the story appears. It also enables us to get the same 'as it happens news' as most of the media; when journalists call us we know what information they have and what slant it has. In battling the multi-million dollar publicity machines of government and big business this kind of capability is priceless.

In June 1987, the Joseph Rowntree Charitable Trust, a Quaker charity, provided a grant of £15,000 to enable GreenNet to make a concerted effort to bring a critical mass of peace groups on-line simultaneously, to develop manuals for novices, and to provide training and support. The Trust had already heard of PeaceNet's work in the United States and their grantees were expressing a desire to access computer networks. They noted "the potential importance of developments such as this for the peace movements should not be underestimated." They cautiously concluded, "the crucial issue is GreenNet's capacity to carry out the work required," but they were reassured by a visit to GreenNet's offices.[21] Once enough groups and individuals had been attracted to use its services, the network became self-financing through a monthly user's charge and connection fees. After a few years, they became one of the first Internet service providers in Britain.

The formation of the Association for Progressive Communications

PeaceNet/EcoNet (IGC) and GreenNet soon started to cooperate and they established the first public transatlantic computer link. GreenNet and PeaceNet were using the same type of host computer, so in November 1987 Weikart was able to copy all the IGC software onto a massive disk, bring it to London and install the same networking system for GreenNet. From this point, IGC and GreenNet were effectively, from the users' perspective, a single network, with transatlantic e-mail communications and common e-conferences. While there were initially network nodes in only two countries, users from many other countries were able to connect via international telephone calls. IGC and GreenNet had each first gone on-line in 1986, yet less than two years later they were able to report they had connected 300 NGOs with "immediate, cost-effective exchange of information between people in 70 countries" using their own servers with gateways to "more than twenty commercial and academic networks." The operations had "no real parallels in the communications industry."[22] By 1990 the US–British joint network had expanded into the Association for Progressive Communications (APC), a global Internet service provider for NGOs.

In order to expand, APC needed to gain funding to buy larger computers and other equipment for the network hubs, to pay for at least a few permanent staff and to cover travel expenses for computer experts to install the first transnational connections. Most NGO computer networks quite quickly became financially viable, because so many groups and individuals were eager to sign up and pay the basic users' fees. Another important source of funding in developing countries, particularly in Latin America, was the UN Development Programme. The IGC had more resources than the others because various large US charities, notably the MacArthur, Ford, and General Service foundations, supported IGC's work to promote networks in other countries. In addition, two rock stars, Peter Gabriel, an internationalist and human rights activist, and Little Stephen, an anti-apartheid activist, performed two concerts in Tokyo in December 1986, with some of the proceeds going to IGC. The name for the APC was chosen in July 1987, when Graham and Mitra met Gabriel and Little Stephen in a New York hotel. Although the APC did not officially exist until 1990, the name was commonly used from this point onwards for the collaborating networks.

The opportunities for innovation were immediately seized by NGOs in Latin America and Africa, but less so in Asia. Developing country networks were started during the immature period of the Internet, using BBS. Some of these rapidly upgraded in the late 1980s to the most advanced systems of the time. This success resulted from a combination of the demand for better access to information and networking facilities from Southern NGOs and the supply of technical knowledge and skills from the Northern NGO networks. Just as key individuals undertook networking initiatives in the United States and Britain, other individuals took the lead in several other countries. In most cases, they were assisted by the staff of IGC, GreenNet, and/or a Canadian network, who became evangelists and advisers for the establishment of new networks.

While the idea of forming a transnational network of NGO networks was under discussion from 1987, because of prevarication by the IGC and divisions between IGC and GreenNet about how structured the organization should be, there were delays in creating a formal organization. The matter was brought to a head when a major Interdoc conference in May 1990 on "Information Exchange for Social Change" was held in the Netherlands. It brought together "a truly worldwide cross-section of information users, information providers and information carriers" including the leaders of the seven networks who were already operating a practical network of networks.[23] IGC and GreenNet have already been discussed. Web Networks in Canada and AlterNex in Brazil were the next networks to collaborate. Because of their special importance, they will be discussed below. The remaining three found-ers of the APC—Nicarao in Central America, NordNet in Scandinavia, and Pegasus in Australia—will then be introduced more briefly.

The Canadian APC member, Web Networks, originated from the envi-ronmental movement. Mike Jensen developed a BBS for the Ontario Environmental Network (OEN), with the support of grants from the Ontario government and the UN World Food Programme. The number of users expanded quickly, not least because participation in a BBS was much cheaper than using the emerging Canadian commercial e-mail mono-nets. Then, OEN created a center to connect all their local members and to provide training, desktop publishing, and hardware supplies for NGOs. In April 1989, Jensen and Mitra upgraded Web Networks, by installing the IGC operating system and linking the Canadian NGOs to IGC and GreenNet. In 1990 Jensen took the IGC "mother system" and specialist hardware to Australia and spent four months linking the Pegasus NGO network to the overall APC network. Later the same year, Jensen worked in Zimbabwe with the local BBS system, Micro-Computing for NGOs (MANGO). This was an NGO coalition led by a news agency, a research centre, and an ecumenical centre, all of which worked on a regional basis with groups in several countries of Eastern and Southern Africa. Their BBS was converted to FidoNet, which then enabled these African NGOs to operate globally. Jensen went on in 1991 to increase the facilities available to FidoNet users, by developing a Fido gateway at GreenNet, which provided access to all the APC e-conferences. Then, costs for communications by Southern African NGOs, within the region and glo-bally, were further reduced, by Jensen spending six months to install another Fido gateway on the UNIX system of WorkNet in South Africa. At the same time, he installed a UNIX-based connection between WorkNet and GreenNet, bringing South Africa into the APC system. By the end of 1991, Jensen had also helped link Senegal, Nigeria, and Kenya to the APC.[24]

The Brazilian Institute for Social and Economic Analysis (IBASE) had been founded in 1981, as part of the development of a progressive civil soci-ety that would eventually bring in democracy and end military influence in Brazilian politics. In 1984, they started to work with Interdoc and, in 1985, they formed a local BBS network. Then one of the IBASE leaders, Carlos Afonso, drafted a proposal in July 1988 for the UN Development Programme to fund the hub for a network in Brazil, which would link to IGC. Afonso estimated at least 50 Brazilian NGOs, plus some 80 individual users, would immediately join the system. In addition, he anticipated the hub would be a focus for transnational networking by some 70 groups in other Latin American and Caribbean countries, particularly members of Interdoc and of the Forum on Debt and Development (FONDAD) campaign on the external debt crisis. The project was approved in December 1988 and funded by UNDP and the

Italian government, via an Italian development NGO, plus a contribution from IBASE. In July 1989, AlterNex started to operate e-mail and e-conferencing, with full connectivity to IGC and the other NGO networks linked to IGC. Initially, there were more foreign users and fewer Brazilian users than expected. In response, IBASE set up "community e-mail agencies" in the larger cities, for use by the smaller NGOs. Susanne Sallin reports that four years later AlterNex was still serving users in as many as 35 other countries. Also, just as AlterNex was assisted by IGC, it went on to assist in the creation of other networks in other Latin American countries.[25]

The story of AlterNex may appear to be no more than a simple account of technological innovation, but it was also a significant contribution to the development of democracy in Brazil. Their formation in 1988–89 required transnational support from IGC and UNDP. Then they faced a political struggle to upgrade their facilities for the 1992 Earth Summit. Government computer scientists, IGC, and the UN summit secretariat all played a role in achieving an end to the government ban on the public use of TCP-IP high-speed Internet connections and an end to the ban on private imports of the more powerful computer equipment. As with many other countries, access to the Internet made Brazil a more open society.

- *NordNet* started under the name FredsNaetet (PeaceNet in Swedish). It was linked to IGC in January 1989 and stimulated networking more generally in the Baltic region. In particular, the European Nuclear Disarmament movement held an East–West conference in July 1990, with half of the conference taking place in Helsinki and half in Tallinn. NordNet established a communication system between the two and also smuggled modems into the Soviet Union. This provided a permanent hole in the border, which allowed Soviet NGOs to communicate freely with the APC network.[26]
- *Nicarao* was established by cooperation between four organizations: IGC, AlterNex, a software cooperative in Managua, and the Regional Co-ordinating Agency for Economic and Social Research (CRIES), an umbrella NGO. CRIES was important in providing administrative support, in being a major user, and in promoting awareness of the computer network within its membership of 34 research organizations in 14 countries. IGC assisted Nicarao to become a full hub and it was connected to IGC in June 1989, making Nicarao the first ISP in Nicaragua. Oxfam-UK used the network to link all its offices in the region.
- *Pegasus*, an Australian network, began operations in September 1989, initially using the name EarthNet. It was started by Ian Peter, an environmental activist, who was well known as a campaigner against the depletion of rainforests. The network quickly signed up all the major

Australian environmental NGOs. Ian Peter had been commissioned in 1986 by the United Nations Environment Programme to create an e-mail network of environmental NGOs in the Asia Pacific Region. He capitalized on this work by making Pegasus an important regional hub, bringing NGOs from Pacific Island countries on-line.

Although the APC as a formal organization only consisted of seven member networks in May 1990, it must be remembered that it was providing global communications for NGOs all around the world. It offered, by far, the most comprehensive e-mail connections available on any system, superior to those on university, commercial, or government networks. It provided e-conferences on all the subjects of interest to NGOs and enabled them to become better informed, both on the substance of the issues and on which other NGOs were active. From the beginning, the APC radically changed the balance between North and South, at least in the world of NGO relations.

A major turning point: the Rio Earth Summit, 1990–92

The developments in NGO networking were fortuitously timed to enable environmental NGOs to make an unprecedented input to the Earth Summit, officially known as the United Nations Conference on Environment and Development (UNCED). In March 1990, Robert Pollard, an American Quaker, environmental activist, and computing expert, put forward a proposal to the secretariat for a set of electronic conferences to enable NGOs around the world to follow the preparations for the summit. This was warmly welcomed by both the UN bodies and the NGOs who were consulted. On 22 April 1990, Maurice Strong, the Secretary-General of the summit, announced the establishment of an UNCED "Global Electronic Network" with access to the system through EcoNet.[27] Then, Robert Pollard and Langston Goree produced a guide for NGOs on how to access the electronic conferences and it was widely circulated at the first session of the UNCED Preparatory Committee in Nairobi in August 1990.[28] The result was an explosion of interest, from both Northern and Southern NGOs.[29] At the time, the only people in Brazil who had any significant experience with and competence in computer networking were AlterNex. At the end of 1990, EcoNet asked AlterNex to take over responsibilities for the APC–UNCED e-conferences and IBASE submitted a detailed proposal to the UNCED secretariat, to link the site for the official diplomatic conference to various sites for NGO activities. The proposal was accepted and included in the general host country agreement negotiated in September–October 1991 between the Brazilian government and the UN. AlterNex capabilities were upgraded, with financial support from the Canadian and Dutch governments, by Sun Microsystems donating a new computer and by the Brazilian university network providing a TCP-IP connection to the United States. UNDP funded AlterNex operations at the summit.[30]

When the summit opened, four local computer centers linked to AlterNex were established at the official UNCED locations in Rio: the main UN conference center, an NGO Communications Center in the Hotel Gloria, the NGO Global Forum, and AlterNex's own operations center. There was also direct access to AlterNex from 40 dedicated lines and from the transnational TCP-IP networks. Conference participants could send e-mail to practically all the available systems (including commercial services, university networks, FidoNet, and all the APC networks), access official UNCED documents and NGO documents, continue participation in the UNCED e-conferences, use word-processing, and print documents. A team of 24 volunteer technicians from seven APC networks staffed the system. Crucial facilities were being used in Brazil for the first time and delays in importing equipment gave very little time to install and test the systems. Against such a background, the AlterNex operation was a major organizational success and an impressive technical achievement.[31]

The AlterNex system made information available not only to diplomats, NGOs, and the media attending the Earth Summit but also to Brazilian NGOs and to the NGOs around the world who were unable to attend. The APC provided open e-conferences for NGOs to debate the issues at UNCED, on which anybody could add their own comments. There were also restricted-access e-conferences, on which authorized NGO participants could hold private discussions. A third facility was a set of read-only e-conferences, for the UN Secretariat to post official documents. The latter was fully utilized by the secretariat, starting with the first posting in April 1990, announcing the initial collaboration with EcoNet. Howard Frederick, writing in early 1992, reported that APC already had over 30 e-conferences covering UNCED.[32] The UN posted background papers and draft negotiating texts, on a server hosted by Antenna, throughout the preparatory process and the main conference, which made them available for the NGO activists present at the meetings and for anybody who had access to one of the APC networks.[33] Such activities were so new to NGO representatives that the APC staff also provided training and computing advice at the main sites, including setting up the first e-mail account for many users. During the conference, nearly 1,400 new accounts were registered with AlterNex. As a result, the new users were inducted into the benefits of networking and there was a permanent effect on NGO activities after UNCED. The ability, for some of the NGOs at Rio, to consult rapidly with their offices at home was seen as a spectacular innovation, enhancing their ability to assess the diplomatic process and generate responses. "This resulted in modifications to resolutions on the basis of contributions from concerned activists from around the world who were unable to attend in person."[34]

At the final UNCED Preparatory Committee (2 March to 5 April 1992 in New York) and the main conference in Rio, there was another major contribution, in the production by Langston Goree (aka Kimo) and Pamela Chasek of the first editions of a new daily newspaper, the *Earth Summit Bulletin*. Each day's edition, covering both the main diplomatic proceedings and the NGO lobbying on the previous day, was printed overnight and distributed in the morning. It combined an accurate informative reporting style, with some investigative reporting, plus "Things to Look For" and "In the Corridors" features. Using a team of doctoral students and other volunteers as journalists, it was able to cover all the various meetings of the plenary and working groups. This was valuable for those small NGOs and small government delegations, who could only attend some of the meetings. All the main political actors, not just the NGOs but also the secretariat and government officials, read the *Bulletin* to gain an overall perspective on what was happening. Each edition was also posted on an e-conference, which enabled daily reporting on the UNCED proceedings to be available around the world. At the main summit the newspaper was renamed the *Earth Negotiations Bulletin*, a title which is now a standard feature of all the main UN meetings on sustainable development. There are still daily printed editions, but web postings have replaced the e-conferences.[35]

Box 4.2 Tributes to APC's work at the Earth Summit

*   "The APC networks delivered a tremendous job during the UNCED Preparatory Process, and during the Earth Summit itself. With their full co-operation, it was possible to reach a very large and important environment-development community worldwide with the information generated during that period in a timely and cost-effective fashion. Without this communication channel, the involvement of non-governmental organizations in the official UNCED process, as well as in the various parallel processes, simply could not have been as effective as they were." (Janos Pasztor, the Information Systems Coordinator for the UNCED Secretariat)

(Box continued on next page)

- "In Rio, each day 2–3 features in English and Spanish were sent out on APC via e-mail and fax to 47 NGOs and media outlets in 19 countries. Without APC, the logistics of this would have been almost impossible and the cost certainly unafford-able. The features were also posted onto APC conferences, thus allowing access to all APC users around the world. The features were picked up from the conferences and reprinted in NGO newsletters and magazines in the United States, Britain, Netherlands, Mexico, Uruguay, Australia and Malaysia. There is no other method by which the features could have been made available to such a wide audience at such low cost." (Patrick McCully, an editor of *Ecologist Magazine*)
- The most dramatic tribute came from Wangari Matthai of the Greenbelt Movement in Kenya. She had been jailed and beaten for her opposition to President Moi's plan to build in Nairobi's Uhuru Park. After news of her plight was posted on the APC Networks, the Kenyan Government was inundated with demands for her release. She said, "Because of all of you I am alive and healing and I have been able to attend the Earth Summit in Rio. So receive my deep-felt gratitude and may you be blessed abundantly."

Source: *APC at the Earth Summit, Statements from the Users*: www.apc.org/summit.htm (as of 1 March 1997).

The comments in Box 4.2 indicate the excitement generated by the AlterNex operation. The impact of APC's work was also recognized in the official diplomatic proceeding of UNCED. *Agenda 21* urged governments, the UN, and NGOs to "*exploit various initiatives for electronic links*, to support information sharing, to provide access to databases, … to facilitate communication … to facilitate intergovernmental negotiations" and the "linkage of different electronic networks." The emphasized phrase was, in diplomatic terms, as near as the UN could come to a specific endorsement of the APC and was giving the UN Secretariat the authority to continue working with the APC.[36] The APC as a whole gained valuable experience from the UNCED operations, which enabled them to establish similar networks at all the major UN conferences in the first half of the 1990s (see Table 4.1).

Table 4.1 APC computing centers at UN conferences, 1992–95

Details of the UN conference	*APC members providing the services*
Rio de Janeiro, Brazil: 3–14 June 1992 United Nations Conference on Environment and Development	AlterNex, Brazil Antenna, The Netherlands
Vienna, Austria: 14–25 June 1993 United Nations Conference on Human Rights	IGC, United States ComLink, Germany
Cairo, Egypt: 5–13 September 1994 International Conference on Population and Development	Chasque, Uruguay
Copenhagen, Denmark: 6–12 March 1995 World Summit on Social Development	NordNet, Sweden Inform, Denmark
Beijing, China: 4–15 September 1995 Fourth World Conference on Women	Ecuanex, Ecuador Nicarao, Nicaragua

After 1995, when the World Wide Web had started to become popular, APC's work was no longer needed to provide communication centers. The United Nations launched its own website on the fiftieth anniversary of the signing of the UN Charter in June 1995. From then onwards, all UN conferences were fully documented by the UN on its own website. Similarly, the major NGOs stopped using e-conferences and made their positions public on their websites. The APC achieved recognition for its pioneering work with the UN, by being granted General Status by ECOSOC in 1995.

The consolidation of the Association for Progressive Communications

The APC entered a new phase in its work in the 1990s, after having demonstrated the benefits for NGOs of cheap, rapid, global communications:

> What the Rio Summit meant for the communications activists was that they were no longer being treated as computer nerds on the fringe, but that non-governmental, non-hierarchical groups could put together and operate an informational distribution and communications system that was more accessible and meaningful than what commercial or government organisations were providing.[37]

While APC had a very active policy of assisting in the creation of new networks, particularly in developing countries, and adding them as nodes to their global network, it expanded its membership very cautiously. It had a formal policy of only accepting one member network in each country. The network had to offer the APC services to all NGOs and to guarantee the free, uncensored flow of information. New networks had to demonstrate their services were "reliable, easy to use, comprehensive, well-supported and inexpensive."[38] The list of the first APC members, until the end of 1993, is given in Table 4.2. This year is chosen to give a picture of the APC network of networks at the point when the World Wide Web commenced operating on the mature public Internet.

In 1990–93 there were still many distinct mono-nets. Although "the Internet" based on NSFNet and other government and university networks had become a very large, transnational set of mono-nets, it was still not open for direct public use. For most people, communication with somebody on a different network was either rather complex or impossible. APC was the only organization ever to address this problem in a comprehensive manner. (After 1995, the problem disappeared because virtually all hosts communicated with TCP-IP and Microsoft included TCP-IP within Windows.) By 1989, five of the original APC members—IGC, GreenNet, Web Networks, AlterNex, and Pegasus—had established gateways to use TCP-IP. This meant NGOs could connect to e-mail services, e-conferences, FTP, Gophers, and, a few years later, to the web pages at universities in many countries, plus the fledgling government systems. APC also provided access to the UN, via UNDP, and to FidoNet. By 1990, there were even connections to 23 commercial e-mail mono-nets, because Mitra developed gateways to them, in some cases without

Table 4.2 The member networks of the Association for Progressive Communications by 1993

Name of network	Location	Connected to IGC/APC	Other countries served by 1993
GreenNet	UK	1987	Telephone and FidoNet
PeaceNet/EcoNet	USA	1987	Direct telephone access
Web Networks	Canada	1988	Telephone and FidoNet
NordNet	Sweden	1989	Nordic and Baltic region
Nicarao	Nicaragua	1989	Central America
AlterNex	Brazil	1989	South America
Pegasus	Australia	1989	South East Asia and Pacific
ComLink	Germany	1991	Austria, Switzerland, Turkey
GlasNet	Russia	1991	Other ex-USSR
Ecuanex	Ecuador	1992	–
Chasque	Uruguay	1992	Paraguay
SangoNet	South Africa	1993	Southern Africa and FidoNet
Wamani	Argentina	1993	–
GLUK	Ukraine	1993	–
Histria and ZaMir	Slovenia	1993	Most parts of ex-Yugoslavia
LaNeta	Mexico	1993	–

the company's knowledge. "He would buy one e-mail account on each, and write a script to log in, download and upload e-mail and deliver it to GreenNet users."[39] No other network was systematically enabling its users to connect to virtually all other networks, in a simple, user-friendly manner. The universities had established the value of a global network for academic use, but APC established the demand for and the practicality of a global public network.

It has already been pointed out that the APC system connected to users in many more countries than the list of members suggests. IGC and GreenNet were open for telephone access from any organization that could afford the cost of long-distance calls. Nicarao was operating as a network for the Central American region and AlterNex covered many countries in South America. GreenNet had special arrangements with NGOs in Africa. While the Soviet Union still existed, several APC members (primarily IGC, GreenNet, and NordNet) were already starting to cross the Cold War divide, by working to establish a network in the Soviet Union, GlasNet, which would formally join APC in 1991. In addition to the members, by February 1993, there were also officially recognized "partner" networks in more than 40 other countries. These were NGOs who promoted civil society communication in their country or region, but lacked the capacity to become APC nodes. Thus, Pegasus was serving a regional network of eight partners, covering Indonesia, Thailand, Malaysia, and five Pacific Island countries. In Southern Africa, there were partners in Tanzania, Zambia, and Zimbabwe, but the SangoNet member in South Africa and the MANGO partner in Zimbabwe provided FidoNet connections to the whole Southern African region. The Kenyan partner, the Environment Liaison Centre International (ELCI), was not just a local electronic network but also worked globally with NGOs interested in the UN Environment Programme in Nairobi. The partner in Senegal, Environment and Development Action in the Third World (ENDA-TM), was important as a regional West African Francophone network. After the collapse of communism, with some financial support from the Soros Open Society Institute, APC strongly supported the development of civil society and the creation of networks in Eastern Europe, which first became partners and then members of APC. However, the coverage was not even throughout the world. While the English-speaking world and the Spanish-speaking world were comprehensively connected to the APC, Francophone Africa was not a strong presence, and the Arab world and much of Asia were excluded for a variety of financial, cultural, and political reasons. This regional bias remains today, both in the APC and in the mature Internet.

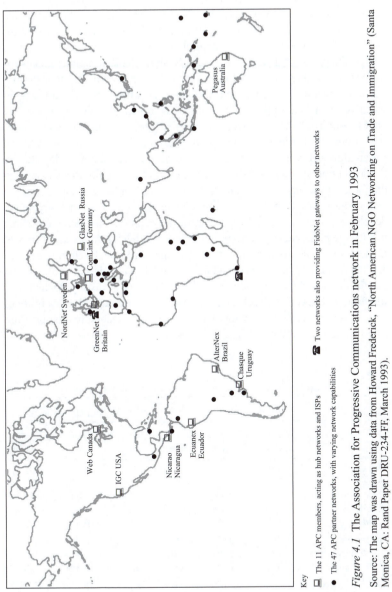

Key

Figure 4.1 The Association for Progressive Communications network in February 1993

Source: The map was drawn using data from Howard Frederick, "North American NGO Networking on Trade and Immigration" (Santa Monica, CA: Rand Paper DRU-234-FF, March 1993).

FidoNet and African NGOs

Throughout the early developments in the creation of the immature Internet in the 1980s, we have encountered FidoNet making a significant contribution. While FidoNet had minimal capabilities, it was particularly valuable for NGOs with limited resources and unreliable telephone systems, notably in Africa. Telephone costs were minimized, by short connection times and use of off-peak tariffs. FidoNet was also very robust: if there was a telephone disconnection, transmission could simply be resumed, after redialing, at the point when the break had occurred. The system was attractive to developing country NGOs, who could have contact with Northern NGOs at much cheaper rates than a normal daytime telephone conversation. FidoNet was also valuable for creating networks in communist countries that could not be detected by the secret police. Table 4.3 shows how the number of Fido nodes expanded dramatically during the immature Internet period. While the absolute increase was greatest in North America, the relative increase was much greater in developing countries and former communist countries. It is safe to assume that a large proportion of American users were individuals pursuing personal interests or linking to local community groups, while the developing country and Eastern European users would mainly be NGO activists pursuing global political issues. We have no direct evidence about the scale of FidoNet activity through the APC networks, but Table 4.3 does indicate the probability of at least hundreds of NGOs, with thousands of users, accessing the immature Internet, before the World Wide Web existed.[40]

Table 4.3 The expansion of FidoNet nodes on the immature Internet

	FidoNet in January 1989			FidoNet in April 1993		
	No. of nodes	*% of nodes*	*No. of countries*	*No. of nodes*	*% of nodes*	*No. of countries*
Africa	20	0.4%	2	93	0.4%	10
Asia	140	3.0%	7	919	4.4%	13
Latin America	32	0.7%	4	288	1.4%	12
USSR, E. Europe	0	0.0%	0	961	4.6%	16
Sub-total	192	4.1%	13	2,261	10.9%	51
W. Europe	894	19.0%	16	5,406	26.0%	20
Australasia	184	3.9%	2	904	4.3%	2
Sub-total	1,078	22.9%	18	6,310	30.3%	22
Not N. America	1,270	27.0%	31	8,571	41.2%	73
N. America	3,434	73.0%	3	12,253	58.8%	6
Global total	4,704	100.0%	34	20,824	100.0%	79

Source: *FidoNews*, 26 April 1993.

Small African NGOs gained access to FidoNet, through a variety of different organizational models. In South Africa, WorkNet was a product of the labor movement and its need for good communications, as part of the anti-apartheid struggle. It was founded in 1987 and soon expanded into a Fido BBS for the whole NGO community in Southern Africa. In 1993, it was renamed SangoNet, upgraded its capabilities, and became an APC member. In Kenya, the ELCI established a Fido BBS in October 1989 to enhance its role as a global network, bringing together Northern and Southern environmental NGOs. In Uganda, an academic network, MUKLA, was formed in December 1990 under the auspices of Makerere University, but it was open to the general public. It was one of the first nodes in a wider project, to link five countries in the region. In Ghana, NGOs were ahead of the universities, with Friends of the Earth starting its Fido node in April 1992. Many more African countries started to use FidoNet in the 1990s. The benefits of FidoNet were so great for those in developing countries that African NGOs continued to use it many years after the mature Internet became available.

A new role for the APC

In the late 1990s, the rapid development of commercial Internet service providers threatened the APC's finances. There were a variety of effects on the different networks. NordNet, GlasNet (Russia), and Pegasus were unable to continue. In the United States, IGC withdrew from being an ISP and became a shell of its former self.[41] However, most members' networks were able to take advantage of their early entry into the market, upgrade their services to full modern ISPs, and maintain enough subscribers to remain viable or even quite profitable. This included two of the African networks, SangoNet in South Africa and ENDA-Tiers Monde. The latter was originally a simple e-mail network based in Senegal and serving much of Francophone West Africa. It became a full APC member in 1997 and expanded its geographical coverage, gaining affiliates in the Maghreb, Asia, and Latin America.[42]

Just as the country networks changed, the APC also needed a new role. It was still involved, for a few years after the fall of communism, with establishing new NGO networks in Eastern Europe, but not elsewhere. In developing countries, APC started assisting individual NGOs with their use of the networks, hosting websites, and developing Internet strategies. It continued training activities, but with a shift from computing skills to communication and political skills. At the annual meeting in 2000 there was a major change in the policy covering membership. The rule that there should be only one member from each country was abandoned and members no longer had to be networks. This brought in some groups that were involved in training or media issues, without running their own networks.

From 2001, APC had a formal Communications and Information Policy Programme to promote civil society interests in global policy-making on information and communication technology (ICT). In particular, APC was a strong presence at the two phases of the World Summit on the Information Society (WSIS) organized by the UN and the International Telecommunications Union, in Geneva in December 2003 and in Tunis in November 2005. The APC advocated the use of ICT for development and action to overcome the North–South digital divide. The WSIS processes made plain the dangers from governments wishing to control the use of the Internet. During 2001–02, the APC developed an *Internet Rights Charter*, emphasizing access for all, freedom of expression, and multilateral democratic Internet governance.[43]

The political impact of computer networking

Graham Lane, the European regional coordinator for Interdoc, wrote a handbook for NGOs in 1990 on how to use electronic communications. In the foreword, Michael Polman, Antenna's Director and Interdoc's computing expert, said, "Networking fits the nature of NGOs like a glove. It supports the informal non-hierarchical exchange of information, it helps lateral communication and decentralized co-operation."[44] We now take e-mail and the web so much for granted that it is difficult to understand how wonderful the benefits seemed when electronic communications were first introduced. It is revolutionary that a small NGO, in a remote place, via a single skilled person, can be a participant in global networks and have some impact on political outcomes. The most important political aspect of APC's early work is that it introduced the rest of the world to the potential of the Internet. The UN's first use of the Internet was via the APC e-conferences for the Rio Earth Summit. A year later, in May 1993, the UN established its own independent presence on the Internet, with a Gopher run by UNDP, on behalf of all parts of the UN. In February 1994, Sallin reported:

> The APC has been chosen by more than 17 United Nations offices as an information provider and communications medium for collecting and disseminating information on global change issues. A few of these UN agencies include: the Food and Agriculture Organization (FAO), the Inter-Governmental Negotiating Committee on a [Framework Convention on Climate Change] (INC/FCCC), and the UN Centre for Human Rights, among others.[45]

Because the APC conferences were simpler to maintain than Gophers and they were well targeted for gaining an NGO audience, the UN continued to use them for some time. As we have already seen, the UN did not start their website until June 1995. The World Bank was similarly heavily influenced by UNCED. Their first use of the Internet was to provide electronic access for NGOs to information on the Global Environment Facility, by posting GEF documents on a GreenNet e-conference in late 1992.[46] It is more surprising that America On-Line had to rely on NGO experience to start a full Internet service. Their transition from being no more than an e-mail provider was undertaken by Mitra Ardron, the founder of GreenNet.[47] The governments of the world followed much later. At the beginning of 1994, even the US government did not use the Internet for political purposes.[48]

Conclusion

Within this complex story, it is evident that NGOs were pioneers in creating the Internet. During the period of the immature Internet, first of all through Interdoc from 1984 and then through the APC from 1987, NGOs were running more advanced networks than anybody else. The NGOs collaborated across all the continents, they offered the widest range of services, and they made more progress than anybody else in connecting different types of networks. If the Internet is a transnational network of networks, with public access, then, for the period from 1989 to 1995, the APC was the core of the Internet. The only way members of the public could have e-mail communications with all types of computer users in all parts of the world was through the APC and the only public access to the full range of e-conferences and Gopher databases on the Internet was through the APC. While the APC was connected to virtually all other networks, they were not all directly connected to each other. Commercial networks offering on-line services for the public were not allowed to provide access to all other networks and university networks did not attempt to do so. From 1993 to 1995, the APC swiftly lost its special position. Websites started to appear, Mosaic became available to browse them, all PCs could access TCP-IP networks, e-conferences and Gophers were transferred to the web, and commercial networks were eventually allowed full access. The mature Internet had arrived by the end of 1995.

Of course, we cannot claim NGOs created the Internet by themselves. At least 14 strands of activity can be identified as having been crucially important.

- The National Physical Laboratory in Britain contributed packet-switching.

- Computer scientists in US universities, building ARPANET with Pentagon funding, defined TCP-IP communication standards and the domain names system.
- Many private individuals developed e-mail and bulletin board systems, in particular Jennings made it possible to connect to NGOs in developing countries through FidoNet.
- UNIX, extensive e-conferencing, and Gopher software came from US universities on a purely civilian basis.
- AT&T developed software to connect UNIX computers, which allowed academics to gain experience with Usenet.
- Developing country NGOs, Pinney, and Polman articulated their demand for global networking and created Interdoc.
- Graham, Weikart, Mitra, Jensen, and Pozar proved incompatible networks could be linked through computers dedicated to act as gateways.
- Human rights NGOs, peace NGOs, and environmental NGOs vigorously pursued the idea of global networking through the Association for Progressive Communications in order to enhance NGO capabilities, especially for developing country NGOs.
- Sir Tim Berners-Lee at CERN in Geneva produced the language for writing web pages.
- Al Gore initiated the High Performance Computing and Communication Act of 1991, which funded the production of Mosaic at the University of Illinois.
- Governments around the world did most of the initial investment in the physical infrastructure over which the messages and computer files were exchanged.
- The innovations by NGOs in bringing all this together would not have been possible without funding from a variety of charities and the UN Development Programme.
- Various parts of the UN Secretariat also provided some of the early information sources that made grass-roots NGOs value APC's technological innovation.
- The vision and the hard work of Maurice Strong, the UNCED Secretariat, AlterNex, and other APC staff staged a powerful public demonstration of the communications revolution for a great number of political actors at the Rio Earth Summit.

In summary, universities, key individual computer experts, the United Nations, and NGOs all made major contributions to creating the Internet as a transnational network of networks, with access for the public.

Equally, it would be wrong to suggest the Internet would never have developed without the NGO contributions. The Internet could have been created by governments. Down this route, various systems of censorship, licensing who could publish on the Internet, and taxation of data transfers would have been attractive to many governments. Alternatively, the Internet could have been created by commercial organizations. Down this route, the initial attempts of Internet service providers to keep users on their own networks could have produced a poorly connected network of a small number of dominant networks in an oligopolistic structure. Costs would have been higher and open-source software would probably have been sabotaged by constructing technical barriers. Down either route, the result would have been many fewer people using the Internet and a minimal presence in developing countries.

In many countries, members of the Association for Progressive Communications were the first commercial Internet service provider, albeit using their profits to promote NGO networking. Some unambiguous examples were AlterNex in Brazil, Pegasus in Australia, SangoNet in South Africa, Chasque in Uruguay, the ELCI in Kenya, and GlasNet in Russia. When we remember the first commercial companies operated limited mono-nets, it can also be argued PeaceNet/EcoNet was the first ISP in the United States and GreenNet was the first in Britain. NGOs recognized the political advantages of information communications technology, *before any other political actors did so*. NGOs were not merely passive adopters of a new technology. They pioneered in the creation of the Internet as a communications system to mobilize the general public to join social and political networks and take political action.

The political leadership of the UN in supporting the development of the Internet made a major contribution to the creation of global advocacy networks and encouraged NGOs to focus on UN policy-making to promote political change. The political leadership of NGOs ensured people from developing countries were participants from the beginning: indeed, Southern NGOs were among the pioneers. There are lower levels of Internet publishing and Internet access in the South than in the North, but it is nevertheless a global Internet and not a Northern Internet from which the South is excluded. The world has an Internet that is radically different from what governments or transnational companies would have created, because NGOs were pioneers in creating a global public Internet.

5 Understanding the place of NGOs in global politics

Having established the importance of non-governmental organizations in politics, law, and communications at the global level, we will now consider how NGOs and their activities can be accommodated in our theoretical understanding of global politics. Most of the literature in the academic discipline of international relations is biased towards the study of "states," neglecting both non-governmental organizations and international organizations. This is based on an assumption that the domestic politics of individual countries is different in nature from international politics. Those who assert there are similarities between politics at all levels of analysis prefer to identify themselves with a pluralist approach, also known as the multicentric approach. This position is signaled in this book and by other pluralist writers, by replacing references to "international relations" with "world politics" or "global politics."

This first part of this chapter outlines a very brief sketch of the four competing approaches to theoretical analysis, in order to demonstrate the need for pluralism. The second part is a full discussion of the structural question, what actors do we study? This starts with an argument that we need to analyze governments and societies rather than states, in order to allow room for consideration of transnational NGOs and transnational companies. It continues by distinguishing the five main ways in which transnational actors combine in global networks to strengthen their political position and to form global coalitions. Then we will examine the advantages and disadvantages of regime theory for analyzing policy-making within all types of international organizations, concluding that regime theory needs to recognize the participation of NGOs in the politics of international regimes.

The third part of this chapter covers the nature of global political processes. It is necessary to change from a focus on power as possession of military and economic capabilities to power as the exercise of influence. It is also necessary to replace the traditional distinctions between high politics and low politics and between interests and values with a wider awareness of the many values, beyond security and wealth, that actors pursue. Then, with an issue-based constructivist analysis, we can move from merely providing interesting descriptions of NGOs to having a theoretical basis for saying NGOs exercise power in global politics. They are crucial agents in the movement of ideas. The fundamental dynamics of political change are the ways in which persuasion, socialization and institutionalization lead to change in the predominant norms. NGOs gain influence by framing debates and linking their values to the concerns of other actors.

NGOs in the four major theoretical approaches

A useful and a successful analytical theory will convert our inability to handle the massive volume of information about the world and our confusion over complexity of the world into an understanding of global politics, by simplifying what we study. All theories can be represented as answering two questions: which political actors do we include or exclude from our analysis and which types of interactions between them do we include or exclude? The dominant theoretical approach of *realism* answers by the spectacular simplification of studying states in conflict over the pursuit of military and economic power. The most sustained challenge to realism, *Marxism*, in all its competing schools, offers an alternative grand simplification of studying the conflict between classes in the global capitalist system over the distribution of economic resources. Although the core concern for Marxists is class conflict, the Marxists are state-centric in their approach to global politics, because they see the dominant class maintaining their control in capitalist societies through control of the state. *Functionalism* was briefly of significance in the 1940s and again in the 1970s but is usually ignored in contemporary textbooks. It answers that we should analyze patterns of cooperation, not conflict, between diverse stakeholders engaged in finding the best way to complete tasks or, in other words, fulfilling social and economic functions. The emphasis is on expertise and experience to find solutions to problems. These ideas still linger on in beliefs that United Nations specialized agencies should be "depoliticized" or that the UN Human Rights Council should be "non-political." The fourth approach, *pluralism*, is concerned with different political actors mobilizing support to achieve their goals in the formation and implementation of public policy. Both functionalists and pluralists depart from a focus on states by giving attention to transnational actors and intergovernmental organizations. However, functionalism is inadequate by neglecting conflict and by assuming governments are losing authority to a self-organizing civil society.[1]

Other authors in recent years have confused the inter-paradigm debate by bringing in normative elements. For a while, the pluralists were labeled as liberals, partly because liberal democracy is based on the pluralism of NGO activity, within the domestic politics of individual countries.[2] Later, in the

United States, there were theoretical developments that resulted in the labels neo-realism and neo-liberal institutionalism being widely used. The use of the word liberal shifted from being a concern with democracy to the neo-liberal free-market ideology of globalization. With these developments, pluralism was forgotten in the "neo-neo debate." Lamy commented, "Both are normative theories of a sort, biased towards the state, the capitalist market and the status quo."[3] John Ruggie has argued the two have converged sufficiently to be discussed together under the label neo-utilitarianism.[4] Since September 2001, the concern with terrorism has breathed new life into security studies, in a modified form, by the addition of "failed states" that provide a haven for transnational terrorist networks. All these developments have effectively reasserted a more sophisticated version of state-centric power theory—realism—as the dominant approach in the study of international relations at the start of the twenty-first century. The alternative theoretical basis for a pluralist, constructivist approach will now be outlined in more detail, as the basis for being able to analyze NGOs in global politics.

Actors in global politics

The pluralist claims about the diversity of actors in global politics are widely understood, because everybody is aware of global actors, such as Amnesty International, the churches, trades unions, and transnational corporations, as well as the United Nations and its agencies. However, there is little understanding that we must reconceptualize states, in order to analyze the contribution of governments and NGOs to diplomacy and policy-making in intergovernmental organizations. Few international relations analysts adopt an explicit pluralist theoretical approach, by disaggregating governments and societies and building NGOs into their theory. In addition, few analysts take a pluralist approach to international organizations and the international regimes within them.

States, nations, governments, and societies

It is essential to refer to states, during any discussion of international law. However, it must be remembered that states as legal entities do not exist in any concrete sense. The legal concept of a state is an abstract fiction, necessary for the purposes of creating and sustaining a legal system. There are two other quite different meanings of "state": the realists' concept of an independent political community and the Marxists' concept of a structure that dominates society. These three meanings have one aspect in common that tends to blur the distinctions between them. They each portray the state as a highly coherent system, a holistic entity, with a common identity and patterns of behavior that are not reducible to the individual people who act as agents of the state. Holism is implied linguistically in newspaper headlines, such as Russia invades Georgia or Israel invades Gaza. Holism becomes explicit whenever politicians or analysts make claims about the existence of a shared national interest.

For lawyers, the state as a system is a sovereign legal entity, entering into legal relationships with other states of an identical nature and being bound by those relationships. For realists, the state is a structured political community, constituted by the common resources, the common identity, and the common goals of a people who support their government. For Marxists in international relations, along with philosophers, sociologists, and political scientists studying comparative government, the state is constituted by the totality of government: the executive, the legislature, the administration, the courts, the police, the armed forces, and the government economic agencies. The legal concept and the realist concept of the state can be treated as being compatible with each other, but it is logically impossible to use the state to encompass all three meanings, because the first two are incompatible with the third. A choice has to be made: for the first two civil society is *an integral component* of the state, whereas for the third civil society is *separate* from the state. When the state is conceptualized as a legal entity or a political community, NGOs cannot be significant transnational actors. When the state is conceptualized as a government, questions can be asked within domestic politics about the relationships between the individual citizen, civil society groups, and the state. Then, within global politics, we can ask when and why do NGOs decide to act in a transnational manner and to what extent they are acting independently. Thus, taking NGOs seriously requires a refusal to treat the state as a coherent, unified political community.

Another problem with use of the term "state" is that it is often used interchangeably with "nation," but the two are quite different concepts. A nation is the sociological phenomenon of a group of people recognizing each other as sharing a common identity. However, the overwhelming majority of the countries of the world are multinational states. Also, some nations or ethnic groups, such as Armenians or Gujaratis, are multi-state nations, with a diaspora spread across many countries. From an empirical perspective, not a single nation-state exists. No country has a resident population who are all from the same national group, with all of the nation living within its boundaries. As a result, we reach the confusing conclusion that nations are important transnational communities. For NGOs dealing with human rights, the distinction between country and nation is crucial, because governments dominated by one national group are often oppressive to citizens from different national groups.

There are three other sources of shared identity that produce a sense of transnational community, connect different societies, and blur the boundaries between states. *Social movements* based on shared values, articulated as policy goals, can be based in a single country or spread across country boundaries to form transnational social movements. The great *religions* differ from social movements in that religious belief systems cover a much wider set of values and can have relevance to a much wider range of policy questions. Christianity, Islam, Judaism, Sikhism, and Hinduism have global importance, because they each have adherents in most countries of the world. A third type of transnational community is an *epistemic community*, which Peter Haas defined as "a network of professionals with recognized expertise and competence in a particular domain and an authoritative claim to policy-relevant knowledge within that domain or issue-area."[5] Among the most influential epistemic communities are natural scientists, as may be seen in the global politics of climate change, but the concept applies equally well to the influence of economists on the World Bank or lawyers in the global politics of human rights. Along with transnational NGOs, the different types of transnational communities are the main components of global civil society. They provide a focus for identities and loyalties that cross-cut the political community in each country. For example, an Armenian, environmentalist, Christian, woman lawyer can be an Argentine citizen, active in Argentine politics. She will probably add non-Argentine perspectives to her political activities within Argentina and Argentine perspectives to her global activities. As Margaret Keck and Kathryn Sikkink put it, actors can "participate in domestic and international politics simultaneously."[6] Transnational communities link global civil society to each country's civil society in a direct, personal manner and NGOs are the strongest channel through which such links are activated.

The pluralist approach goes further, by not only separating state from society but also disaggregating the government itself. In the study of politics within countries, nobody would ignore the different perspectives and procedures adopted by different government ministries nor the rivalries between ministries and ministers over the claims for resources and prestige. Graham Allison has shown how both organizational processes and bureaucratic politics can offer understanding of foreign policy.[7] Robert Keohane and Joseph Nye extended this analysis in one of the most important, but least consulted, articles ever written about global politics. They define "transgovernmental relations as sets of direct interactions among sub-units of different governments that are not controlled or closely guided by the policies of the cabinets or chief executives of those governments."[8] The crucial point is that each ministry can, to some extent, have its own independent foreign policy. Frequent contacts at intergovernmental organizations, such as health ministers at the World Health Assembly or finance ministers at the International Monetary Fund (IMF), offer opportunities for personal communications, an appropriate agenda, and a legitimate situation for specialized discussions. We need to go one step further and take as the starting point for all analysis the assumption that NGOs will also be involved: government ministries, NGOs and secretariats of international organizations interact in global policy networks to determine political outcomes.

From now on, the three concepts of the state will be distinguished, rather than conflated. We can use "state" in a strictly legal context, use "country" for the political community, and use "government" in its broadest sense, to cover not just the executive but any part of the authority structure. Under any of the three meanings, a state is a systemic structure, but traditional approaches have ontological inconsistency (not being consistent about the nature of what exists). They overestimate the coherence of states and underestimate the coherence of global systems. When a pluralist approach is adopted, consistency can be maintained. Countries are relatively open political systems, with government ministries, national groups, and other sectors of civil society having cross-border relations. In addition, international organizations and transnational communities can be analyzed as open global systems, which generate distinct political interactions and affect their constituent elements. This pluralist ontological position is essential for the inclusion of NGOs in the analysis of global politics.

Transnational corporations

There are many mechanisms by which a large company may move beyond the confines of one country and become a transnational corporation (TNC). Strictly speaking, on the standard academic definition of transnational activity, a company becomes transnational when it imports or exports goods or services. However, involvement in trade is not normally regarded as sufficient to warrant the label TNC, and a company that does no more than trade will rarely engage in transnational political activity. The United Nations defines a TNC as the combination of a parent enterprise and its foreign affiliates, which may be under the direct or indirect control of the parent.[9] In political terms, indirect control, such as McDonald's relationships with the independent restaurants operating under its franchise, has much the same impact as direct transnational control.

It is beyond the scope of a book on NGOs to discuss all the complex ways in which TNCs become transnational political actors. In summary, their main impact is through their involvement in production, trade, employment, investment, and taxation within individual countries. The impact of TNCs on global policy-making is much less extensive. We have seen they do not have direct access to consultative status at the UN, but they can have indirect access through international NGOs. In some cases, such as the Oil Companies International Marine Forum, they behave no differently from other

NGOs: OCIMF uses its consultative status with the International Maritime Organization, in collaboration with Greenpeace and Friends of the Earth, to minimize oil pollution at sea. In other cases, such as the International Council of Infant Food Industries, coalitions of TNCs can be in deep-seated conflict with a wide range of other NGOs. In UN specialized agencies, individual TNCs also can have more privileged informal direct access to the secretariat and government delegates. The greatest influence is through private trans-national banks participating in the corridors of the IMF and sustaining "the Washington Consensus" on global financial policy. On the other hand, since July 2000, through the Global Compact the UN has attempted to co-opt TNCs into support for human rights, maintenance of labor standards, protection of the environment, and opposition to corrupt practices.

It is important to note here that, in theoretical terms, the political activities of TNCs cannot be encompassed within any state-centric approach. Within the domestic politics of individual countries, it is intrinsic to the nature of TNCs that they challenge the sovereignty of states and the political independence of governments, in a fundamental manner.[10] Within global politics, TNCs can have a considerable impact, either via their influence on the foreign policies of key governments, such as the US government on the question of climate change, or via lobbying in intergovernmental organizations, primarily on questions affecting employment conditions in the International Labour Organization (ILO), production standards in technical UN agencies, and on trade in the World Trade Organization. All these complexities require both TNCs and business international NGOs to be placed alongside other NGOs in a pluralist analytical approach.

International non-governmental organizations and transnational NGO networks

NGOs organize themselves into a variety of different types of coalitions, to exchange information, to mobilize support, to coordinate strategy, to share costs, and to gain greater political weight through joint action. There are five main types of structure through which NGOs may operate at the global level: "umbrella" international NGOs, information networks, advocacy networks, issue caucuses, and governance networks. It will be remembered that TNCs can be members of umbrella international non-governmental organizations at the UN. It is unlikely they will ever be involved in the other types, except occasionally via their umbrella INGOs joining other networks or caucuses.

Umbrella INGOs arise when different NGOs and/or TNCs based in different countries share common goals and decide to create a formal institutional structure, with a secretariat and a regional or global headquarters. This can be done by sharing a common identity expressed in a common name, such as

Friends of the Earth International, or it can be done by similar organizations giving priority to different local concerns, but finding benefits from close collaboration, such as the International Council on Social Welfare. INGOs may be highly centralized and coherent. For example, Amnesty International operates as a single institution, with the National Sections following policy set by the International Council. Alternatively, an INGO may be a multi-level hierarchy. For example, the International Planned Parenthood Federation adopts common policy at the global level, but its member associations pursue very different programs in the different countries. More complex relations can also occur when some INGOs have both single-country NGOs and other INGOs as members.

The concept of a network has been used to describe much looser arrangements. The NGOs that join a network do not acquire a common identity nor become part of an institutional structure. As an analytical ideal type, the simplest form is an *information network* that enables its members to communicate, without undertaking any form of joint political action. Information networks are now easy to establish through the Internet, by the use of websites and e-mail list servers. Often they are created as independent NGOs, in order to service the needs of many NGOs for reliable, well-researched, up-to-date information. Two prominent examples are the Bretton Woods Project, which monitors, reports on, and analyzes the activities of the World Bank and the IMF; and the International Centre for Trade and Sustainable Development, which does similar work on trade policy issues and the activities of the World Trade Organization.

The most important writing on networks in the academic literature is derived from Keck and Sikkink's concept of *transnational advocacy networks*, which they define as "networks of activists, distinguishable largely by the centrality of principled ideas or values in motivating their formation."[11] In their discussion, it becomes plain they are referring to activists as representatives of NGOs. The strength of the networks derives from the fact that the activists are the focal point for mobilizing their organizations to promote the network's values and engage in the network's campaigns, rather than participating on their own behalf as individuals. Advocacy networks are constituted by NGOs, but Keck and Sikkink suggest "parts of" IGOs or government agencies should be included as potential participants in these networks. In so doing, they are implicitly (but not explicitly) referring to Keohane and Nye's transgovernmental actors.[12] NGOs often identify with the network by being listed on its web pages and/or endorsing campaign activities and joint policy statements issued by the network. Transgovernmental actors do not, and cannot, identify themselves with advocacy networks in any of these ways. On the other hand, specialist sections of IGO secretariats and government agencies do give ad hoc political support to NGOs in policy-making fora and they may also provide funding. It is more appropriate to say transnational advocacy networks are solely composed of NGOs (plus individuals) and these NGO networks at times act in coalition with transgovernmental actors.

Issue caucuses are similar to, but different from, advocacy networks. The term caucus comes from US politics and is used to describe groups of politicians who meet to decide joint strategy within a policy-making forum. The term is used at the global level, by NGOs when they hold strategy meetings during the sessions of UN bodies and other IGO fora. Issue caucuses differ from advocacy networks in being focused on a single forum rather than pursuing an issue across all relevant fora. In most cases, they are also temporary, having no life once the intergovernmental session has ended. There can be some continuity of action. Thus, there is a Women's Caucus at many UN bodies, but its composition depends on who chooses to attend at that particular time and place. There may sometimes be minimal organizational continuity, when one NGO acts as the convener for a series of sessions over several years. Issue caucuses are very difficult to analyze. On the one hand, they can be highly ephemeral and leave little trace of their activities, outside the memories of their participants. On the other hand, their daily meetings can be crucial in achieving NGO influence on policy outcomes.

Another type of network is much less common and does not have a standard name. I will call them *governance networks*. They exist to promote the participation of a diverse range of NGOs in a particular policy-making forum. The ideal type has two defining features: they are open to *all* NGOs who are accredited to the forum and they do *not* engage in any advocacy. When they are related to a major UN conference, they are often known as the NGO Facilitation Committee. When they relate to a permanent institution, they may be known as the NGO Steering Committee or the NGO Network for that institution. Governance networks inform their members about the timing and the agenda of meetings of the relevant institution. They assist NGO representatives to gain accreditation to participate in the meetings and may raise funds to assist with travel and accommodation costs for members with limited resources. They coordinate with the official secretariat on such tasks as obtaining the institution's documents, organizing orientation sessions for new participants, booking rooms for NGO strategy meetings, and facilitating exchanges with government delegates. The network does not take positions on substantive issues, but usually assists issue caucuses within the network to make their lobbying more effective. However, all governance networks will act collectively and forcefully if they encounter any downgrading of the status of NGOs or restrictions on their participation rights. The core impact of governance networks is to increase the level and quality of the participation of NGOs in the policy-making process. They are crucial for smaller NGOs and those with limited budgets.

The five types have been outlined as analytical ideal types. The distinction between advocacy coalitions and caucuses is less a dichotomy than the end points on a spectrum, determined by the degree of continuity and organization across time. In practice, information networks and governance networks may engage in a limited amount of advocacy, while advocacy networks may sometimes promote research or address governance questions. INGOs can be the coordinators for advocacy networks or the conveners of governance networks. Nevertheless, despite the blurring of the boundaries, the distinctions are of great importance, not least because furious antagonism can be generated within and between NGOs when the roles are confused. The greatest dangers arise when attempts are made to use governance networks as advocacy networks. If policy statements are published in the name of all NGOs, without each NGO explicitly endorsing the joint statement, the network can be subject to such political conflict that it disintegrates.

Intergovernmental organizations, hybrid international organizations, and regimes

Just as governments are the focus of most, but not all, politics within countries, intergovernmental organizations, such as the UN, are the focus of most politics at the global level. Government ministries are located at an intersection of domestic politics and global politics. Domestic politics will affect the positions governments advocate in IGOs, while the decisions of intergovernmental organizations will feed back into domestic politics, via the media, via domestic NGOs, and via ministries tabling legislation to implement the decisions. We saw in Chapter 2 how NGOs interact with government delegations in virtually all parts of the UN system. However, most international relations theory neglects the UN as much as it neglects NGOs.

Hybrid international organizations, composed of both governments and NGOs or TNCs, were defined and discussed in Chapter 3. Now we will note their theoretical significance. The fact that governments are willing to take the steps of negotiating and establishing such organizations, becoming members, participating in the policy-making processes, using their votes, implementing the decisions, and producing further legally binding conventions is totally incompatible with the concept of sovereign states. Only a pluralist approach can handle the existence of global political systems in which *both* governments and non-state actors possess decision-making authority.

Regime theory is one body of theory that does give serious consideration to the possibility of global policy-making. All writers start from Stephen Krasner's definition of regimes as "sets of implicit or explicit principles, norms, rules, and decision-making procedures around which actors' expectations converge in a given area of international relations." Krasner's following sentences introduce a slight confusion, because principles are stated to be "beliefs of fact, causation and rectitude."[13] It would have been better to have separated the two meanings of "principles": the beliefs of fact and causation, which cover understanding of how the world works, and rectitude, which covers the moral values used to determine policy goals. Then, regimes are sets of principles, values, and norms.

This may be illustrated by the regime to prevent pollution of the seas run by the International Maritime Organization (IMO). Biology and chemistry provide the principles to understand pollution. Beauty, conservation of biodiversity, and wealth creation (in industries such as fishing and tourism) are the general, abstract values promoted by the regime. Marine habitats should not be polluted by oil is the original specific, applied norm (with other types of pollution being covered by later additional norms). Then, rules requiring discharge of oily waste water in reception facilities at ports are attempts to control behavior, in order to achieve the norms. Finally, the IMO Marine Environment Protection Committee provides the procedures for deciding the rules. As with this illustration, regimes are usually seen as being embedded within international organizations. More than one regime may be created and managed within a single organization. In the case of the IMO, there is also a maritime safety regime, designed to prevent loss of life at sea.

Krasner's definition is an ideal starting point for a pluralist, but the predominant approach to regimes of the neo-liberal institutionalists perversely ignores NGOs. There are also other strong biases: towards rational choice theory and towards applications in international political economy. There are some departures from classical realism by considering institutions as modifying international anarchy, by recognizing multiple issue-areas rather than a single international system, by seeing behavior as being structured by actors' expectations, by assuming economic resources are in normal circumstances more important determinants of political outcomes than military capabilities, and by accepting transnational corporations can be important political actors. Despite all this, neo-liberal institutionalist regime theory remains closer to realism than pluralism by being state-centric and, perversely, by paying insufficient attention to the principles, values, and norms which define the nature of regimes.[14]

Because virtually all regimes are embedded within international organizations and all international organizations (apart from the global economic organizations) include NGOs as significant political actors, it is essential to have a pluralist approach to explain what happens in regimes. Steps have been made in this direction. Haas has put values and knowledge at the center of his analysis of adaptation and learning by international organizations.[15] Oran Young has asserted "institutional arrangements are important determinants of collective outcomes" and "important constraints on the behavior of individual actors." He has addressed questions of compliance with regimes by governments, under the impact of social pressures to avoid becoming pariah countries. He utilizes bureaucratic politics and transgovernmental relations: "[I]ndividual agencies within national governments sometimes come to define their roles, at least in part, in terms of administering and maintaining the provisions of one or more international regimes." Finally, Young also assumes "favorable records of compliance" require "continuous pressure" from NGOs on the responsible agencies.[16] Empirical work on environmental politics cannot avoid including NGOs in the analysis of behavior in regimes. For example, *Institutions for the Earth* concludes NGOs play an active role, embarrass governments, and criticize their policies. "Under these conditions, international institutions are part of a complex network of governments, international institutions, non-profit NGOs, the mass media, and industry groups, in which public pressure may overwhelm industry and government resistance."[17]

With authors such as Haas and Young, and with work on environmental regimes, there is a clear move towards an alternative, pluralist regime theory. Krasner himself made values and norms "the basic defining characteristics of a regime" and said "changes in principles and norms are changes of the regime itself."[18] While much of the work on regimes has focused on institutions, little attention has been given to the values which define regimes. Recognition that the prime activity of NGOs is the mobilization of support for values gives a theoretical basis for putting NGOs at the center of regime theory. Also, we can see empirically NGOs are involved in creation of norms, definition of rules, and participation in decision-making procedures.

Almost all the work on regimes locates them within intergovernmental organizations. They also occur within hybrid international organizations. For example, the Red Cross contains one regime to regulate the laws of war and a second regime providing humanitarian assistance in disaster situations. Young has gone further from state-centric assumptions and referred to transnational regimes within global civil society. He cites governance of the World Wide Web as an example. Stronger examples of transnational regimes are the international NGOs for sports, such as the International Olympic Committee or the Fédération Internationale de Football Association (FIFA), which govern within their limited domains with full regulatory authority.[19] Thus, with all types of international organizations regimes involve NGOs, but with hybrids and transnational regimes NGOs have decision-making authority.

The nature of global political processes

The international relations literature is biased towards the study of power, defined in terms of the ability to exercise coercion or to control economic resources. This makes it difficult to imagine NGOs or international organizations can exercise influence. Study of politics as actors trying to win support for their ideas or, more formally, as contention over the allocation of values has to be incorporated in the pluralist approach for us to take NGOs seriously and to be able to explain how they can affect political outcomes. This section will argue the case for a constructivist, issue-based approach to global politics.

Sovereignty, authority, power, and legitimacy

International politics is commonly distinguished from domestic politics by the myth of sovereignty. This is a legal concept suggesting states can exercise authority within their territory and are free from external authority. However, in practice, nearly all states have to some extent lost sovereignty, by joining intergovernmental organizations. In traditional terms, sovereignty was violated when the domestic policies of governments were subject to external review, as they now are under human rights treaties and other compliance monitoring mechanisms. Unambiguous transfer of sovereignty occurs when a government is legally obliged to obey an IGO's decision even when it is not a member of the decision-making body or when it opposes the decision. This applies under the dispute settlement process of the World Trade Organization, under the treaties covering the activities of the European Community, under the Statute of the International Criminal Court, and under the UN Security Council. Also, since 1996, the ECOSOC NGO Statute has a minor element of supranationality, in that a national NGO can, in theory, be awarded consultative status against the wishes of its home government. (National NGOs may be accredited "after consultation with the Member State concerned," but the "consultation" does not provide a veto.)

A more subtle argument arises about the political decisions taken in international regimes. On environmental questions, when global commons are at stake or when ecosystems cross country boundaries, an independent policy is inherently impossible. On health questions, when there are global epidemics, or on questions of safety in international travel, such as preventing collisions of aircraft or ships, an independent policy may be possible, but with very high risks of it failing. On innumerable questions of professional activities, the design of goods, the provision of services, the definition of quality standards, and the communication of knowledge, harmonization is a highly valued goal often only achievable by collective decision-making, while an independent policy would be inefficient and costly. On all these types of questions, legal sovereignty may remain, but political independence has effectively been lost.

The study of politics requires a wider concept than sovereignty or legal authority. As James Rosenau has put it, the exercise of authority also occurs in informal settings, in decisions that invoke compliance even though the right to make them has not been stated in legal form. ... Authority relations are thus to be found wherever people undertake collective tasks ... and any such relationships that have consequences across national boundaries can be considered part of world politics.[20]

Authority is not a fixed possession of a political actor but a role in a relationship. It may derive from legal provisions, from pragmatic benefits of compliance, from the possession of expert information and understanding, or from widely accorded respect and status, which at its strongest is charisma. The UN has supranational legal authority for peace enforcement, but depends upon expertise and status for peace-keeping. The UK government has sovereignty over its currency but not over trade. The Pope has high charismatic authority over Roman Catholics, including some government leaders, but not over non-Catholics. Amnesty International has expert authority on human rights but not on other questions. As Rosenau points out, the exercise of authority in each case is conditional upon the acceptance of its legitimacy.[21] For each actor and for each policy question, authority is dependent on the status of the actor exercising authority, the nature of the claim to authority and the values invoked by the policy question.

The pursuit of power by governments has been central to realism. Power has been seen as having two aspects. The prime emphasis is on capabilities, the attributes of actors. For traditional realists, this was possession of military resources, which can be used to gain control over territory. Neo-realists have expanded capabilities to include the possession of economic resources. Marxists have a similar approach in seeing power as the possession of capital, but they also emphasize coercion by the major capitalist "states." The second aspect of power is the relationship of influence, when one actor brings about change in the behavior of another actor. The two aspects are merged into a single concept of power, by assuming the possession of capabilities will lead to influence. Sovereignty is linked to this conceptualization of power, by the assumption that the exercise of sovereignty depends on the capability to exercise force, through control of the military or the economy. However, possession of capabilities does not always result in influence, as the US government found in the Vietnam War.

An alternative approach to power is to lay the prime emphasis on influence. Politics concerns how actors relate to each other, debate and bargain with each other, and arrive at collective decisions. Any contrast between having "real power" and "only" having influence is meaningless. In terms of the dynamics of day-to-day global politics, power *is* influence: the exercise of power is, *by definition*, influence over outcomes. David Easton has defined politics as the authoritative allocation of values.[22] Richard Mansbach and John Vasquez have amended and extended Easton's approach to a pluralist issue paradigm: "Politics from this perspective consist not so much of a struggle for power, but of contention over issues."[23] Global politics is then the process of actors mobilizing support for their own values and seeking to influence a collective decision more or less in accord with their preferred outcomes. Thomas Risse has argued there are three logics of social action. In addition to bargaining and institutionalized rule-guided behavior, there is argument, "with the aim of reaching a mutual understanding based on a reasoned consensus."[24] It is clear that a body of literature such as this can encompass NGOs arguing and bargaining, usually with governments within global institutions, to influence the authoritative allocation of values.

Power, as military or economic capabilities, has limited impact unless it can be legitimized by widespread acceptance of its use. Legitimacy is the fundamental basis for influence. It is more difficult to understand than the more concrete and more measurable variables of military and economic resources. Legitimacy is subject to change across time: for any political actor, it may increase or decrease quite rapidly. The legitimacy of a government or an NGO operates at four interrelated levels. An influential actor will have internal legitimacy among its own administrators and executives, support legitimacy among the people who are its immediate constituency, domestic legitimacy in the wider political system in which it operates and global legitimacy in its external political environment. Legitimacy is also complex in specific political relationships, because it is composed of two analytically separate dimensions. The legitimacy of each political actor is the actor's status. The legitimacy attached to their policy proposals is the degree to which the proposals embody values that are widely endorsed by the relevant target audience.

NGOs do not have any military capabilities and have quite limited or insignificant economic resources, but many of them do possess communication capabilities. By presentation of political information and by making their values salient to other political actors, NGOs seek to enhance their own status and promote the legitimacy of their policy proposals. Amnesty International, for example, "derives global legitimacy both from its very high status, one recognition of which was the award of the Nobel Peace Prize in 1977, and from the high moral value that so many people attach to the policies it is pursuing."[25] From this perspective, NGOs do have power, because they can mobilize support for values to exercise influence over policy decisions.

High politics, low politics, interests, and values

All analysts of global politics recognize that different issues are treated with differing levels of priority. Stanley Hoffmann, a simplistic realist, has been credited with making a widely used distinction between the "high politics" of sovereignty and defense questions and the "low politics" of economic and social questions.[26] This implies a very static and uniform view of politics. In practice, different governments have very different types of policy questions to which they give priority. For Israel it may be their relations with the Palestinians; for Burundi it may be the price of coffee; for the Maldives, the ocean covering their land; for Colombia, the trade in cocaine; for Iceland, the solvency of their banks; and for Niger, the impact of drought. It is false to assume that all governments have the same priorities, with strategic security at the top of the list. The "low politics" questions of health or the environment become high-priority security questions when we face the threat of global pandemic diseases or the impact of climate change.[27]

A more general concept of the saliency of an issue can be used to replace the high/low politics distinction. Saliency has two components: it reflects the importance attached to the values evoked in a political debate and it reflects the extent to which the political actor expects to be affected by the outcome. Saliency allows for recognition of items on the current global political agenda being of higher or lower priority for governments or NGOs, but the priorities can vary from one actor to another and for the same actors across time. For example, some actors' priorities change suddenly when an earthquake or a hurricane occurs. Saliency can also be used to compare different issues. Human rights questions generally have more saliency than environmental questions to ministries of justice, Amnesty International, Microsoft, and the Council of Europe than they do to environment ministries, Friends of the Earth, Exxon, and United Nations Environment Progamme. The high/low politics categories are imposed by the analyst upon the world. Saliency can be investigated, without any preconceptions about what values are actually used by actors to rank the importance of issues. International relations is not the study of "great powers" and "superpowers": "the system of interest for the study of an issue consists of all those actors for whom the issue is salient."[28]

The famous quote from Palmerstone, "[W]e have no eternal allies and we have no perpetual enemies. Our interests are eternal and perpetual, and those interests it is our duty to follow," implies interests are static.[29] It is also common to contrast interests with values or moral principles, in such a way as to assume that supposedly objective interests must take priority over subjective values. As Hans Morgenthau put it in a lecture in 1979 on US foreign policy, "you cannot be consistent in the defense of human rights, since it is not your prime business as a state among other states to defend human rights."[30] This approach is similar to claims to objectivity and primacy of interests, when politicians invoke "the national interest." In fact, the term is merely used to persuade the listener to agree with the speaker. Usually, it privileges the values of security and economic wealth over other values. Society actually consists of various groups making differing claims about interests, based on different value preferences. For activists in human rights NGOs, security is not an absolute priority over freedom nor a justification for torture. For environmentalists, wealth should not always be pursued at the expense of the environmental values, beauty, health, biodiversity, and animal welfare.[31] Indeed, when the export of arms is a policy question, pursuit of security may be incompatible with maximizing wealth, if the valuable purchase is by a potential enemy. Just as there is no theoretical basis to distinguish between high politics and low politics, there is also no basis to distinguish interests from values. Interests are merely the values that have, or are claimed to have, higher priority than other values. The contention over values in domestic politics continues in global politics.

Constructivism

In a magisterial review of the literature, Martha Finnemore and Kathryn Sikkink summarize constructivism as

> an approach to social analysis that asserts the following: (a) human inter-action is shaped primarily by ideational factors, not simply material ones; (b) the most important ideational factors are widely shared or 'intersubjec-tive' beliefs, which are not reducible to individuals; and (c) these shared beliefs construct the interests and identities of purposive actors.[32]

The development of constructivism started as a reaction against rationalism, a position that takes the existence of actors and their interests as given. John Ruggie took rationalism as one of the defining features of neo-realism and neo-liberalism: "[B]oth assume that states are rational actors maximizing their own expected utilities, defined in such material terms as power, security and welfare."[33] Rationalists assume the nature of political actors, their properties, their goals, and their actions can be fully understood solely by considera-tion of the interactions of the individual actors, without any reference to the properties of the social system in which the interactions occur. Rationalists are reductionists: for them social outcomes are reducible to the combined behavior of individuals. Constructivists are holists: for them social outcomes are produced by the social system as a collective entity. Rationalists are pri-marily materialists, who see political behavior as determined by possession of military and economic resources and focused on security and wealth as outcomes, while constructivists analyze ideational phenomena that exist as shared beliefs determining social and political behavior.

There are three problems with rationalism. First, all analysis of rational choice is static and reductionist, whereas constructivism is dynamic and holistic. It ceases to be a question of rational choice when we consider the ways in which actors *change* their value preferences (their utilities) in response to *collective* social processes. Second, while rational choice can in principle be used to analyze the maximization of any value, in practice rationalists only analyze material values. There is no rational choice theory of the pursuit of freedom in the global politics of human rights or beauty in global environmental politics. Third, rationalists predominantly analyze the pursuit of just one or two values, such as security or wealth. In practice, all human beings have complex patterns of value preferences, desiring some balance between security, freedom, wealth, justice, equity, equality, beauty, health, and other values. This complexity prevents elegant simple analysis, because of the problem of incommensurability: there is no common standard of measurement to enable rational comparison of multi-dimensional value choices. Of course, political actors may *attempt* to act rationally, but analysis of decision-making must go beyond rationalism.

Constructivism makes the realm of ideas, the way we perceive the nature of the world and the evolution of norms central to politics. However, constructivism cannot be simply equated with pluralism. The problem is that constructivism is compatible with the four different analytical approaches. Alexander Wendt in arguing "Anarchy is What States Make of It" is a constructivist realist.[34] Ruggie, in arguing for the existence of socially constructed global systems, does not offer any theoretical criticisms of neo-realism nor neo-liberal institutionalism to match his ontological criticisms and remains almost completely state-centric.[35] The Marxists in their conceptualization of capitalist systems, especially in using "false consciousness" as an explanation of the proletariat failing to rebel against their exploitation, are constructivists. Neo-functionalists in explaining Western European integration as processes of learning and changing loyalties from the country to the European level are constructivist. Finally, Keck and Sikkink in discussing advocacy networks as the source of new ideas, norms, and identities are pluralist constructivists.

Keck and Sikkink have developed the pluralist concept of advocacy networks within a constructivist ontology (a constructivist view of the nature of political actors). They discuss the historical examples of the anti-slavery and women's suffrage campaigns and have contemporary case studies of transnational activism on human rights in Latin America, on environmental politics, and violence against women. They draw on the sociology of social movements to emphasize advocacy as a process of framing issues within a context that enhances support for the network's values; the role of information, NGO leaders, and finance in resource mobilization; and the utilization of the political context or opportunity structure to decide the targets for action. "Campaigns are processes of issue construction."[36] Unfortunately, Keck and Sikkink do not fully transfer these concepts from sociology, which were developed to analyze individual societies, to elaborate a *global* pluralist position. In the same way as Ruggie, they still use the static rationalist language of "states" and "national interests" more often than using "governments" and their "values" and "policies." They also say NGO networks can "persuade, pressure and gain leverage over much more powerful organizations and governments." This is self-contradictory: when advocacy networks influence policy-making, the NGOs are at that very moment exercising power over governments.

Keck and Sikkink concentrate on the impact of the networks upon individual governments and they have minimal reference to advocacy within intergovernmental organizations. This is partly explained by much of their book being concerned with human rights, which are ultimately protected or abused by governments. However, even in this field, the UN has been crucial and NGOs have made considerable effort to influence global standard-setting in UN declarations and human rights treaties. We can extend the logic of Keck and Sikkink's theoretical position by modifying their famous diagram on the use of the boomerang effect by NGOs.

In the original diagram, copied as Figure 5.1, NGOs in State A, who cannot obtain access to their government, obtain support from NGOs in State B. The

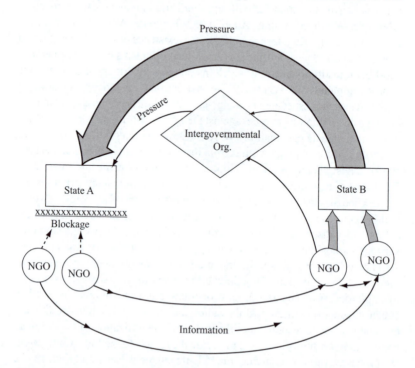

Figure 5.1 Keck and Sikkink's "boomerang pattern" of NGO pressure

advocacy network is not portrayed in the diagram and the NGOs in State A are not shown as appealing to the intergovernmental organization. Presumably, the diagram should be interpreted as asserting the main boomerang effect occurs via State B putting pressure on State A. (There is no discussion of the reason for the bilateral boomerang route being portrayed by an arrow of much greater weight than for the IGO route.) A revised global pluralist version of this diagram is given in Figure 5.2. It shows a greater number of potential flight paths for the boomerang. Indeed, it offers ten hypothetical paths. If the news media were also incorporated in the diagram, it would reflect the full complexity of the range of transnational routes to challenge the most obdurate governments, such as the Burmese generals.

In using the social movements literature, Keck and Sikkink have primarily paid attention to the framing of issues and have given little explicit attention to opportunity structures. Nevertheless, they do say "conferences and other forms of international contact create arenas for forming and strengthening networks."[37] From this perspective, the United Nations and other intergovernmental organizations are crucial. By establishing systems of consultative status, they have provided permanent opportunity structures for NGOs to promote their values at the global level. Also when specialized diplomatic conferences or specialized institutional bodies hold meetings, the relevant NGO networks and individual NGOs gain direct access to a forum where their advocacy will be perceived to be highly salient. This relationship is so strong that most

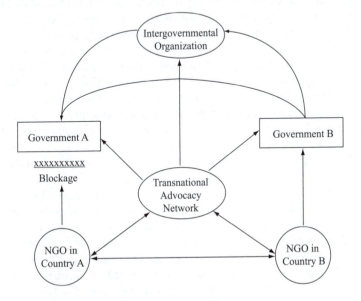

Figure 5.2 Multiple routes for the boomerang effect

transnational advocacy networks were created for the specific purpose of lobbying an IGO or using an existing IGO to create a new intergovernmental institution. The global environmental movement cannot be understood without reference to the UN's conferences at Stockholm in 1972, at Rio de Janeiro in 1992, and at Johannesburg in 2002. The Jubilee 2000 campaign to cancel developing country debt cannot be understood without reference to the IMF and the World Bank. The Coalition for an International Criminal Court, the International Campaign to Ban Landmines, and the Cluster Munition Coalition were each focused on specific existing UN bodies, with the purpose of creating new global legal norms and new intergovernmental structures. Smith has noted three key functions performed by these relationships: networks provide constituencies to promote the legitimacy of multilateral institutions, they generate new proposals for multilateral cooperation, and they strengthen the transfer of global norms to national and local practices.[38]

The dynamics of political change

In the 1980s, when the word constructivist had not yet been coined, I argued that the sources of strength, which contribute to the success of NGOs, are the intense personal commitment of their members, the specialist knowledge of issues possessed by NGO leaders, the flexibility of action provided by the lack of bureaucratic constraints, the low administrative costs, the professional skill in the use of information to sustain their arguments, and the high trust for the accuracy of their information. The corresponding weaknesses are the dependence on individual leaders, the danger of intense conflicts about personalities or activities, and the lack of shared economic activities that can maintain the group's cohesion. NGOs subject governments to international pressures, which are reinforced through the domestic political system, producing "a global political system from which no society can remain isolated." It had become commonplace for political debate within countries to be littered with external references: in particular, a UN resolution could be presented as embodying "a global norm which it is deviant to reject." The unique power of NGOs is the communication of political ideas and they are "producing political interdependence within the global system."[39]

In subsequent work, I argued there were three distinct types of processes during which NGOs could affect the contention over issues: agenda-setting, policy formulation, and policy implementation. Governments suffer from agenda overload, so NGOs are the dominant influence upon new items being added to the agenda. There are two senses in which there is a political agenda: the public agenda of debate in the news media and the formal agendas of legislatures and intergovernmental policy-making bodies. The UN generates "interactions between the public agendas in different countries, the formal agenda of the UN institution and the formal agendas of domestic legislatures."[40] The ability of NGOs to influence policy formulation at the UN is greatest at the beginning of the policy-making process, which is akin to agenda-setting, but after the opening stages they will have less impact on the broad goals being set by governments. NGOs can also influence the detailed text towards the end of the negotiations on a treaty or a resolution. Finally, NGOs affect the implementation of policy by monitoring its effectiveness and influencing governments to commit the necessary resources.[41] Keck and Sikkink elaborated the policy formulation stage by separating out three aspects. NGO networks may influence the discursive positions that set the limiting parameters on the available policy options. This matches my own suggestion that there is more room for influence in the opening stages. Networks may persuade IGOs to introduce new procedures, as when the World Bank established an Independent Inspection Panel for its projects. This is a point of overlap between policy formulation and policy implementation. NGOs may also change the specific policies of governments or international institutions.[42] The actual policy process is often not as linear as this analysis suggests and the term "issue cycle" aptly captures the twists and turns that may occur.[43]

Finnemore and Sikkink have moved from the macro-level of the issue cycle to concern with the micro-level of how actors behave, what norms are, and how norms change. The literature has mainly given attention to regulative norms, which constrain behavior, and constitutive norms, "which create new actors, interests or categories of action." Finnemore and Sikkink argue for more attention to evaluative or prescriptive norms, which set standards of "oughtness" for proper behavior. If norms are shared, the question arises "how many actors share the assessment before we call it a norm."[44] This is the key to discussing the dynamics of change. Finnemore and Sikkink suggest norm entrepreneurs promote the emergence of new norms. Gradually, they obtain a critical mass of supporters, so that the system reaches a tipping point, when the norm cascades through the population, achieving widespread support. The third stage arises when the new norm is no longer contested: it is internalized and taken for granted.[45]

It is surprising to see Finnemore and Sikkink are still quite state-centric in their discussion of norm dynamics. They refer to "a critical mass of states" becoming norm leaders. They do acknowledge the role of individuals leading international campaigns to promote change, in the case of the creation of the laws of war and the spread of women's suffrage. They also refer to NGOs, advocacy networks, and IGOs, such as the World Bank, the UN, and the ILO, as organizational platforms for norm promoters. However, they seem to be reluctant to visualize that NGOs could, by themselves, promote a new norm and provide a critical mass of support, which later generates a cascade of support through the world of government diplomacy.[46] In the 1970s, the International Baby Foods Action Network (IBFAN) did create a critical mass, consisting of NGOs concerned with health, children's rights, development, exploitation by TNCs, community action, poverty alleviation, and women's rights, plus sections of the UN and World Health Organization secretariats. This coalition persuaded all the world's governments, except the Reagan administration in the United States, to adopt the norm that public marketing of dried milk for babies was unacceptable. Furthermore, it is impossible to imagine a situation in which a critical mass consists solely of governments, without NGOs and IGO secretariats being part of the coalition promoting change.

Finnemore and Sikkink offer different mechanisms for change during the different stages of the norm life cycle.[47] The norm entrepreneurs promote norm emergence by persuasion. During the cascade stage, there is a mixture of persuasion, socialization, and the impact of institutions. When institutions adopt norms, individual actors follow suit to gain in legitimacy, to comply with pressures for conformity, and to enhance their esteem. They suggest psychological processes of reducing cognitive dissonance, which explain acceptance of group norms by individuals, can also exist as "an analogue … at the level of the state."[48] Finally, in the internalization stage, the professions and "state bureaucracies" systematically promote norms by institutionalized socialization processes, such as professional training, and repeated patterns of behavior generate norm acceptance.[49] The next questions are which norms will be adopted and under what conditions.[50] Finnemore and Sikkink argue a domestic need for international legitimation, the prominence of "the states promoting the norm" and various intrinsic characteristics of the norm, including the clarity and specificity of its formulation and its content, determine the recruitment of support for a norm.[51] They also refer to change resulting from "adjacency claims" when emergent norms are related to existing norms, and the "world time-context" when crises may discredit a political actor and the norms associated with that actor.[52]

Again, we should add the caveat that Finnemore and Sikkink are remaining too state-centric: the processes of persuasion, socialization, and institutional pressures can be extended from explaining change by governmental actors to the adoption of new norms by NGOs, TNCs, or any type of international organization. In addition, they tend to reify norms, by stating "norms are *agents* of stability or change."[53] Of course, only people can be agents of change. This error matches the tendency to underemphasize the significance of norm entrepreneurs, who are predominantly from NGOs, as the agents of change. In particular, they do not make any mention of norm entrepreneurs or NGOs, except for professional associations, during the third stage when norms are internalized. There are at least three processes whereby NGOs are significant actors in this final stage. First, when government bureaucracies move towards the institutionalization of change, they often have to recruit individuals from NGOs, giving them temporary or even permanent appointments within the bureaucracy. Second, government officials often retire at a relatively young age and continue an active engagement with policy processes, by joining relevant NGOs. As a result of both these mechanisms, specific specialized NGOs can have privileged access to the relevant bureaucracies. Third, some NGOs work hard as norm entrepreneurs, monitoring government activities and policy outcomes, to ensure policy is implemented effectively.

All this work on policy-making processes, norms, and political change needs to be supplemented by more systematic consideration of persuasion. Even processes of socialization, institutionalization, and habit formation, which occur at the structural level, still require agents of norm change and norm reinforcement, acting within the structural context, who persuade individuals and groups to support and implement norms. The focus on norms is too specific and too much at the micro-level to analyze major processes of change. Before there could be a norm that prisoners should not be subject to sleep deprivation, there first had to be the development of a global politics of human rights and then the institutionalization of a prohibition on torture. Before there could be a norm that energy efficiency should be maximized, environmental change had to be placed on the global political agenda and then the institutionalization of processes to minimize climate change. Norm change is embedded within changing value preferences. Norm entrepreneurs seek to persuade other actors to change their value systems. Occasionally, this will be by the adoption of new values.

At the grand macro-level, the history of political change since the mid-seventeenth century can be portrayed as the entry into politics and the spread of the value of equality, with the consequent effect on religious freedom, slavery, female suffrage, decolonization, and the global spread of democracy. Change at this level requires the analysis of persuasion by the mobilization of social movements. Once the value of equality had become institutionalized within democracies, the prohibition of discriminatory practices, on grounds such as race, gender, or disability, became a question of giving greater priority to the value of equality for the victims of discrimination over the value of freedom for the perpetrators of discrimination. Change at this level requires the analysis of persuasion by the mobilization of the support for values within domestic and global policy-making processes.

The term "issue-areas" has been widely used in the study of global politics, particularly with reference to interdependence and to international regimes. It is useful to distinguish two separate meanings to issue-areas. First, an issue-system is a set of political actors who contest the priority to be given to a specific value. Second, there are policy-systems, which consist of policy-making organizations, along with the actors that are actively seeking to influence their decisions. They involve contention over the authoritative allocation of values, in the form of policy outcomes that endorse behavioral norms. Issue-systems are relatively abstract and concern how actors perceive and give priority to a value in politics. Policy-systems are more concrete, being located within an organization, and being the focus for contention of several different issue-systems. Thus, the global financial policy-system is primarily located in the IMF. It lies at the intersection of several issue-systems, because financial policy affects economic growth, social relations, the environment, and gender questions.[54]

This distinction allows us to conceptualize framing as a process of introducing an issue into a policy-system and perhaps displacing the previously dominant issue. For example, Charlotte Epstein has analyzed the International Whaling Commission. It was established as a policy-system to regulate a resource-based approach to whaling, dominated by contention over the allocation of wealth. Due to pressure from NGOs, it made a fundamental shift to a policy-system regulating the conservation of whales, dominated by contention over biodiversity conservation and respect for the allure (the beauty) of whales.[55] Equally, framing may take the form of contestation to locate a policy question within a policy forum that is dominated by consideration of the value to be prioritized. For example, IBFAN could not have achieved an International Code to restrict the marketing of baby foods within the WTO (with the value of wealth being dominant), but were assured of victory when policy-making was located in the World Health Organization (where health was the dominant value).

NGOs and other political actors mobilize support for values by transmitting messages to a target audience. There are four fundamental features to this interaction process: the status of the actors, the content of the message, the political environment in which it occurs, and the non-political environment. Each of these provides a basis for a norm entrepreneur to persuade others to adopt the underlying values and hence to make the new norm more salient to the target audience. Each defines a distinct category of issue linkages, which can be pursued to embed a value and hence a specific norm in a policy outcome. These four types of issue linkages are outlined in Box 5.1.

Box 5.1 How political actors win support by persuasion

People from NGOs, participating in formal debates or informal political discussions, try to gain support by winning an argument. This is not just a matter of rational argument. It will also be a process of persuading others to change the goals that they support. This can be achieved by making one of the following four linkages from the NGO's goals to the other person's values and norms.

Actor linkages

Communications from high-status actors will receive more attention than communications from low-status actors. In addition, evaluation of the content of communications will be partially determined by the status of the actor. For this reason, NGOs work hard to maintain their status, in particular their reputation for reliability in the information they provide. They also make prominent any external recognition of their status, such as the receipt of the Nobel Peace Prize by several NGOs over the years. Similarly, NGOs will attempt use status to increase support, by obtaining endorsements for their goals from high-status public figures, such as pop stars, comedians, or film stars. For example, Amnesty International has held major pop concerts and several shows with prominent comedians, while the film star George Clooney has been a key figure working with other NGOs to raise awareness of genocide in Darfur.

Value linkages

The content of a political message will explicitly or implicitly invoke values. NGOs gain support for a goal by linking it to a value which has widespread support. Keck and Sikkink suggest both avoidance of physical harm to vulnerable people and invocation of legal equality provide an effective value linkage.[1] However, their list of widely-shared values is too short. In addition, all human beings have the need for some wealth to provide food, clothing, and shelter. This means we will all respond to an argument that links our own wealth to a policy question. Also, most of us have sufficient

(Box continued on next page)

empathy with others to respond to wealth as a question of the alleviation of absolute poverty. Similarly, security, freedom, and justice are widely-shared values. Appreciation of beauty is also universal, but the application of this value can be highly varied between different cultures.

Bargaining linkages

A policy-making forum, such as a parliament, an intergovernmental body, or a diplomatic conference, provides a political environment in which individual actors must win a majority for any policy outcome they desire, by forming alliances with other actors. Thus, bargains are made to support a set of policy positions. This can only occur by actors changing the values they support, to some extent, in favor of the value preferences of other actors. NGOs will find it easier to encourage bargaining in a policy-system dealing with a range of different issues, either through separate agenda items or through a single policy question being complex. For example, the WTO Doha Development Agenda involves many wealth questions in the regulation of tariffs, quotas, and other barriers to trade, plus equity and equality in measures to promote development, plus health questions in whether trade norms should apply to AIDS drugs, plus environmental values in the relations between the WTO and global environmental bodies, and these policy questions will all have to be agreed as a single outcome.

Functional linkages

The non-political environment for policy-making provides linkages between different issues, independent from any political process. This can be true whether or not the political actors are aware of any linkage. Thus, policy towards drug addicts was linked to the spread of HIV (via shared use of needles by addicts) and this was true even before HIV was known to exist. A variety of biological, chemical, physical, environmental, economic, and social processes can affect politics and link political issues. For example, many resource-use questions invoke environmental issues through functional linkages, such as pollution effects or habitat change. Because these linkages

(Box continued on next page)

are not produced by political interactions, but are inherent to the implementation of policy, the task, or function being undertaken, it is appropriate to call them functional linkages. NGOs emphasize positive effects of the goals they support or negative effects of the goals they oppose, by publishing research reports establishing functional linkages.

Note

1   Keck and Sikkink, *Activists Beyond Borders*, 27.

Persuasion is achieved by two related processes. The aim is to increase the saliency of a policy question for the target political actor and/or redefine the values that are used to assess the question. Change in saliency of existing values or adoption of new values is achieved by making new issue linkages through articulating actor, value, bargaining, or functional linkages. Actor or bargaining linkages may not achieve long-term change, because they are vulnerable to changes in circumstances. Actors who are friends or allies may suddenly become unacceptable, because of a change in their status, such as revelation of corruption or aggressive behavior. Bargaining linkages may be broken, if a deal is renegotiated or is not fully implemented. The strongest impact is through value or functional linkages. They are likely to have a long-term effect, because change is made in normative or analytical perceptions of the world and this change is internalized. Often individuals who undergo a significant shift in their values become lifelong campaigners. While this may sometimes be a feature of government leaders, it is a common feature of those who work for NGOs. Norm entrepreneurs are driven by values and use the other linkages as tools for persuasion.

Persuasion is predominantly an explanatory process at the personal level, although great speeches, such as Martin Luther King Jr.'s "I Have a Dream" speech in August 1963, can be major social events. We also need explanation of political change at the systemic level. Change can arise from outside the political realm and have an impact upon politics, from four sources. Technological change can present new problems or offer new opportunities. Economic change can occur with uneven social effects and hence affect the relationships between those who gain and those who lose. Demographic change can have similar differential effects, with a shift in the age balance within societies. Population growth also has had a massive effect on the politics of development. Environmental change affects both perceptions of the world around us and the resources available for the economic system.

These analytical categories are not totally distinct. Technological change and economic change are closely related and global health pandemics result from and affect both environmental change and demographic change.

For these changes to affect politics, they must impact upon the articulation of political ideas. Change can arise from within the political system from three sources of new information. New images of the world, from photographs and films, can make well-known information seem more immediate and dramatic. For example, in October 1984, Michael Buerk's BBC TV film on the Ethiopian famine immediately transformed the global politics of food aid. New research can result in the re-evaluation of established questions for political debate or put new items on the agenda. For example, Rachael Carson's book *Silent Spring*, published in 1962, dramatically shifted perceptions of the damage caused by pollution. New models for change can arise through the development of new perceptions of what is possible, followed by demands for such changes to be made. For example, changes in Poland and Hungary in 1988–89 destabilized all the communist regimes of Eastern Europe.

The effects of technological, economic, demographic, and environmental change, with the exception of natural disasters, generally occur slowly, sometimes taking decades. Political change can be much faster. However, it requires the active engagement of norm entrepreneurs, usually NGO activists, to turn new information into an instrument of value change, followed by changes in norms. The media experts within NGOs concentrate in public debate on making value or functional linkages between their own values and other people's responses to the new information. The aim is to increase the saliency of the policy questions and to push them up the public agenda and hence to greater priority on institutional agendas. Within policy-making institutions, all four types of linkages—value, functional, actor, and bargaining—may be used by NGO lobbyists to generate the adoption of new policy norms. Often critical events are seized upon by NGO activists to achieve change. The Chernobyl disaster of April 1986 was used by environmental NGOs to prevent further building of civilian nuclear reactors in many countries. Critical events can crystallize a growing awareness by many individuals that they wish to see change and convert this potential into collective political actions. Critical events are not defined by major changes in the underlying policy question. They have symbolic significance in encapsulating an image of the desire for change and providing a collective reference point for political debate about change.

Conclusion

Through the above review of the structures and processes of global politics, the case has been argued for a constructivist pluralist understanding of global politics and the role that NGOs can have in promoting political change. The argument has both theoretical and empirical components. Theorizing about actors and structures both goes back many decades and is relatively simple to understand. The only complexity is to assert the reality of structures: intergovernmental organizations, international NGOs, transnational networks, and hybrid international organizations do have to be analyzed as policy-systems, each with their own dynamics of change. This chapter, along with the previous chapters on NGO access to policy-making and on NGOs in international law, has suggested the empirical evidence shows NGO engagement in global political structures is not unusual and anomalous. NGOs are a central presence in all aspects of global politics.

Theorizing about global political processes from a constructivist perspective is more recent, more complex, and more contentious. Yet, if we stop to think why we study politics and why we become engrossed with politics, we realize each of us is deeply concerned with our own values and those of our friends and contacts, along with the values being adopted by the institutions in which we participate. There is already an extensive body of literature illustrating how NGOs have achieved change in values and norms, notably in such fields as human rights, peace, environmental politics, and development. More work is needed in other policy domains. This chapter concentrated on the theoretical argument about values in global political processes. The case has been made that values cannot simply be dichotomized into high and low politics, nor into "objective" interests and "subjective" moral concerns. At the heart of politics is the contention between different actors over the priority to be given to their values. The crucial patterns of interaction are about the establishment of issue-systems in which particular values are under contention and the way in which these issue-systems impact upon policy-systems. All the arguments in this chapter are tentative and exploratory, but they do provide a theoretical basis for understanding how NGOs, lacking in traditional power capabilities, can exercise influence in global politics. NGOs act as norm entrepreneurs and persuade other actors to adopt their values and norms. Because they are agents in a social process, they too are subject to change under the pressure of the collective construction of issues and policy outcomes. Just as nobody would study the politics of one country without considering the interaction of society and the government, we cannot study global politics without consideration of the engagement of NGOs in the global contention over issues.

6   The creation of global governance

This book has so far progressed from discussing what is meant by a non-governmental organization in the world of global diplomacy to outlining NGO participation rights in global policy-making, their increasing role in the international legal system, and their impact on global communications. In each of the three domains of politics, law, and communications, NGOs have initiated change, made demands to be considered part of the international system, and have brought about a restructuring of relationships. Global politics, law, and communications are no longer confined to governments: they are multi-actor systems. In order to understand the activities of NGOs and the influence they achieve, it was necessary to reject an orthodox state-centric power-based approach and adopt an issue-based approach, focusing on a diverse range of actors engaged in contention over the translation of values into norms that govern behavior. Now we must bring together all these ideas and ask what has been the overall impact of NGOs on global politics.

The question will be addressed in two ways. At the overall structural level, NGOs have contributed to a transformation of the system. The nineteenth century was a world of inter-state relations, in which NGOs and intergovernmental organizations were few in number and their impact on diplomacy was relatively limited. The twenty-first century is a multicentric world, in which many transnational and transgovernmental actors from each country interact within a diverse range of international organizations and networks. These interactions are sufficiently important and sufficiently constraining to be described as a system of global governance. Thus, one answer will be to claim NGOs have been the leading actors in transforming the nature of global politics. In addition, NGOs have reframed the debates about global issues, participated in global policy-making, and influenced policy implementation. Thus, the second answer will be to demonstrate the extent of the impact of NGOs in several major policy domains: women's issues, population policy, development, human rights, environmental change, and arms control.

What is global governance?

Traditional approaches to power and authority lay emphasis on hierarchical structures and the ability of those at the top to utilize coercion to maintain their authority. On this basis, the only alternative to international anarchy is for all countries to become subject to some higher supranational authority—a world government—that can impose order through an international legal system ultimately backed by centralized use of force. A variety of concepts has been developed to assert there are alternative possibilities to the choice between anarchy and world government. In the 1970s, interdependence was used by politicians and academics to indicate the policy options of governments were constrained by complex interactions with many other actors. In the 1980s, the concept of an international regime was focused on order and predictability in behavior within specific issue-areas. From the 1990s, globalization has been used to indicate economic, financial, and technological change has embedded each country in an interconnected global system that is beyond the control of individual governments. The research work on interdependence, regimes, and globalization has in each case been biased towards international economic relations rather than global politics in general. They have each replaced the traditional emphasis on international anarchy with an assertion of the existence of a global system, which includes non-state actors. Interdependence was usually bracketed with transnational relations; regimes were strongly associated with epistemic communities and to a lesser extent NGOs and transnational corporations; globalization was conceived as being driven by TNCs. They combine systemic thinking with pluralism. Nevertheless, each approach did little more than make a temporary dent in state-centric power theory, partly because the theorizing was insufficiently ambitious.

Global governance is the latest concept used to offer a third alternative to the anarchy–supranationalism dichotomy. The concept has emerged from those in the world of global diplomacy who wish to strengthen and revitalize the United Nations and other global institutions. When the Cold War ended, there was a ferment of optimistic discussion about improved prospects for international cooperation. In January 1990, Willi Brandt brought together the members of four eminent global commissions—the Brandt Commission on development, the Palme Commission on disarmament, the Brundtland Commission on sustainable development, and the South Commission on cooperation among developing countries, at Königswinter in Germany. This led to the creation of a Commission on Global Governance in September 1992, which reported in August 1994 with wide-ranging proposals on global security, economic interdependence, reform of the UN, and strengthening international law. The analysis was based on the assumption of a new situation, in which the "interdependence of nations is wider and deeper" and there has been a "shift of focus from states to people" with a "growth of international civil society." They asserted "the world's arrangements for the conduct of its affairs must be underpinned by certain common values" but they were "not proposing movement towards world government."[1] Governance was defined as the combined effect of "the many ways individuals and institutions, public and private, manage their common affairs." It was a process by which diverse interests achieve cooperation, both through formal institutions and in informal arrangements. While global politics used to be seen primarily as consisting of intergovernmental relationships, global governance must now be understood as involving NGOs and TNCs. "There is no single model …. It is a broad, dynamic, complex process of interactive decision-making that is constantly evolving."[2]

During the time the Commission on Global Governance was working, the academic community launched a new journal, *Global Governance: A Review of Multilateralism and International Organizations*. It is noteworthy this was the product of a group of academics who have communicated closely with the diplomatic world through the Academic Council on the UN System, the UN University, their research, and their career appointments. The link was demonstrated in the first article being by the serving UN Secretary-General, Boutros Boutros-Ghali. He argued that the promotion of democracy was integral to the UN's work on development, on peace-building, and on human rights. More radically, he also called for increased democratization of the UN itself, by wider involvement with the media, NGOs, parliamentarians, and international lawyers. In particular, NGOs are "an indispensable part of the legitimacy without which no international activity can be meaningful."[3] Boutros-Ghali's writing was not theoretical, but it clearly embodied the two components of systemic thinking and pluralism.

The first theory article in the new journal was by James Rosenau, the most important pioneer of pluralist writing over the last 40 years. He clearly and explicitly discussed governance as a systemic concept. He rejected the idea of command mechanisms in his disavowal of hierarchy and adopted the idea of control from cybernetics: "[S]ystems of rule can be maintained and their controls successfully and consistently exerted even in the absence of legal or political authority." It must be emphasized that this cybernetic concept of control covers feedback through complex networks of communication. It does not mean control as threatening acts enforcing reluctant obedience: it means processes of inhibiting deviant behavior and encouraging socially accepted cooperative behavior, which result in "the evolution of intersubjective consensuses." Unlike more idealistic writers, Rosenau does acknowledge some organizations "defy steerage and resort to violence" but fails to mention that, on his own logic, such defiance will generate countervailing feedback.[4]

Rosenau stresses the turbulence of dynamic change in the contemporary world. This provides a strong basis for his assertion that new forms of authority are evolving: there are many nascent mechanisms for rule-making, some of which will eventually become fully institutionalized. Governments are challenged from above by the development of authority at the global level and from below by the increased importance of cities and micro-regions. It is in such a context that Rosenau describes social movements as "constituent parts of the globalizing process" and highlights "regimes as important sources of global governance." He departs from the state-centric bias in the regime literature, by asserting NGOs are joint sponsors of regimes and help sustain their control mechanisms. Rosenau also includes the United Nations and the European Union as examples of steering mechanisms that have taken an institutional form. Unfortunately, Rosenau is so overwhelmed by his emphasis on turbulence that he concludes he cannot see "the final chapter of this story of a disaggregated and fragmenting global system of governance."[5]

Lawrence Finkelstein responded to Rosenau by objecting his broad use of the term makes it difficult to know what is excluded: global governance "appears to be virtually anything." Finkelstein insists governance is not an institution, but it is an activity. This is a false contrast, because the structures (Rosenau's steering mechanisms) and the processes (Finkelstein's governance activity) are two sides of the same coin. All systems have both a structure and interaction processes occurring within the structure. Finkelstein offers a formal definition: "[G]lobal governance is governing, without sovereign authority, relationships that transcend national frontiers."[6] It is difficult to see exactly what distinguishes this from Rosenau's "systems of rule … in which the pursuit of goals through the exercise of control has transnational repercussions."[7] The difference between the two articles is mainly one of style rather than substance, but Rosenau is more insistent on pluralism than Finkelstein. Rosenau has pointed out that, despite the acknowledgment of "the transformation of boundaries, the erosion of state authority, and the proliferation of NGOs," Finkelstein's definition "falls back on old ways of thought" in being implicitly state-centric.[8] The one way in which no other writers have followed Rosenau is in his claim that globalization and localization are equally important, "so simultaneous and interactive as to collapse into an erratic but singular process" that he calls "fragmegration."[9] All the literature on global governance is highly indebted to Rosenau, except it remains exclusively focused on global, or sometimes regional, multi-country political systems.

Other academic work on global governance has mainly divided into three streams. There are empirical studies that usually take the concept for granted and apply it, without comment, to research on politics within international organizations.[10] Then there are theoretically informed empirical studies. Thomas Weiss and Leon Gordenker have edited a collection of essays stressing the significance of the UN's relations with NGOs by locating them within the context of global governance.[11] Oran Young has edited a strong volume on environmental regimes, using global governance to produce a pluralist version of regime theory.[12] Robert O'Brien, Anne Marie Goetz, Jan Aart Scholte, and Marc Williams have used global governance as the basis for exploring the engagement of the international economic institutions, the World Bank, the International Monetary Fund (IMF), and the WTO, with global social movements.[13] A collection of studies edited by Rorden Wilkinson and Stephen Hughes covers a much wider range of policy domains but asserts "it is premature to speak of a complete and fully coherent system of global governance" and concludes "global governance is poorly done, and equally poorly understood."[14] Finally, there are theoretical studies that are sympathetic to the systemic approach, but react against the language of management and "problem-solving" that is often associated with writing on global governance. These writers are critical of the emphasis on global civil society and international organizations. Their impact is to push global governance back towards an international political economy approach to globalization.[15]

Although the ideas of the Commission on Global Governance are not well developed and Rosenau's theorizing is too focused on turbulence rather than governance, the Commission and the journal do both challenge orthodox perspectives on international relations and in so doing justify the introduction of the new term, global governance. Their approach contains two key components. First, "global governance" is referring to a global political system that is more than the sum of the actions of the separate governments of the world. There is some degree of holism at the global level: systemic interactions produce coherent behavior rather than anarchy. Sovereignty is increasingly giving way to authoritative collective action. Patterns of expectations, desires for efficiency, and avoidance of costs can constrain behavior at the global level and promote order without government. Global governance designates relationships that maintain non-hierarchical, non-coercive processes of governed behavior, without the existence of government structures. Second, unlike the previous systemic concepts (interdependence, regimes, and globalization), it is central rather than peripheral to global governance that NGOs and TNCs are part of the global system. The interactions of governments with global civil society contribute to global policy-making. Many NGOs and TNCs identify themselves as global actors. They positively seek to promote expansion of global civil society and coherence in global politics. Hence, global governance is a pluralist concept. After the above discussion, we arrive at the following definition. *Global governance consists of policy-making and policy implementation in global political systems, through the collaboration of governments with actors from civil society and the private sector.* The policy-making and policy implementation will not always be coherent nor successful in achieving the agreed goals. Nevertheless, global governance is at a minimum the political process of attempting to agree upon coherent and effective collective action. The actual balance between governments, their various ministries, national NGOs, networks of NGOs, TNCs, various types of international organizations, and their secretariats will vary between different policy domains, but all types of actors are involved to some extent in all policy domains.

In addition to the defining features of holism and pluralism, I would identify five further characteristics in the use of the concept of global governance.

1   Analysis of global governance is focused on decision-making in international organizations. Most of the writing concerns intergovernmental organizations, particularly the United Nations or the wider UN system, including its specialized agencies. Other global IGOs outside the UN system, such as the World Trade Organization and the Global Environment Facility, and regional IGOs also receive attention. However, global governance can also occur through the international NGOs, such as the International Olympic Committee, or through hybrid international organizations, such as the International Conference of the Red Cross.[16]

2   There is not a single system of global governance: there are many distinct systems. Because different political issues greatly vary in their salience to different political actors, global governance is seen as being structured in different ways in different policy domains. Thus, the politics of human rights, climate change, or global financial stability each involves distinct actors focusing on separate international organizations, with minimal overlap between the policy domains.

3   Global governance occurs in all policy domains, whereas writing on interdependence, on regimes, and on globalization has been predominantly from a global political economy perspective. Regime theory has also been used in research on environmental politics and to a lesser extent on human rights. A section of the globalization literature has been devoted to debating whether media TNCs based in the United States have created a cultural hegemony. However, none of this earlier work touched the core concerns of orthodox realist power theory. In contrast to this, global governance is equally applicable to questions of arms control, nuclear proliferation, peace-keeping, peace-building, genocide, war crimes, and debate about the responsibility to protect.

4   Global governance is not reducible to rule-making in regimes. It is also the process by which regimes are created and, as Finkelstein pointed out, it covers the consequences of policy-making, "allocative effects, programs and projects, efficacy, compliance and domestic implementation."[17] From the constructivist literature, we can add agenda-setting, the framing of issues and the emergence of norms. Global governance also covers the allocation of status to global political actors, when decisions are made

to admit governments, NGOs, or TNCs to membership, observer status, or consultative status with international organizations or to elect such actors to councils or committees.

5   Global governance implies acceptance of the argument that power is not just the ability to exercise coercion. It is also achieving influence by mobilizing support for the endorsement of values and the adoption of norms in policy formulation and implementation. There are few writers who make direct links between the two, but global governance belongs within constructivist theory.

Thus, global governance refers to systemic processes of interactions between governments and global civil society, primarily focused on the policy outcomes of international organizations, each operating within their own distinct set of structured political relationships, to establish norms, formulate rules, promote the implementation of rules, allocate resources, or endorse the status of political actors, through the mobilization of support for political values.

The structures of global governance

Under all definitions of global governance, including the one above, a global political system that excludes civil society would be a system of intergovernmental diplomacy and not one of global governance. Thus, it might appear to be a tautology, true by definition, to say NGOs have created global governance. However, it is not that simple. The move from intergovernmental systems to pluralist systems could have occurred in three ways: under the initiative of governments; by the secretariats of intergovernmental organizations recruiting NGOs; or because of the demands made by NGOs knocking on the doors. In practice, the change has occurred to some extent along all three routes, but NGO demands have been the major driving force.

Various governments have contributed at different times. The Soviet government gave substantial backing to trades unions when the UN first established consultative status. The Canadian government on many occasions has strongly supported participation by NGOs in environmental negotiations. Developing country governments have encouraged NGO engagement in debates on development questions at the UN. On the other hand, all governments have predominantly been pragmatic, endorsing NGO participation when they expect to gain support for their own policies and being neutral or hostile on other occasions. Furthermore, governments have merely been supporting NGO demands. The one exception when a government took the lead was when the US government put significant effort into achieving NGO participation at the San Francisco conference that created the UN.

The desire of IGO secretariats to co-opt NGOs to provide resources, skills, information, and political prestige in support of the IGO as a collective institution has been of real and increasing importance. In the early years of the UN, this was a strong feature of the work of the specialized agencies and programs. The United Nations Educational, Scientific and Cultural Organization (UNESCO) positively required collaboration with educational, scientific, and cultural NGOs to give credibility to its activities in these domains. We have seen that they subsidized key NGOs by providing facilities at UNESCO's Paris headquarters and they even promoted the creation of one scientifically oriented, environmental, hybrid international organization, the World Conservation Union (IUCN). Similarly, the Office of the United Nations High Commissioner for Refugees (UNHCR) and United Nations Children's Fund (UNICEF) had intense cooperation with NGOs in their field operations. At other times, various secretariats have established strong relations with NGOs for more political reasons. From 1962 to 1994, the UN Centre Against Apartheid collaborated closely with the Anti-Apartheid Movement, to appeal to public opinion over the heads of the US and UK governments, for stronger action by the General Assembly and the Security Council against the apartheid government. In the run-up to the UN Conference on the Human Environment in Stockholm in 1972, Maurice Strong took the lead in mobilizing first the scientific community, then women and young people, and finally the environmental movement as a whole, to increase public awareness of and engagement with the conference.

Despite these contributions, the main reason NGOs have become part of the structures of global governance has been their continual pressure to be heard. We saw in Chapter 2 that, in the first years of the UN's existence, a far greater variety of NGOs applied to the UN for consultative status with Economic and Social Council (ECOSOC), in far greater numbers and far more quickly, than had been expected. The NGOs made strong demands for a wide range of participation rights and gained much of what was requested. At various times, governments have tried to limit NGO activity, notably in the 1968 review of the NGO Statute, at the start of the preparatory process for the 1992 Earth Summit and on many occasions in the history of the UN's handling of human rights questions. Yet, the NGOs have always been able to defend their participation rights successfully. Indeed, since the early 1970s, they have steadily expanded the range of bodies in which they participate and the type of activities in which they engage. In addition, the amount of time allocated to NGOs during formal diplomatic proceedings and the prestige of level at which they can speak (from subsidiary committees, to main committees, to plenary) has increased. While governments and international secretariats, at various times, have made their contributions, the main reason NGOs are able to participate in the global politics of policy-making has been their insistent and incessant demands to be heard on the issues that are salient to each of them.

In the field of international law, individual governments and international secretariats have been of minimal significance in enhancing the status of NGOs to that of legal persons. We saw in Chapter 3 that the NGOs individually and separately have gained rights and responsibilities under treaty law, because the value and the quality of their work have been of such a standard as to make recognition and incorporation of the NGOs essential for the success of the treaties. Often a major reason for recognition of the NGOs has been the leadership role they have played in pushing forward the negotiation of treaties. This applies to treaties establishing international humanitarian law, setting and monitoring standards for human rights, and protecting the environment. The work of the International Committee of the Red Cross is integral to the Geneva conventions; the human rights treaties would be a charade without the contributions made by a variety of human rights NGOs; and all environmental treaties depend to some extent on the knowledge, the expertise, and the resources provided by NGOs, to enhance effective implementation of the treaties. Similarly, a set of constitutional treaties establishing hybrid international organizations have given legal status to NGOs, because their contribution has been regarded as essential to the success of the organization. While all these processes are in varying ways the result of NGO initiatives and the political status NGOs have accumulated, in each case the achievement of legal status did require the collective endorsement of the governments who ratified the treaties. In addition, the general argument that NGOs have acquired legal personality through the ECOSOC Statute on NGOs becoming customary international law is completely dependent upon its endorsement in UN resolutions and in diplomatic practice by governments.

All the literature on global governance includes the revolution in global communications as one of the features of the contemporary global political system and a technological foundation for the existence of global civil society. We saw in Chapter 4 that the high connectivity of e-mail systems, the open collaborative ethos of the Internet, the spread of Internet use to the general public, the creation of public electronic information systems and the establishment of the UN and the World Bank on the Internet were all achieved by NGOs, especially through the work of the Association for Progressive Communications in the late 1980s. The Rio Earth Summit of 1992 generated an immense excitement among those who participated in it, directly or indirectly. It was widely regarded as an "unprecedented" UN event. The APC had created the summit as the first political event linking global diplomacy to global civil society through the Internet in real time: it was then and remains today the paradigm of global governance. Before the summit "global governance" was rarely discussed, but a few months after the summit the Commission on Global Governance was established.[18]

The three major dimensions of change, in politics, law, and communications, reinforce each other. The political impact of NGOs in global governance is now impossible to block because their legal right to participate in most (but not all) bodies in the UN system is unchallengeable. The chair of a committee might on rare occasions exclude NGOs from a specific meeting, but they cannot be excluded from the corridor outside nor from all other UN bodies that discuss the same issue. The legal status of NGOs is maintained because it is inconceivable that a political majority could be found to reduce the rights defined in the NGO Statute. Both the political status and the legal status of NGOs are difficult to challenge, because their access to global communications means their voice cannot be silenced. The political influence of NGOs in diplomacy started in the nineteenth century. Their legal rights evolved after the addition of Article 71 to the UN Charter in 1945. Their global communication capacities also began through post and travel in the nineteenth century, but underwent a revolutionary upgrade with the development of the Internet in the 1980s. The three dimensions combined have integrated global civil society into global diplomacy, to such a degree that the inter-state system was transformed into a system of global governance in the 1990s.

For each aspect of global governance in which relations were transformed, the incorporation of global civil society required significant normative change. Providing participation rights in policy-making forums required a general normative shift from expectations that diplomacy could be secret and foreign relations are exempt from the normal processes of democratic debate. It also required a more specific normative shift that NGOs could be allowed to engage in political behavior in the committee rooms and the corridors of intergovernmental organizations. Giving NGOs legal rights under international treaties required amendment of the fundamental normative presumption that international law only concerns the relations of states and IGOs. In creating the Internet, NGOs converted the intellectual property and physical infrastructure of the various separate computer networks into a global public good, a network of networks with open public access.[19] In terms of the promotion of values, the creation of the constitutive norms that constructed the Internet was more the product of the sharing, cooperative culture of computer scientists than it was of NGOs. However, the translation of this potential into a working system with behavioral norms of open access and inter-network connectivity was the achievement of NGOs. Thus, in the language of constructivist theory, NGOs constructed global governance, by promoting and achieving major normative change in global political, legal, and communication systems.

The impact of NGOs on global issues

Civil society, acting at the global level through NGOs, has not only promoted the constitutive norms to create a system of global governance, but also it has operated within that system to change the major norms that define the policy options on global issues. However, the extent to which NGOs have been norm entrepreneurs or have had a secondary role varies considerably from issue to issue. Six major areas of NGO activity and influence will now be considered, in the historical order in which they arose. These can only be sketched very briefly and readers are referred to the Selected Bibliography offering references to more detailed studies on some of the issues.

NGOs and women's issues

Women first organized transnationally, notably on suffrage questions and then on peace questions, a century ago. A variety of women's groups actively influenced the League of Nations on social welfare questions. Lobbying at San Francisco resulted in text on non-discrimination in five articles of the UN Charter and in the following year a Commission on the Status of Women was achieved. The government delegates to the CSW have often been appointed from women's NGOs or been women officials who collaborate very closely with their domestic NGOs. The CSW promoted several treaties on specific women's questions in the 1950s and a general declaration in 1967, which was expanded into a Convention on the Elimination of Discrimination Against Women in 1980. From the 1960s, the CSW and women's NGOs shifted their focus from women's rights to the role of women in development. This resulted in a series of UN special conferences on women in development, in 1975, 1980, 1985, and 1995, which produced a massive global mobilization of women's NGOs, substantial impact of national and local women's NGOs from different parts of the world upon each other, and an increased intensity of global networking. Remarkably strong feminist positions have been endorsed as UN policy goals for development.

In recent years, the biggest impact of the women's movement has been in the dramatic heightening of awareness of violence against women. The International Tribunal on Violations of Women's Human Rights organized at the NGO Forum for the World Conference on Human Rights, in Vienna in June 1993, had a substantial impact on delegates' perceptions of the nature of human rights and on the text of the Vienna Declaration. In the next year, the question was taken up by the Commission on Human Rights, which appointed a Special Rapporteur on Violence Against Women and gains were consolidated in the texts from the Beijing conference in 1995. The result was a major change of direction for several important human rights NGOs, such as

Amnesty International and Human Rights Watch. In 1998, through women's lobbying, systematic use of violence against women was included in the Statute of the International Criminal Court as a crime against humanity. Then, in October 2000, the least accessible global forum was conquered with the passage of Security Council Resolution 1325, not only calling for protection against gender-based violence but also urging a range of practical policy measures to incorporate a gender perspective and the involvement of women: in conflict resolution and peace processes, in training for and deployment of peace-keeping operations, in the design of refugee work, in the application of sanctions, and in negotiating and implementing peace agreements.

On all these issues, the women's NGOs have been the norm entrepreneurs, initiating and achieving change in global policy-making and in international law, through the energy and skill of their lobbying. No other section of global civil society has been organized for so long, has been so effectively organized, and has achieved such a substantial impact.

NGOs and global population growth

The initial struggle for the provision of contraception, sexual education, and reproductive health was undertaken by courageous pioneering women. They often had to go to jail, even in countries like the United States, Sweden, and India, to establish the right to run clinics and to publish information. Eight national associations came together in 1953 and agreed to establish the International Planned Parenthood Federation, now one of the world's largest NGOs. At this time, the overall issue was so controversial that ECOSOC's Population Commission limited itself primarily to a scientific and statistical approach to demography. IPPF applied for consultative status in 1955 but was rejected. Attempts were made to frame family planning in terms of health, but Catholic governments threatened to leave the World Health Organization if it so much as discussed family planning.

IPPF expanded rapidly, with many more national associations joining, service activities being established in local communities, and global collaboration between its members increasing. Gradually, the Federation and related NGOs succeeded in framing population growth as a cause of hunger and an impediment to development. The advent of the contraceptive pill in 1960 led to a rapid change in attitudes and behavior in many countries. By August 1964, IPPF was on ECOSOC's NGO Register; by 1969 it was promoted to Category II and by 1973 it gained Category I status. In the mid-1960s, development NGOs, such as Oxfam, became willing to support family planning projects, the WHO obtained a mandate to provide "technical assistance" and the UN Secretary-General established a UN Fund for Population Activities. At the International Conference on Human Rights in Teheran in May 1968, the IPPF delegation lobbied for and achieved a special resolution on family planning, declaring couples have "a basic human right" to decide their family size and a right "to adequate education and information." Soon afterwards the IPPF became the first NGO to receive a direct grant from the World Bank.

UN conferences on population issues were held in 1974, 1984, and 1994. The 1974 conference in Bucharest was highly controversial. The IPPF had a strong presence both as an NGO and within the official government delegations. They circulated a professionally produced daily newspaper, *Planet*; ran the Population Tribune, a large NGO forum; and lobbied vigorously to overcome divisions between Western and developing country governments. The outcome was a synthesis in which development and population policies were agreed to be mutually dependent. By 1984 in Mexico City, the Reagan administration was making a sustained attack on population NGOs and UN programs. Similarly, in 1994 in Cairo, the Bush administration was hostile to family planning, this time with much more active support from the Holy See and some Catholic governments. In each case, the IPPF was able to maintain strong endorsement of the right to family planning and reproductive health facilities. However, the IPPF lost out severely when they failed to maintain a lobbying presence at the UN Millennium Summit in September 2000 and access for all to reproductive health services was deleted from the Millennium Development Goals. Despite this setback, IPPF has driven through substantial change against a varied pattern of opposition from governments and strong opposition from religious groups.

NGOs and development

In the UN's first decades, NGOs had no influence on development questions, for the simple reason that no development NGOs, as we now know them, then existed. While Oxfam and CARE had been formed in 1943 and 1945, respectively, they were initially concerned with relief for refugees and the destitute in war-torn Europe. It was not until African countries became independent and the UN and the World Bank started substantial development programs in the early 1960s that a variety of humanitarian, welfare, and professional NGOs started to engage with development questions and started to fund projects.

In the 1970s, operational NGOs realized small projects had minimal impact within global economic structures that inhibit development. A series of UN conferences and General Assembly special sessions provided platforms for NGOs to challenge orthodox thinking. The concept of development shifted from growth of gross national product (GNP) by industrialization to meeting "basic needs." Progress on development was linked to the environment, population growth, subsistence agriculture, and trade. While the NGO world, academics in development studies, and some development officials made this intellectual shift, it did not become integral to most multilateral and national policy-making until a second round of UN conferences in the 1990s.

An exception to the early lack of interest in development among NGOs was the creation of War on Want in Britain in 1951. This contributed to Britain being, in 1964, the first donor country to have a separate development ministry. War on Want was crucial in converting a wider range of development NGOs into global campaigning NGOs. In 1974, they published a report, *The Baby Killer*, which brought the death of babies due to bottle-feeding onto the global public agenda. A very wide-ranging coalition of NGOs learnt the techniques and the benefits of using a network, the International Baby Foods Action Network, for global campaigning.

The most spectacular NGO campaigning on development arose from an imaginative individual, Martin Dent, using the biblical concept of jubilee to frame a call for debt forgiveness. His idea was taken up by the Debt Crisis Network and Christian Aid serviced a global Jubilee 2000 campaign. The outcome was enhancement of the Heavily Indebted Poor Countries Initiative of the IMF and the World Bank, which has now provided substantial debt reduction for 35 countries. Similarly, the Global Call to Action Against Poverty, which operated in Britain as Make Poverty History and in the United States as the ONE Campaign and was supported by Live 8 concerts in each of the G8 countries, achieved a substantial impact on the G8 Summit in Scotland in July 2005. The G8 leaders pledged to double the level of Official Development Assistance (ODA) from $25 to $50 billion, but in practice did not deliver on this promise.

We are now in a situation where the pessimists could claim that development has failed, particularly in the majority of African countries. On the other hand, the Millennium Development Goals, based on the policies adopted by the UN conferences of the 1990s, have set standards for the global political system as a whole to meet. While insufficient resources have been mobilized and global structures still present barriers to development, NGOs have undoubtedly achieved a massive shift in development thinking and development policy targets.

NGOs and human rights

NGOs influenced the UN's handling of human rights in the most fundamental manner from the beginning. In 1945, they ensured the draft UN Charter was amended at San Francisco to make it mandatory for ECOSOC to create a Commission on Human Rights (CHR) and they contributed to the drafting of the 1948 Universal Declaration on Human Rights (UDHR). For decades thereafter, their ability to push the agenda forward was blocked by Cold War antagonisms and the attitude that responding to complaints would violate sovereignty.

In the 1960s a process started of negotiating treaties on various aspects of human rights. First of all there were two general covenants that converted the UDHR into legal commitments. In addition, there was a series of more detailed, specific conventions. They covered discrimination against people on grounds of race, discrimination against women, torture, and the rights of children, migrant workers, and disabled people. The legal revolution these developments have embodied was outlined in Chapter 3. The UN's role in human rights was expanded when the CHR was given the authority, under ECOSOC Resolution 1503 in 1970, to examine and hence to comment on the worst situations of persistent human rights violations. Then, the CHR developed a series of "special mechanisms" to report on violations in specific countries and on specific themes, such as torture, disappearances, food, health, or housing. For all these treaties and mechanisms, NGOs have been central to their creation and their operations. In particular, NGOs provide the evidence for the 1503 procedures and for treaty committees, and individual campaigners have been appointed to many of the special rapporteur posts.

With all these developments, it became more apparent that the human rights section of the UN Secretariat was understaffed and had insufficient status. Amnesty International took the lead in campaigning for creation of a UN High Commissioner for Human Rights and, in December 1993, the General Assembly defined a mandate for the new post. NGOs were very disappointed by the appointment of Ayala-Lasso as the first High Commissioner, because he was a diplomat, who wished to avoid controversy and operate in a low-key manner. After trying to work with him, they pressed Kofi Annan for a new appointment; Lasso resigned and Mary Robinson took over. Her term of office established the principle of strong, independent leadership by a prestigious UN official, who would collaborate with NGOs.

The greatest political achievement by NGOs has been the creation of the International Criminal Court (ICC). In 1995, a small group of the major human rights NGOs, led by Amnesty International, approached William Pace of the World Federalist Movement to form the Coalition for an International Criminal Court. They mobilized "like-minded" governments to ensure a drafting conference was convened. At the Rome conference in 1998, they lobbied to block several attempts by the US administration to weaken the independence of the court. Once the ICC Statute was agreed, the Coalition continued to lobby to obtain the necessary 60 ratifications. There is no comparable event in modern times to the Clinton and Bush administrations using every form of political influence at their disposal (except the direct use of military force), in order to prevent something happening, yet being defeated.

NGOs have dominated the international diplomacy of human rights. It is difficult to imagine that governments would have established any international standards or monitoring mechanisms, without the pressure and the detailed specialist work from NGOs.

NGOs and global environmental change

There has been a strand of environmental politics involving NGOs since the nineteenth century, but the language was of conservation and the approach was scientific. The hybrid international organizations, the World Conservation Union, and the International Council for Science were important in the development of the international law on conservation of habitats, birds, endangered species, biodiversity, and climate change. Apart from these two hybrids, environmental NGOs did not exercise any leadership role at the global level until the 1970s. This changed when they were recruited by Maurice Strong to attend the UN Conference on the Human Environment, in Stockholm in 1972. NGOs then produced one significant shift in the global agenda, by obtaining a resolution calling for a moratorium on commercial whaling.

The Stockholm conference led to the creation of a UN Environment Programme, which operated in a low-key manner, mainly coordinating scientific monitoring of environmental change. Its headquarters were established in Nairobi, which led to a new NGO network, the Environment Liaison Centre International, being based there. NGOs remained predominantly focused on local and national politics until the mid-1980s. Discovery of the ozone hole, satellite photographs of burning rainforests, the decline in African elephants, and increased worries about climate change, combined with the impact of the Brundtland Report, *Our Common Future*, published in 1987, pushed environmental questions up the global agenda and led to the convening of the Rio Earth Summit in 1992. This produced two structural changes. First, the UN established a Commission on Sustainable Development, which became the central forum for global environmental politics. As we saw in Chapter 3, NGOs are mobilized into nine Major Groups for multi-stakeholder dialogues each year with the governments at the CSD. Second, the Global Environment Facility (GEF) became the funding mechanism for the global and regional conventions on biodiversity, climate change, international waters, land degradation, ozone depletion, and persistent organic pollutants. In the GEF, a global GEF-NGO Network is given privileged access to policy-making and to a Small Grants Programme for NGO projects. Since the late 1990s, global environment politics has been dominated by climate change. The Climate Action Network and very many other NGOs, including industrial interests, are a substantial presence at the Conferences of the Parties to the Framework Convention on Climate Change (FCCC).

A unique feature of environmental politics is that civil society can be mobilized to act unilaterally through green consumerism. There are two notable global governance organizations combining NGOs, producers, and retailers: the Forest Stewardship Council and the Marine Stewardship Council, certifying sustainable timber production and fisheries management. These are interesting in being effective structures for global governance that do not contain governments and have an impact without the need for governmental action.

There can be no clear overall conclusions about the role of NGOs in global environment governance. Sometimes they are in the lead, but sometimes they are only following governments. At certain points they have been a major presence in global governance, but at other points they have been weak. Sometimes they confront TNCs and sometimes they collaborate with them. Their main political impact has been by the authoritative impact of scientific research, but there are occasions when they influence policy because of widespread public support. Since 1992, they have had high status as participants in all forums for global environmental governance.

NGOs and arms control

During early stages of the Cold War, it was politically very difficult for the peace NGOs to gain public support. Only communist front organizations and a few Christian groups, notably the Quakers, could breach the East–West divide. The first substantial challenge came from nuclear scientists, who became increasingly worried by the dangers of nuclear war. Starting in July 1957 under the leadership of Joseph Rotblat, the annual Pugwash Conference on Science and World Affairs brought together eminent scientists from all major countries. After each conference, they discreetly passed on their combined views to decision-makers in both the East and the West, to promote peace. In the West, scientists also contributed, in the late 1950s and early 1960s, to the development of a mass peace movement that focused on the radioactive fall-out from nuclear tests. The combination of Pugwash making technical progress with detection of underground tests and the pressure of public opinion, especially in Britain, contributed to agreement on a nuclear test-ban treaty in 1963. After that, the strength of the Western peace movement was inversely related to East–West tension and the arms race. There was a steady decline, when détente occurred, and a more dramatic increase in support, when many new missiles were deployed in the early 1980s. However, this second phase was different in that the Western peace movement was able to make some links with dissidents in Eastern Europe and the Soviet Union. The massive scale of public concern in the West and the political importance of dissidents in the East, combined with work by Pugwash, contributed to several further arms control agreements. Pugwash subsequently was awarded the Nobel Peace Prize in 1995.

The International Campaign to Ban Landmines (ICBL) was launched in October 1992 by a diverse group of six NGOs, with Jody Williams of the Vietnam Veterans of America as the coordinator. They soon gained prestigious support from UNICEF and the ICRC, and expanded rapidly. After five years, there were more than 1,300 NGOs from 85 countries in the network. Some of the major governments tried to prevaricate by treaty work on the "eventual elimination" of landmines, while some other governments acted unilaterally to destroy all their own landmines. The ICBL pushed the process by reframing an arms control question as a humanitarian issue. In October 1996, the Canadian government circumvented the UN Conference on Disarmament, by convening a conference in Ottawa that was solely open to the 50 governments who were willing to commit themselves to a total ban on landmines. In December the following year a comprehensive treaty was completed and signed by 122 governments, entering into force in March 1999. Recognition of the contribution made by the ICBL and the Red Cross Movement was given in the text of the treaty and the 1997 Nobel Peace Prize was awarded jointly to Jody Williams and the ICBL. One loophole in the landmines treaty was the ability of the military to drop cluster bombs, containing many smaller bombs, from the air. Several NGOs, including the ICBL, took up this question and in November 2003 launched the Cluster Munition Coalition. In a process that was very similar to that for the landmines treaty, a convention was adopted in May 2008 and signed in December 2008. NGOs and governments of smaller countries completely outmaneuvered opposition from the major governments in constructing both these treaties.

Conclusion

The impact of NGOs has varied considerably from one policy domain to another. In the field of human rights, very little diplomatic action would have been taken or international law developed without the sustained political pressure from NGOs. The same is true for women's issues: whether it is women's rights, the politics of population and family planning, the relationship between women and development, or violence against women, women's NGOs have been at the forefront of placing the issues on the global agenda, generating change in policy goals and achieving some movement towards equity and equality. In the field of global environmental politics, governments have been willing and able to exercise leadership, but NGOs have also been major participants in expanding awareness of environmental issues, disseminating research findings, tabling policy proposals, and monitoring policy implementation. Governments have been dominant in deciding about the transfer and utilization of Official Development Assistance, the structure of international trade, and questions of arms control. This does not mean governments have been dominant in setting the agenda on development and arms control questions nor in framing how the issues are perceived nor in establishing the norms that determine their policy choices. However much the balance between NGOs, governments, and international organizations may vary between different policy domains or across different time periods, at no point since the UN was created has it been possible to understand the global politics of any issue without considering the influence of NGOs and governments upon each other. Academic literature or diplomatic history may at times attempt to reduce events to inter-state relations. However, there always is another story of domestic politics, transnational relations, and inter-actions in international organizations, which is essential to full understanding of global politics.

Only a pluralist constructivist approach can allow for the possibility of NGOs being major participants in politics, law, and communications and explain the influence they achieve. Virtually all the pluralist constructivist writing is applied to demonstrating the impact of specific NGOs or specific types of NGOs on particular issues. It is hoped that the reader will be convinced by the general argument of this book that NGOs have not only exercised influence in specific ways. They have been crucial participants in the creation of the structures of global governance in the contemporary world. NGOs are neither under the control of sovereign governments nor are NGOs supplanting the role of governments. We live in systems of global governance, in which governments and NGOs interact with each other and influence each other. NGOs do not have any military capabilities nor significant economic resources, but they do mobilize support for values and norms. NGOs have constructed global governance, raised new issues, framed issues, and participated in the construction of global norms. NGOs are crucial components in the politics of global governance.

Notes

Foreword

1 Peter Willetts, *Pressure Groups in the Global System: The Transnational Relations of Issue-Oriented Non-Governmental Organisations* (London: Pinter, 1982) and *"The Conscience of the World": The Influence of Non-Governmental Organisations in the UN System* (London: Hurst, 1996).
2 These numbers are based on Peter Willetts, "Transnational Actors and International Organizations in Global Politics," in *The Globalization of World Politics*, 4th edn., eds J. Baylis, S. Smith, and P. Owens (Oxford: Oxford University Press, 2008), 330–47.
3 Boutros Boutros-Ghali, "Foreword," in *NGOs, the UN, and Global Governance*, eds Thomas G. Weiss and Leon Gordenker (Boulder: Lynne Rienner, 1996), 7.

1 NGOs, social movements, and civil society

1 League of Nations Information Section, *Essential Facts about the League of Nations* (Geneva: League of Nations, 1938), 305.
2 Interim Committee of Consultative Non-Governmental Organisations, *Consultation between the United Nations and Non-Governmental Organisations* (Westport, CT: Greenwood Press, 1978, reprint of a 1949 study), 12–13.
3 The consultative arrangements were developed in ECOSOC Resolution 4 (I) of 16 February 1946; Resolution 3 (II) of 21 June 1946; Resolution 17 (III), of 1 October 1946; Resolution 57 (IV) of 28 March 1947; and through various practices in the early years. They were consolidated as a Statute in ECOSOC Resolution 288 B (X) of 27 February 1950. The Statute was revised by Resolution 1296 (XLIV) of 23 May 1968 and again by Resolution 1996/31 of 25 July 1996. Much of the text has remained unchanged since 1946. In this and the next chapter, when these resolutions are quoted, they are simply referenced by the respective date when they were passed.
4 Harold Paine and Birgit Gratzer, "Rev. Moon and the United Nations: A Challenge for the NGO Community," Global Policy Forum, November 2001. Available at: www.globalpolicy.org/ngos/credib/2001/1101moon.htm.
5 *We the Peoples: Society, the United Nations and Global Governance* (General Assembly document, A/58/817), 11 June 2004, paras. 15 and 24. Hereafter the "Cardoso Report."

6 "Remarks by Andrew S. Natsios, Administrator USAID," InterAction Forum, 21 May 2003. Available at: www.usaid.gov/press/speeches/2003/sp030521. html

7 Decision 1/1 of the Preparatory Committee for UNCED, 14 August 1990, reprinted in Peter Willetts, *"The Conscience of the World"* (Washington, DC: Brookings, 1996), 302–03. See also Peter Willetts, "From Stockholm to Rio and Beyond: The Impact of the Environmental Movement on the United Nations Consultative Arrangements for NGOs," *Review of International Studies* 22 (1996): 57–80.

8 *List of Non-Governmental Organisations in Consultative Status with the Economic and Social Council as at 31 August 2005* (ECOSOC document E/2005/INF.5).

9 The companies were Solar Energy Systems Ltd of Australia (ECOSOC document E/CN.17/2002/PC.2/16, item 139), 22 January 2002; and First for Foodservices, UK, and Body Shop International, UK (General Assembly document A/CONF.199/PC/6, items 1 and 159), 19 March 2002.

10 *Report of the Commission on Sustainable Development acting as the preparatory committee for the World Summit for Social Development, Fourth Session* (General Assembly document A/CONF.199/4), paras. 27–29, and *Earth Negotiations Bulletin*, 22, no. 31, 28 May 2002.

11 Jane Nelson, *Building Partnerships: Cooperation between the United Nations System and the Private Sector* (New York: UN Department of Public Information, 2002), chapter III; the UN Global Compact Office (www.unglobalcompact.org); and John Ruggie, "global-governance.net: The Global Compact as Learning Network," *Global Governance* 7 (2001): 371–78.

12 "NGO Documents on UN and Business," Global Policy Forum, is a list of key documents. Available at: www.globalpolicy.org/reform/business/ngoindex.htm

13 UN Non-Governmental Liaison Service, "Joint Civil Society Statement at the Global Compact Counter-Summit," 23 June 2004. Available at: www.un-ngls. org/cso/cso3/joint.html.

14 *Report of the World Summit for Social Development* (General Assembly document A/CONF.166/9), 19 April 1995. Note: "civil society organization" does not appear in the Copenhagen Declaration or the Programme of Action or in this report.

15 Francesco Mezzalama, *Report of the Joint Inspection Unit on the Involvement of Civil Society Organizations other than Non-Governmental Organizations and the Private Sector in Technical Cooperation Activities* (General Assembly document A/57/118), 27 June 2002, para. 12.

16 For contrasting views, see Gordon Laxer and Sandra Halperin, eds, *Global Civil Society and Its Limits* (Houndmills, UK: Palgrave, 2003), which largely discounts the concept, and Gideon Baker and David Chandler, eds, *Global Civil Society: Contested Futures* (Abingdon, UK: Routledge, 2005), which is more convinced of its value.

17 *Report of the World Summit for Social Development* (General Assembly document A/CONF.166/9), 19 April 1995. The Declaration Commitment 6(k), and the Programme of Action, paras. 34(g), 52 (b), 79(e), and 85 all juxtapose NGOs and local communities or community organizations.

18 The earliest writers in this field were James Rosenau, ed., *Linkage Politics: Essays on the Convergence of National and International Systems* (New York: Free Press, 1969); Robert Keohane and Joseph Nye, eds, *Transnational Relations and World Politics* (Cambridge, MA: Harvard University Press, 1972); Richard Mansbach, Yale Ferguson, and Donald Lampert, *The Web of World Politics:*

Non-State Actors in the Global System (Englewood Cliffs, NJ: Prentice Hall, 1976); James Rosenau, *The Study of Global Interdependence: Essays on the Transnationalisation of World Affairs* (London: Pinter Publishers, 1980); and Peter Willetts, ed., *Pressure Groups in the Global System* (London: Frances Pinter, 1982).

19 Robin Broad, ed., *Global Backlash: Citizen Initiatives for a Just World Economy* (Lanham, MD: Rowman & Littlefield, 2002); Katharine Ainger *et al.*, eds, *We Are Everywhere: The Irresistible Rise of Global Anti-Capitalism* (London: Verso for Notes from Nowhere, 2003); Tom Mertes, ed., *A Movement of Movements* (London: Verso, 2004); and Louise Amoore, ed., *The Global Resistance Reader* (London: Routledge, 2005). The first three of these books are from the perspective of activists and the fourth is academic.

20 The reference to turtles was to a WTO dispute over trade in shrimps, caught in nets that killed turtles. The International Brotherhood of Teamsters is a North American trades union.

21 Sidney Tarrow, *Power in Movement* (Cambridge: Cambridge University Press, 1994), 3–4.

22 See for example, André Drainville, "Québec City 2001 and the Making of Transnational Subjects," in *The Global Resistance Reader*, ed. Amoore, 169; Emir Sader, "Beyond Civil Society," in *A Movement of Movements*, ed. Mertes, 253–55; and Immanuel Wallerstein, "New Revolts Against the System," in *A Movement of Movements*, ed. Mertes, 269–70.

23 Tarrow, *Power in Movement*, 21.

24 Cardoso Report, paras. 43, 53, 97, 98, and 172.

25 Cardoso Report: contrast the terms of reference in Annex I with the entry for "constituency" in the Glossary.

26 For example, Michael Waltzer, ed., *Toward a Global Civil Society* (Providence, RI: Berghahn Books, 1995), which, despite its title, is solely concerned with civil society at the country level, locates economic activity within civil society, while Robert Fine and Shirin Rai, eds, *Civil Society: Democratic Perspectives* (London: Frank Cass, 1997), distinguishes state, market, and civil society. Michael Edwards, *Civil Society* (Cambridge: Polity Press, 2004), provides a review of different meanings attributed to civil society.

27 Kumi Naidoo and Rajesh Tandon, eds, *Civil Society at the Millennium* (West Hartford, CT: Kumarian Press for Civicus, 1999), 5, 9, 11, 12–13.

28 Richard Falk, *On Humane Governance: Toward a New Global Politics, A Report to the World Order Models Project* (Cambridge: Polity Press, 1995), chapter 8 title, 17, 35, 254. Later, Falk modified this position, saying he had "no illusion that the social forces emanating from civil society are inherently benevolent"; Richard Falk, "Global Civil Society and the Democratic Prospect," in Barry Holden, ed., *Global Democracy: Key Debates* (London: Routledge, 2000), 163. Having made this caveat, Falk then continued much as before.

29 Neera Chandhoke, "The Limits of Global Civil Society," in *Global Civil Society 2002*, eds Marlies Glasius, Mary Kaldor, and Helmut Anheier (Oxford: Oxford University Press, 2002), 41.

30 This is the central concern of David Chandler, *Constructing Global Civil Society: Morality and Power in International Relations* (Houndmills, UK: Palgrave Macmillan, 2004).

31 Chandler, *Constructing Global Civil Society*, 6.

32 Helmut Anheier, Marlies Glasius, and Mary Kaldor, eds, *Global Civil Society 2001* (Oxford: Oxford University Press, 2001), 15–16.

33 Fine and Rai, eds, *Civil Society: Democratic Perspectives*, 25.
34 John Keane, *Global Civil Society* (Cambridge: Cambridge University Press, 2003), 142.
35 *Note by the President of the General Assembly* (A/60/CRP.2), 22 March 2006, approved by General Assembly Decision 60/554 of 27 March 2006.

2 The access of NGOs to global policy-making

1 ECOSOC Resolution 288 B (X) of 27 February 1950; Resolution 1296 (XLIV) of 23 May 1968; and Resolution 1996/31 of 25 July 1996.
2 In 1993, only two regional NGOs had Category I status. One more regional NGO and two national NGOs were added under ECOSOC Decision 1995/305 of 27 July 1995.
3 See the list at www.staff.city.ac.uk/p.willetts/NGOS/NGO-2005.HTM. Another 18 of the 136 General Status NGOs, from their names, were not obviously global, so only 89 were clearly global in scope. Where to draw the line between general concerns and specialist concerns would be very subjective.
4 Eleanor Roosevelt and William De Witt, *UN: Today and Tomorrow* (Puttiers, NY: Harper & Brothers, 1953), 144.
5 UN Press Release ECOSOC/5876 of 26 October 1999 and ECOSOC Decision 1999/292 of 26 October 1999.
6 See Report of the NGO Committee for May and June 2000 (ECOSOC document E/2008/88 Part I and Part II), 5 July 2000 and 13 July 2000; ECOSOC Decision 2000/224B of 25 July 2000; the Report of the NGO Committee covering meetings on 21 and 27 July 2000 (ECOSOC document E/2008/88 Part II/Add.1), 27 July 2000; ECOSOC Decision 2000/295, 28 July 2000; Report of the NGO Committee covering a meeting on 27 September 2000 and the committee's procedural vote (ECOSOC document E/2008/88 Part II/Add.2), 4 October 2000; and UN Press Release ECOSOC/5934 covering the final Council vote, 18 October 2000.
7 *We the Peoples: Civil Society, the United Nations and Global Governance* (General Assembly document, A/58/817), 11 June 2004. For a highly negative critique of this report, see Peter Willetts, "The Cardoso Report on the UN and Civil Society: Functionalism, Global Corporatism or Global Democracy?," *Global Governance* 12 (2006): 305–24.
8 CONGO does not include within its membership all the recognized NGOs.
9 See Michael Longford, "NGOs and the Rights of the Child," in Peter Willetts, ed., *"The Conscience of the World": The Influence of Non-Governmental Organisations in the UN System* (London: Hurst and Washington, DC: Brookings, 1996).
10 The UNPFII was established by ECOSOC Resolution 2000/22 of 28 July 2000 and held its first session in May 2002. Note that indigenous peoples' organizations object to being described as NGOs (see Chapter 1).
11 For a wider background on the institutions, see Julie Mertus, *The United Nations and Human Rights: A Guide for a New Era* (London: Routledge, 2005 and 2009) and Bertrand Ramcharan, *UN Human Rights Council* (London: Routledge, forthcoming).
12 In each case, the current name of the fund, institute or program is given and the year is when the General Assembly authorized their establishment. In several cases, they operated initially under a different name. The list is not comprehensive.
13 *Arrangements and Practices for the Interaction of NGOs in All Activities of the UN System* (General Assembly document A/53/170), 10 July 1998, para. 47.

14 For more details, see Alba Zizzamia, *NGO/UNICEF Co-operation: A Historical Perspective* (UNICEF History Series, Monograph V, March 1987). Available at: www.unicef.org/about/history/files/CF-HST-MON-1986–005-ngo-cooperation-mono-V.pdf.

15 Compare the *Draft Proposal by the Chairman of the Open-Ended Working Group on the Rules of Procedure* (ECOSOC document E/ICEF/1994/L.18), 15 April 1994, rules 50 and 51 with the *Rules of Procedure* (ECOSOC document E/ICEF/177/Rev.6), adopted 6 May 1994, Rule 50(2) and Annex, paras. 1–2.

16 *Rules of Procedure of the Executive Board of the United Nations Development Programme and of the United Nations Population Fund* (UNDP document DP/1997/32), May 1997.

17 For wider institutional coverage, see Stephen Browne, *United Nations Development Programme (UNDP)* (London: Routledge, forthcoming); and Richard Jolly, *UNICEF (United Nations Children's Fund)* (London: Routledge, forthcoming).

18 For an overview of conferences, see Michael G. Schechter, *United Nations Global Conferences* (London: Routledge, 2005) and Paul Taylor and A. J. R. Groom, *Global Issue in the United Nations' Framework* (London: Macmillan, 1989).

19 Peter Willetts, "From 'Consultative Arrangements' to 'Partnership': The Changing Status of NGOs in Diplomacy at the UN," *Journal of Global Governance* 6 (2000): 191–212.

20 *Report of the World Summit for Social Development, Johannesburg, 26 August– 4 September 2002* (General Assembly document A/CONF.199/20).

21 For wider institutional coverage, see Elizabeth R. DeSombre, *Global Environmental Institutions* (London: Routledge, 2006); and Peter Newell and Harriet Bulkeley, *Governing Climate Change* (London: Routledge, 2010).

22 Mertus, *The United Nations and Human Rights*, 108. These arrangements are credited "in some instances" with causing "the Government concerned to review its policies affecting children": *Statement submitted by Action Aid*, ECOSOC document E/AC.70/1994/NGO/7, 21 June 1994, para. 13.

23 Willetts, "From 'Consultative Arrangements' to 'Partnership'," 198–99.

24 *Rules of Procedure of the Conference on Disarmament* (UN document CD/8, last revised as CD/8/Rev.9), 19 December 2003, Rule 42.

25 *Report of the Conference on Disarmament* (General Assembly A/59/27), para. 19, decision taken on 12 February 2004.

26 Paul James, *The Arria Formula*, revised October 2003. Available at: www.global-policy.org/publications-mm/all-policy-papers-articles-and-statements-mm/40088.html.

27 *NGOs and the Council*. Available at: www.globalpolicy.org/security-council/ngos-and-the-council.html.

3 The status of NGOs in international law

1 "Reparation for Injuries Suffered in the Service of the United Nations" in *International Court of Justice Reports, 1949*, 178–79, reproduced in Tim Hillier, *Sourcebook on Public International Law* (London: Cavendish Publishing, 1998), 175–81.

2 There are differences between the 1969 Convention and the 1986 Convention in the "Miscellaneous Provisions." Note that these conventions have not yet entered into force.

3   Constitutional Charter. Available at: www.orderofmalta.org/site/pdf/Constit._ Charter_and_code.pdf, Article 2.

4   Observer status was granted by General Assembly Resolution A/48/265, 24 August 1994.

5   Menno Kamminga, "The Evolving Status of NGOs under International Law: A Threat to the Inter-State System," in Philip Alston, ed., *Non-State Actors and Human Rights* (Oxford: Oxford University Press, 2005), 99. For wider coverage of the ICRC, see David Forsythe and Barbara Rieffer-Flanagan, *The International Committee of the Red Cross: A Neutral Humanitarian Actor* (London: Routledge, 2007).

6   General Assembly Resolution 45/6, 16 October 1990, covered the ICRC; Resolution 48/265, 24 August 1994, covered the Sovereign Military Order of Malta; and the Holy See became a Permanent Observer from 6 April 1964 by agreement with the UN Secretary-General.

7   Observer status for the International Federation was proposed on 16 August 1994 (General Assembly document A/49/100/Add.1), 11 October 1994. The United States response came on 19 September 1994 (General Assembly document A/49/231). Observer status was granted by General Assembly Resolution 49/2, 19 October 1994. The block on further NGOs was placed by General Assembly Decision 49/426, 9 December 1994.

8   *Report on the First Session of the Commission* (ECOSOC document E/259), 2 October 1947, para. 22; repeated in ECOSOC Resolution 728 F (XXVIII), 30 July 1959.

9   *Agenda 21* (General Assembly document A/CONF.151/26), 14 August 1992, paras. 1.1, 23.1 and 23.2.

10 *Convention Concerning the Protection of the World Cultural and Natural Heritage*, 16 November 1972, articles 8 (3), 13 (7) and 14 (2), respectively.

11 "Notes of Meeting of International NGO/PHC Group, Palais des Nations, 1 May 1995," circulated as a memorandum among NGOs concerned with primary healthcare, 12–14.

12 All the following fail to discuss INGOs: David Armstrong, *The Rise of the International Organisation: A Short History* (London: Macmillan, 1982); Giuseppe Schiavone, *International Organizations. A Dictionary and Directory* (London: Macmillan, 1983); Paul Taylor, *International Organization in the Modern World* (London: Pinter, 1993); and Nigel White, *The Law of International Organisations* (Manchester: Manchester University Press, 1996).

13 David Armstrong, Lorna Lloyd, and John Redmond, *International Organisation in World Politics* (London: Palgrave, 2004); and Volker Rittberger and Bernhard Zangl, *International Organization: Polity, Politics and Policies* (London: Palgrave, 2006).

14 Harold Jacobson, *Networks of Interdependence. International Organizations and the Global Political System* (New York: Alfred Knopf, 1979); Werner Feld and Robert Jordan, *International Organisations: A Comparative Approach* (New York: Praeger, 1983); and Margaret Karns and Karen Mingst, *International Organizations: The Politics and Processes of Global Governance* (Boulder, CO: Lynne Rienner, 2004).

15 Clive Archer, *International Organizations* (London: Routledge, 2001, 3rd edn.), 39–40.

16 The lists of recognized NGOs, as at 31 July of each year, are given in ECOSOC documents E/1998/INF/6 and E/1999/INF/5, and the debate on 17 December 1999 is reported in General Assembly document A/54/PV.84.

17 I originally referred to iquangos, international quasi-non-governmental organiza-
    tions. See Peter Willetts, "Transactions, Networks and Systems," in *Frameworks
    for International Co-operation*, eds John Groom and Paul Taylor (London: Pinter,
    1990), 275–76.

18 The World Commission on Environment and Development, *Our Common Future*
    (Oxford: Oxford University Press, 1987). For the Commission's reliance on the
    Villach conference, see pp. 175–76.

19 Membership data as of January 2009, from *ISO members*. Available at: www.iso.
    org/iso/about/iso_members.htm.

20 See the ANSI entry, on *ISO members*, for the US member. For wider coverage,
    see Craig N. Murphy and Joanne Yates, *The International Organization for
    Standardization (ISO): Global Governance through Voluntary Consensus*
    (London: Routledge, 2008).

21 George Pring, *International Law and Mineral Resources* (Geneva: UNCTAD,
    2003). Available at: http://commdev.org/content/document/detail/1214.

22 *Convention No. 14 of the International Commission on Civil Status (CIEC)*, signed
    on 13 September 1973. Available at: http://web.lerelaisinternet.com/CIECSITE/
    Conventions/Conv14Angl.pdf.

23 "Agreement on Technical Barriers to Trade," in WTO, *The Legal Texts: The
    Results of the Uruguay Round of Multilateral Trade Negotiations* (Cambridge:
    Cambridge University Press, 1999), articles 1.1–1.2, 2.4, and 2.6.

24 *IUCN Statutes and Regulations*. Available at: http://cmsdata.iucn.org/downloads/
    statutes_en.pdf (last amended in November 2004).

25 *Convention on Wetlands of International Importance Especially as Waterfowl Habitat*,
    adopted at Ramsar, Iran, on 2 February 1971. Available at "Documents": www.
    ramsar.org. This quote is from the "Partner Organizations" link on the "About
    Ramsar" page. *What is the Ramsar Convention on Wetlands?*. Available at: www.
    ramsar.org/about/info2007–02-e.pdf.

26 *Memorandum of Understanding,* between the CITES Secretariat and IUCN, July
    1999. Available at: www.cites.org/ common/disc/sec/CITES-IUCN.pdf.

27 Steve Charnovitz, "Non-Governmental Organizations and International Law,"
    The American Journal of International Law 100 (2006), 348–72: 355–56; and
    Anthony Judge, "Legal Status of International NGOs: Overview and Options,"
    in *International Associations Statutes Series*, Union of International Associations
    (Munich: K G Saur Verlag, 1988), Appendix 1.

28 Ian Brownlie, *Principles of Public International Law* (Oxford: Oxford University
    Press, 2008, 7th edn.).

29 Malcolm Shaw, *International Law* (Cambridge: Cambridge University Press,
    2008, 6th edn.), 196–97. Shaw does acknowledge the ICRC has international
    legal personality: see 261–62.

30 Shaw, *International Law*, 1,283 and 1,295–96.

31 Kamminga, "The Evolving Status of NGOs," 110–11.

32 David Ettinger, "The Legal Status of the International Olympic Committee,"
    Pace Yearbook of International Law 4 (1992): 97–120.

33 Shaw, *International Law*, 116. A more conservative view is taken in Christopher
    Joyner, ed., *The United Nations and International Law* (Cambridge: Cambridge
    University Press, 1997), see 5–6 and 443–45.

34 Hurst Hannum, "The Status of the Universal Declaration of Human Rights
    in National and International Law," *Georgia Journal of International and
    Comparative Law* 25 (1995/96): 287–398.

35 *Rules of Procedure* for the Dublin conference (document CCM/52); *List of Delegates* (document CCM/INF/1); and the text of the Convention (document CCM/77), are all available from the Irish Department of Foreign Affairs web page. Available at: www.clustermunitionsdublin.ie/documents.asp.

36 It is notable that the WHO has endorsed a strong statement that the list of subjects of international law "now includes non-state actors, such as individuals, non-governmental organizations (NGOs), and multinational corporations (MNCs)." See David Fidler, "International Law," Section 7 of *Global Public Goods for Health—A Reading Companion*, a WHO distance learning module. Available at: www.who.int/trade/distance_learning/gpgh/en.

37 For a much more sophisticated legal discussion, see Anna-Karin Lindblom, *Non-Governmental Organisations in International Law* (Cambridge: Cambridge University Press, 2005). However, this book is odd in that Part I concludes by explicitly saying "no … attempts will be made" to address the central question discussed here, "to measure NGOs against the concepts of 'subject of international law' and 'international legal personality'," 117.

4 NGOs, networking, and the creation of the Internet

1 I am indebted to Ian Peter's discussion. Available at: www.nethistory.info/History of the Internet/origins.html, dated 2004.

2 Barney Warf and John Grimes, "Counterhegemonic Discourses and the Internet," *The Geographical Review*, 87 (1997): 259–74. Manuel Castells, *The Information Age: Economy, Society and Culture, Volume 1, The Rise of the Network Society* (Oxford: Blackwell, 2nd edn., 2000), 45 and 371. See also Howard Rheingold, *The Virtual Community. Homesteading on the Electronic Frontier* (Reading, MA: Addison-Wesley Publishing, 1993; and MIT Press, 2000), xxi.

3 On ARPA see Katie Hafner and Matthew Lyon, *Where Wizards Stay Up Late: The Origins of the Internet* (London: Simon & Schuster, 1996).

4 *Paul Baran and the Origins of the Internet.* Available at: www.rand.org/about/history/baran.html; and Philip Elmer-Dewitt, "First Nation in Cyberspace," *Time*, 6 December 1993.

5 Ian Peter, *The History of Email.* Available at: www.nethistory.info/History of the Internet/email.html.

6 *An Interview with Robert E. Kahn*, 22 March 1989. Available at: www.archive.org/stream/AnInterviewWithRobertKahnOh158/RK108.txt.

7 Michael Hauben and Ronda Hauben, *Netizens: On the History and Impact of Usenet and the Internet* (Washington, DC: IEEE Computer Society Press, 1997), 44.

8 Hauben and Hauben, *Netizens*, 41.

9 John Quarterman, *The Matrix: Computer Networks and Conferencing Systems Worldwide* (Bedford MA: Digital Press, 1990), 230–31.

10 The text of the policy as of 18 June 1990 is in *CSNET-Forum*, 6, no. 3, 23 August 1990. Available at: http://stuff.mit.edu/afs/athena/reference/net-directory/documents/csnet-forum.

11 For the history of Fido, FidoNet, and a collection of *FidoNews*, see the website of Tom Jennings. Available at: http://wps.com; see also Rheingold, *The Virtual Community*, xxiv and 138–42. For developments in Africa, see www.africa.upenn.edu/Global_Comm/Global_Networks_10165.htm.

12 Chip Berlet, *When Hate Went Online*. Available at: http://simson.net/ref/leaderless/berlet_when_hate_went_online.pdf, April 2001.

13 Brian Murphy, "Interdoc: The First International Non-Governmental Computer Network," *First Monday*, 10 (May 2005) and Graham Lane, *Communications for Progress* (London: Catholic Institute for International Relations, 1990), 47–49.

14 Laurie Wiseberg, "Protecting Human Rights Activists and NGOs: What More Can Be Done," *Human Rights Quarterly*, 13 (1991): 533.

15 Susanne Sallin, *The Association for Progressive Communications*, 14 February 1994. Available at: www.ciesin.columbia.edu/kiosk/publications/94-0010.txt.

16 Andrew Garton. Available at: http://agarton.org/1994/01/good-causes-on-the-information-highway, 26 January 1994.

17 Association for Progressive Communications, *Annual Report 2000*. Available at: www.apc.org/en/system/files/apc_ar_2000+en.pdf; and Peregrine Wood, *Putting Beijing Online*. Available at: www.apcwomen.org/netsupport/sync/toolkit1.pdf.

18 Sallin, *The Association for Progressive Communications*, 9; Howard Frederick, "Computer Networks and the Emergence of Global Civil Society," in Linda Harasim, ed., *Global Networks: Computers and International Communication* (Cambridge, MA: MIT Press, 1993), 283–96; and Graham's CV. Available at: www.well.com/~mgraham.

19 *Partial list of organisations on APC networks, December 88*. Available at: http://www.mitra.biz/apchistory/apc_dec88_organisations.pdf.

20 *Join Us In Celebrating A Story*. Available at: http://anniversary.gn.apc.org, posted in 2006; *GreenNet. Over 20 Years of Networking for Social Change*. Available at: www.gn.apc.org/about/history; APC, *Annual Report 2000*; and Mitra Ardron's archives. Available at:www.mitra.biz/apchistory.

21 Thanks are due to Stephen Pittam, the JRCT Secretary, for providing the grant papers.

22 Mitra Ardron and Deborah Miller, *Why the Association for Progressive Communications is Different*. Available at: www.mitra.biz/apchistory/apc_ica_1988.pdf, May 1988.

23 Sallin, *The Association for Progressive Communications*; Murphy in APC, *Annual Report 2000*, 30; and Lane, *Communications for Progress*, 48. The quote is from Lane.

24 APC, *Annual Report 2000*; Sallin, *The Association for Progressive Communications*; and *Rory O'Brien, Curriculum Vitae*. Available at: www.web.net/~robrien/rorycv.html.

25 See three reports on Brazil at www.mitra.biz/apchistory, and Sallin, *The Association for Progressive Communications*, note 40.

26 Jim Walch, *In the Net. An Internet Guide for Activists* (London: Zed Books, 1999), 110–16.

27 Robert Pollard, *United Nations Conference on Environment and Development: Information, Public Participation and Communication System. A Preliminary Proposal* and e-mail exchanges in March–April 1990 on the draft proposal. Available at: at http://habitat.igc.org/docs/ippcs.htm.

28 Shelley Preston, "Electronic Global Networking and the NGO Movement: The 1992 Rio Summit and Beyond," *Swords and Ploughshares: A Chronicle of International Affairs*, 3 (Spring 1994); and Langston Goree and Robert Pollard, *Computer Communications and the 1992 United Nations Conference on Environment and Development*. Available at: http://habitat.igc.org/docs/cc-unced.htm.

29 See Roberto Bissio, "Occupying New Space for Public Life," in John Foster and Anita Anand, eds, *Whose World is it Anyway? Civil Society, the United Nations and the Multilateral Future* (Ottawa: United Nations Association in Canada, 1999), 423 and 438–39.

30 See the article by AlterNex's founder, Carlos Afonso, *The Internet and the Community in Brazil: Background, Issues, and Options*. Available at: www.cgi.br/publicacoes/artigos/artigo9.htm. For more about APC's work at UNCED, see Rory O'Brien and Andrew Clement, *The Association for Progressive Communications and the Networking of Global Civil Society*. Available at: www.apc.org/about/history/apc-at-1992-earth-summit; and Carlos Afonso, *UNCED Information Strategy Project in Rio: a Final Report*. Available at: www.nsrc.org/db/lookup/country.php?ISO=BR, 6 September 1992.

31 This paragraph is based on Afonso, "UNCED Information Strategy Project ..." Note that Afonso referred to Chasque as NGONET.

32 Frederick, "Computer Networks and the Emergence of Global Civil Society," 293.

33 At this stage, Antenna was not a member of the APC, but it did join for a few years in the 1990s.

34 O'Brien and Clement, "The Association for Progressive Communications and the Networking of Global Civil Society."

35 See the *ENB* archive. Available at: www.iisd.ca/voltoc.html.

36 *Agenda 21* (General Assembly document A/CONF.151.26), para. 40.25, emphasis added.

37 Walch, *In the Net*, 42 and 45, a single quote.

38 *Notes for People Interested in Setting Up and Running APC Nodes*. Available at: www.mitra.biz/apchistory/apc_setup_notes_1mar89.pdf, March 1989.

39 Quote from APC, *Annual Report 2000*, 29. Twenty e-mail systems are listed on *Gateway Addresses to and from the IGC Networks*, see www.mitra.biz/apchistory, July 1990. Sallin, *The Association for Progressive Communications*, has a somewhat different list. Delphi and Prodigy seem to be the important omissions from both lists.

40 Willetts, *"The Conscience of the World"*, p. 46.

41 Data summarized from Don Daniels, "Tabulation of FidoNet Nodes by Country," *FidoNews*, 10, no. 17, 26 April 1993. See also data for 19 June 1992, in *FidoNews*, 9, no. 39, 28 September 1992. Note that in Table 4.3 North America includes US colonies and the Caribbean includes UK colonies.

42 For the attempts by IGC to adapt in the late 1990s, see Craig Warkentin, *Reshaping World Politics: NGOs, the Internet and Global Civil Society* (Lanham, MA: Rowman & Littlefield, 2001), 145–56.

43 See Mark Surman, *Balancing Mission and Money: Building Sustainable Electronic Networks for Civil Society*. Available at: www.commons.ca/articles/fulltext.shtml?x=429, 10 September 1999.

44 *APC's Recommendations to the WSIS on Internet Governance, November 2005*. Available at: www.apc.org/en/system/files/apc_recommendations_ig_EN.pdf; and APC, *Internet Rights Charter*. Available at: www.apc.org/en/node/5677.

45 Michael Polman "Foreword," in Lane, *Communications for Progress*, xii–xiii.

46 Sallin, *The Association for Progressive Communications*. The FCCC was misnamed by Sallin.

47 Bissio, "Occupying New Space for Public Life," 434, and *GreenNet News*, Winter 1992/93 (published circa October 1992). Available at: www.mitra.biz/apchistory/gn_news_winter92.pdf. The conference was named gef.report.

48 *Some of Mitra's Past Projects and Clients.* Available at: www.mitra.biz/project-sandclients.htm.
49 Blake Gumprecht, *Government Information on the Internet*, Second Edition, in four parts. Available at: at www.faqs.org/faqs/us-govt-net-pointers/part1 and … /part2, etc. There are no US government websites (just Gophers) in parts (1) and (2) dated 26 February 1994, but five in parts (3) and (4) dated April 1994.

5 Understanding the place of NGOs in global politics

1 Many authors classify the different theoretical paradigms in a similar manner, but they sometimes use different labels for one or more of the four approaches. For examples of this classification see Michael Smith and Richard Little, eds, *Perspectives on World Politics* (London: Routledge, 1991); Richard Mansbach and John Vasquez, *In Search of Theory: A New Paradigm for Global Politics* (New York: Colombia University Press, 1981); James Rosenau, "Order and Disorder in the Study of World Politics," in *Globalism versus Realism*, ed. Ray Maghroori and Bennett Ramberg (Boulder, Col.: Westview Press, 1982), 1–7; Peter Willetts, ed., *Pressure Groups in the Global System* (London: Frances Pinter, 1982); and Paul Viotti and Mark Kauppi, eds, *International Relations Theory* (New York: Macmillan, 1993). Unfortunately, there is some inconsistency with language: Maghroori and Ramberg use "globalism" to mean pluralism, while Viotti and Kauppi use "globalism" to mean the Marxist approach. Rosenau does not recognize functionalism to be a distinct approach and hence only uses three categories.
2 Ole Wæver, "The Rise and Fall of the Inter-Paradigm Debate," in *International Theory: Positivism and Beyond*, eds Steve Smith, Ken Booth, and Marysia Zalewski (Cambridge: Cambridge University Press, 1996), 149–85.
3 Steven Lamy, "Contemporary mainstream approaches: neo-realism and neo-liberalism," in *The Globalization of World Politics*, eds John Baylis, Steve Smith, and Patricia Owens (Oxford: Oxford University Press, 2008, 4th edn.), 125.
4 John Ruggie, "What Makes the World Hang Together? Neo-Utilitarianism and the Social Constructivist Challenge," in *Constructing the World Polity: Essays on International Institutionalization* (London: Routledge, 1998), 1–39.
5 Peter Haas, ed., *Knowledge, Power, and International Policy Co-ordination* (Columbia: University of South Carolina Press, 1997), 3.
6 Margaret Keck and Kathryn Sikkink, *Activists Beyond Borders: Advocacy Networks in International Politics* (Ithaca, NY: Cornell University Press, 1998), 4. The quote refers to transnational networks, but it can also apply to transnational communities.
7 Graham Allison, *Essence of Decision: Explaining the Cuban Missile Crisis* (Boston, MA: Little, Brown & Company, 1999, 2nd ed.).
8 Robert Keohane and Joseph Nye, "Transgovernmental Relations and International Organizations," *World Politics* 27 (1974): 39–62. The authors first introduced the concept of transgovernmental relations in *Transnational Relations and World Politics* (Cambridge, MA: Harvard University Press, 1972), 379–84.
9 "Definitions and Sources" in United Nations Conference on Trade and Development, *World Investment Report, 2009* (Geneva: UNCTAD, 2009), 243.
10 See the section on "Transnational companies as political actors" by Peter Willetts, in *The Globalization of World Politics*, ed. John Baylis and Steve Smith (Oxford: Oxford University Press, 2008, 4th edn.).
11 Keck and Sikkink, *Activists Beyond Borders*, 1.

12 Keck and Sikkink, *Activists Beyond Borders*, 9. They do not mention Keohane and Nye's 1974 article.

13 Stephen Krasner, ed., *International Regimes* (Ithaca, NY: Cornell University Press, 1983), 2.

14 The clearest example is Robert Keohane, *International Institutions and State Power: Essays in International Relations Theory* (Boulder, CO: Westview Press, 1989). Keohane explicitly abandons his work with Nye on transnational relations and implicitly abandons their transgovernmental relations article.

15 Ernst Haas, *When Knowledge is Power: Three Models of Change in International Organizations* (Berkeley, CA: University of California Press, 1990).

16 Oran Young, "The Power of Institutions: Why International Regimes Matter," in *International Co-operation: Building Regimes for Natural Resources and the Environment* (Ithaca, NY: Cornell University Press, 1989), 68, 70, 77, and 78.

17 Marc Levy, Robert Keohane, and Peter Haas, eds, *Institutions for the Earth: Sources of Effective Environmental Protection* (Cambridge, MA: MIT Press, 1994), 399–400. Here Keohane seems to be changing his position yet again: see note 14.

18 Krasner, *International Regimes*, 3–4.

19 For studies of these three non-governmental regimes see John Mathiason, *Internet Governance: The New Frontier of Global Institutions* (London: Routledge, 2008); Jean-Loup Chappelet, *The International Olympic Committee and the Olympic System: The Governance of World Sport* (London: Routledge, 2008); and Alan Tomlinson, *FIFA (Fédération Internationale de Football Association)* (London: Routledge, forthcoming).

20 James Rosenau, *Turbulence in World Politics: A Theory of Change and Continuity* (Hemel Hempstead, UK: Harvester Wheatsheaf, 1990), 187.

21 Rosenau, *Turbulence in World Politics*, 190. The list of sources of authority has been expanded by myself to include expertise and status, at a lower level than charisma.

22 David Easton, *A Framework for Political Analysis* (Englewood Cliffs, NJ: Prentice Hall, 1965) and *The Political System* (New York: Knopf, 1953).

23 Mansbach and Vasquez, *In Search of Theory*, 30.

24 Thomas Risse, "'Let's Argue:' Communicative Action in World Politics," *International Organization*, 54 (2000), 1–39: 1–2.

25 Willetts, *Pressure Groups*, 24.

26 Stanley Hoffmann, "Obstinate or Obsolete: The Fate of the Nation-State and the Case of Western Europe," *Daedalus* 95 (1966): 862–915.

27 On human security, see Peter Hough, *Understanding Global Security* (London: Routledge, 2008).

28 Willetts, *Pressure Groups*, 23. At this point, I was explicitly pluralist, but only implicitly constructivist, through my emphasis on systems.

29 *Quotations on Diplomacy and Foreign Policy*. Available at: www.fco.gov.uk/en/about-the-fco/publications/historians1/history-notes/the-fco-policy-people-places/quotations-diplomacy-foreign.

30 Hans Morgenthau, *Human Rights and Foreign Policy*. Available at: www.cceia.org/resources/publications/1979_lecture_by_morgenthau/index.html.

31 Peter Willetts, "Who cares about the environment?" in *The Environment and International Relations*, eds John Vogler and Mark Imber (London: Routledge, 1996), 120–37.

32 Martha Finnemore and Kathryn Sikkink, "Taking Stock: The Constructivist Research Program in International Relations and Comparative Politics," *Annual Review of Political Science* 4 (2001), 391–416: 392–93.

33 Ruggie, "What Makes the World Hang Together?", 9.

34 Alexander Wendt, "Anarchy is What States Make of It: the Social Construction of Power Politics," *International Organization* 46 (1992): 391–425.

35 Ruggie, "What Makes the World Hang Together?" only mentions NGOs once, on p. 27.

36 Keck and Sikkink, *Activists Beyond Borders*, 2–8.

37 Keck and Sikkink, *Activists Beyond Borders*, 12.

38 Jackie Smith, *Social Movements for Global Democracy* (Baltimore, MA: Johns Hopkins University Press, 2008), 90–91.

39 Willetts, *Pressure Groups*, 185–88 and 192–96. This work was followed by a sustained research program, exploring a pluralist constructivist approach to global intergovernmental organizations. I did not refer to constructivism, but to an issue-based approach to global politics.

40 Peter Willetts, ed., *"The Conscience of the World": The Influence of Non-Governmental Organisations in the UN System* (Washington, DC: Brookings Institution, 1996), 45–49.

41 Keck and Sikkink, *Activists Beyond Borders*, 25–26.

42 The term issue cycle comes from chapter 4 of Mansbach and Vasquez, *In Search of Theory*.

43 Martha Finnemore and Kathryn Sikkink, "International Norm Dynamics and Political Change," *International Organization*, 52, no. 4 (1998): 887–917, quote from 891–92.

44 Finnemore and Sikkink, "International Norm Dynamics," 895–905.

45 Finnemore and Sikkink, "International Norm Dynamics," 895, 896–97, and 899.

46 Points on the norm life cycle abstracted from Finnemore and Sikkink, "International Norm Dynamics," 896–905.

47 Finnemore and Sikkink, "International Norm Dynamics," 904.

48 Finnemore and Sikkink, "International Norm Dynamics," 905. Their reference to "state bureaucracies" is coupled with "international organizations," but the presumption must be they mean intergovernmental organizations, rather than all types of international organizations.

49 Points on which norms matter abstracted from Finnemore and Sikkink, "International Norm Dynamics," 905–09.

50 Finnemore and Sikkink, "International Norm Dynamics," 906.

51 Finnemore and Sikkink, "International Norm Dynamics," 908–09.

52 Finnemore and Sikkink, "International Norm Dynamics," 891, emphasis added. Note also "they exercise influence" (888), "work their influence" (893), "influence … behavior" (894), relationships between norms "influence … their influence" (908), norms "compete for support" (895), norms can be "powerful" (904 and 907 twice), "influential" (905 and 906), "effective" (907 twice) and "successful" (907 twice).

53 Peter Willetts, "The Issue of Issues," a paper at the British International Studies Association annual conference, December 1991. A revised version (December 1996) is available at: www.staff.city.ac.uk/p.willetts/ARTICLES/ISSOFISS.DOC.

54 Charlotte Epstein, *The Power of Words in International Relations: Birth of an Anti-Whaling Discourse* (Cambridge, MA: MIT Press, 2008).

6 The creation of global governance

1 Ingvar Carlsson and Shridath Ramphal, in *Our Global Neighbourhood: The Report of the Commission on Global Governance* (Oxford: Oxford University Press, 1995), xiv and xvi.

2 *Our Global Neighbourhood*, 2–5.

3 Boutros Boutros-Ghali, "Democracy: A Newly Recognized Imperative," *Global Governance* 1 (1995), 3–11: 10.

4 James Rosenau, "Governance in the Twenty-First Century," *Global Governance* 1 (1995), 13–43: 15–16.

5 Rosenau, "Governance in the Twenty-First Century," 24, 29, and 39.

6 Lawrence Finkelstein, "What is Global Governance?" *Global Governance* 1 (1995), 367–72: 369.

7 Rosenau, "Governance in the Twenty-First Century," 13.

8 James Rosenau, "Toward an Ontology for Global Governance," in *Approaches to Global Governance Theory*, eds Martin Hewson and Timothy Sinclair (Albany: State University of New York Press, 1999), 287–301, 288.

9 Rosenau, "Toward an Ontology for Global Governance," 293.

10 For example, Paul Diehl, ed., *The Politics of Global Governance. International Organizations in an Interdependent World* (Boulder, CO: Lynne Rienner, 2005, 3rd edn.) contains no discussion of the concept.

11 Thomas Weiss and Leon Gordenker, eds, *NGOs, the UN and Global Governance* (Boulder, CO: Lynne Rienner, 1996).

12 Oran Young, ed., *Global Governance: Drawing Insights from the Environmental Experience* (Cambridge, MA: MIT Press, 1997).

13 Robert O'Brien, Anne Marie Goetz, Jan Aart Scholte, and Marc Williams, *Contesting Global Governance. Multilateral Economic Institutions and Global Social Movements* (Cambridge: Cambridge University Press, 2000).

14 Rorden Wilkinson and Stephen Hughes, eds, *Global Governance: Critical Perspectives* (London: Routledge, 2002): 2 and 13.

15 For example, Hewson and Sinclair, eds, *Approaches to Global Governance Theory*, and the readings in Timothy Sinclair, ed., *Global Governance* (London: Routledge, 2004).

16 Rosenau, in "Governance in the Twenty-First Century," acknowledged transnational actors in global governance but did not recognize that his examples, credit-rating agencies, are themselves subject to governance by the European Community and global organizations.

17 Finkelstein, "What is Global Governance?," 369.

18 Even Rosenau did not address questions of global governance until he prepared three background papers for the Commission. The words "global governance" only appear three times, without any discussion, in James Rosenau and Ernst Czempiel, eds, *Governance without Government: Order and Change in World Politics* (Cambridge: Cambridge University Press, 1992).

19 For a discussion of the Internet as a global public good, see Debora Spar, "The Public Face of Cyberspace," in *Global Public Goods: International Cooperation in the 21st Century*, eds Inge Kaul, Isabelle Grunberg, and Marc Stern (Oxford: Oxford University Press, 1999).

Selected bibliography

The strong claims in this book, about non-governmental organization influence in global policy-making, are substantiated by the case studies, covering a diverse range of policy domains, in the following six volumes. Peter Willetts, ed., *Pressure Groups in the Global System* (London: Frances Pinter, 1982), asks why groups based in the politics of one country seek to engage in activities in other countries and at the global level. Thomas Weiss and Leon Gordenker, eds, in *NGOs, the UN and Global Governance* (Boulder, CO: Lynne Rienner, 1996), focus on organizational and strategic aspects of NGO engagement in global governance. Peter Willetts, ed., *"The Conscience of the World"* (Washington, DC: Brookings, 1996), provides detailed empirical studies of the outcomes achieved by NGOs in global policy-making. Ann Florini, ed., *The Third Force: The Rise of Transnational Civil Society* (Washington, DC: Carnegie Endowment, 2000), seeks to assess the strengths and limitations of transnational networks at the global level. Margaret Keck and Kathryn Sikkink, *Activists Beyond Borders* (Ithaca, NY: Cornell University Press, 1998), develop the concept of transnational advocacy networks and focus more on the country and the regional level than the global level. Michael Edwards and John Gaventa, eds, *Global Citizen Action* (Boulder, CO: Lynne Rienner, 2001), raise questions about the nature of global civil society and the ethics of campaigning.

Shamima Ahmed and David Potter, *NGOs in International Politics* (Bloomfield, CT: Kumarian Press, 2006), have produced the only general textbook on the subject and it is pitched at an introductory level. Srilatha Batliwala and David Brown, *Transnational Civil Society* (Bloomfield, CT: Kumarian Press, 2006), offer a committed sociological perspective. (However, the reader should be aware that this volume is not reliable. There are as many as three factual errors on the first page.) Two other general books have been written to assist NGOs in understanding how to gain influence: John Foster and Anita Anand, *Whose World is it Anyway?* (Ottawa: United Nations Association in Canada, 1999); and Felix Dodds, *How to Lobby at Intergovernmental Meetings* (London: Earthscan, 2004).

The most comprehensive evidence and analysis of NGO influence are in the issue-area of human rights. William Korey, *NGOs and the Universal Declaration of Human Rights* (New York: Palgrave, 1998), gives an impressive, detailed, historical account of NGO activities from 1945 to 1998. It should be the first port of call for any events in this time period. The following five volumes are strongly analytical: Ann Marie Clark, *Diplomacy of Conscience: Amnesty International and Changing Human Rights Norms* (Princeton, NJ: Princeton University Press, 2001); Kerstin Martens, *NGOs and the United Nations* (Houndmills, UK: Palgrave, 2005); Peter Baehr, *Non-Governmental Human Rights Organizations in International Relations* (Houndmills, UK: Palgrave, 2009); Thomas Risse, Stephen Ropp, and Kathryn Sikkink, *The Power of Human Rights* (Cambridge: Cambridge University Press, 1999); and Philip Alston, *Non-State Actors and Human Rights* (Oxford: Oxford University Press, 2005), which primarily addresses international legal questions.

Much of the writing on the International Criminal Court gives little attention to NGOs, but they are properly acknowledged in Marlies Glasius, *The International Criminal Court: A Global Civil Society Achievement* (London: Routledge, 2006); Benjamin Schiff, *Building the International Criminal Court* (Cambridge: Cambridge University Press, 2008); and Michael Struett, *The Politics of Constructing the International Criminal Court* (New York: Palgrave Macmillan, 2008). It is also important to use the website of the Coalition for the International Criminal Court, www.iccnow.org, and read William Pace's accounts of the Coalition's work.

There is a strong literature on the global women's movement. The most comprehensive study is Mary Meyer and Elisabeth Prügl, *Gender Politics in Global Governance* (Lanham, MD: Rowman & Littlefield, 1999). The global women's conferences and their impact on the UN are covered by Hilkka Pietilä and Jeanne Vickers, *Making Women Matter* (London: Zed Books, 1996); Anna Snyder, *Setting the Agenda for Global Peace*, (Aldershot, UK: Ashgate, 2003); and Hilkka Pietilä, *The Unfinished Story of Women and the United Nations* (New York: Non-Governmental Liaison Service, 2007). The global women's networks are analyzed in Valentine Moghadam, *Globalizing Women* (Baltimore, MD: Johns Hopkins University Press, 2005); Myra Ferree and Aili Tripp, *Global Feminism* (New York: New York University Press, 2006); and Kimberly Jensen and Erika Kuhlman, *Women and Transnational Activism in Historical Perspective* (Dordrecht, the Netherlands: Republic of Letters, 2010). The impact of women's networks on peace and conflict resolution is covered by Catherine Foster, *Women for All Seasons: The Story of the Women's International League for Peace and Freedom* (Athens, GA: University of Georgia Press, 1989); Harriet Alonso, *Peace as a Women's Issue* (Syracuse, NY: Syracuse University Press, 1993); and Cynthia Cockburn, *From Where*

We Stand (London: Zed Books, 2007). Ironically, most feminist writing on international politics pays little attention to the global women's movement.

A number of books are devoted to the impact of NGOs within a single policy domain: Keith Suter, *An International Law of Guerrilla Warfare* (London: Frances Pinter, 1984); Andy Chetley, *The Politics of Baby Foods* (London: Frances Pinter, 1986); Maxwell Cameron, Robert Lawson, and Brian Tomlin, *To Walk Without Fear: The Global Movement to Ban Landmines* (Oxford: Oxford University Press, 1998); Bas Arts, *The Political Influence of Global NGOs: Case-Studies on the Climate and Biodiversity Conventions* (Utrecht: International Books, 1998); Robert O'Brien, Anne Marie Goetz, Jan Aart Scholte, and Marc Williams, *Contesting Global Governance: Multilateral Economic Institutions and Global Social Movements* (Cambridge: Cambridge University Press, 2000); and Charlotte Epstein, *The Power of Words in International Relations: Birth of an Anti-Whaling Discourse* (Cambridge, MA: MIT Press, 2008).

Those who hold the mistaken belief that NGO influence is a new phenomenon should read Thomas Davies, *The Possibilities of Transnational Activism: The Campaign for Disarmament between the Two World Wars* (Leiden: Martinus Nijhoff, 2007), or the works, cited above, on the women's movement.

A wealth of primary source materials can be found on the websites of NGOs and of intergovernmental organizations. Unfortunately, many NGOs and some IGOs are appallingly bad about keeping archives, so readers are advised to download any interesting web pages onto their own computer. It is useful to keep a bibliographic file, listing each web page title, its original URL, the date when it was downloaded and its filename on your own computer, along with a few words indicating what was of interest about the page. Caution should be exercised about the use of non-academic websites. NGO web pages and Wikipedia articles cannot be assumed to be accurate about all the specific information they present. However, for a political scientist, an NGO's web page can always be offered as sound evidence of what the NGO itself wished to communicate to the public and how it framed its appeal for support. IGOs generally keep comprehensive archives and are continually expanding them both forwards and backwards in time. Except in rare cases, their web pages are completely reliable. However, one frequent bias on IGO web pages, especially in their archived records, is to omit information about the NGOs involved in the IGO's activities. The deficiencies of both NGO and IGO websites are best remedied by comparing and contrasting pages covering a specific issue or a specific event from a range of NGO, IGO and news websites.

To investigate a particular issue start with the index web pages of the Global Policy Forum, available at: www.globalpolicy.org, or the UN

Non-Governmental Liaison Service, available at: www.un-ngls.org. In addition, the OneWorld Network provides a guide to global issues, country-specific information and a global directory of NGOs. Navigation is not easy, but start from the "What Is OneWorld?" links, available at: http://us.oneworld. net and the "About" links, available at: http://uk.oneworld.net. Finally, many of the sources for this book are available from the author's website, www. staff.city.ac.uk/p.willetts.

Index of NGOs and hybrid international organizations

* Indicates the organization is a hybrid
Note: page numbers in **bold** refer to figures and tables.

Subject index